日本人の考え方を英語で説明する辞典

本名信行
ベイツ・ホッファ　編

An English Dictionary of Japanese Ways of Thinking

有斐閣
YUHIKAKU

AN ENGLISH DICTIONARY OF JAPANESE
WAYS OF THINKING
by
Nobuyuki Honna & Bates Hoffer, eds. 1989
First published in Japan
by
YUHIKAKU PUBLISHING CO., LTD.

はじめに

　現在，日本は確実に国際化の道を歩んでいます。また，国際化
の只中にあって，日本人は異文化理解が不得手だと思われがちで
すが，けっしてそんなことはありません。外国の風物や生活を紹
介したテレビ番組や，外国人の生き方や考え方を説明した書物が
人気を集めているのは，これまで外国の思想や様式を自国の繁栄
のためにどんどん取り入れてきた日本人の，異文化理解への興味
と関心の高さを示すものといえるでしょう。

　この意味では，日本人の国際感覚も日に日に磨かれつつあると
いえましょう。しかし，もう一歩前進しなければならないでしょ
う。日本人はこれまで異民族と個人的にまじわることなしに，異
文化を映像と文献を通して抽象的に理解してきました。これだけ
では，不充分なのです。

　これからは，違った文化的背景をもつ人々と直に，そして緊密
に交流する経験をしなければなりません。同じ人間として，相互
にふれあう経験を通して，自分と相手を公平にながめる態度を習
得する必要があります。日米関係の問題ひとつとってみても，こ
ういったコンテキストのなかでしか，解決できないところまで来
ていると思います。

　ところが，文化的背景の異なる人々と交際すると，どうしても

了解事項に差異が生じます。そこで，合理的，明示的に説明しなければならなくなります。これはとてもやっかいなことですが，異文化との出会いでは避けて通ることはできません。こういうめんどうなことがあるから，国際交流などといったむずかしいことは専門家とか有資格者にまかせればよい，という意見もあります。しかし，今や異文化コミュニケーションは専門家だけの仕事ではなく，市民レベルで日常に生じる出来事になっています。また，そうでなければならないのです。

　日本人は日本のことを英語で外国人に説明するのがどうも苦手なようです。日本文化はまったく独特のもので，これを合理的に，あるいは一般的に説明することは不可能であり，外国人にはとうてい理解できるものではないと信じているふしさえあります。これはどうみても，こまったことです。外国の人々がせっかく日本人を理解しようと努力しはじめたときに，日本人のほうが相変わらず，狭い殻にとじこもっていたのでは，国際感覚にいっそうの磨きをかけることにはなりません。

　説明は説得とは違います。こちら側の考え方，感じ方を相手に提示できれば成功なのです。質問に沈黙で応えるのではなく，相手が前提を共有していないということを念頭に，順序正しく説明しようとする姿勢が，相手に好感をあたえます。そして，この過程のなかで，お互いに今まで気がつかなかった自分を知るようになるのです。異文化体験とは，そういうことを自覚することともいえましょう。

　最近，外国人の口から日本語がポンポン飛び出してきますし，活字にも現れます。そして，それがタイムやニューズウイークのような一般誌にのって，世界中に広まっています。以前は，kabuki, noh, haiku といった伝統芸術や，kimono, happi, sukiyaki, tempura, tatami のような衣食住に関係したものが多かったようです。いわゆる「目に見える文化」が関心のまとであったわけです。今は，nemawashi, haragei, sogo-sosha, wa のように，「目に見えない文化」にも注意が向いています。つまり，日本人の行動様式，社会組織，考え方，感じ方にも関心がよせられているのです。

　本書は，外国人に日本人の考え方，感じ方を英語で説明する際の，ひとつの方向を示したものです。内容は，政治，経済，法律等を含む社会生活全般にわたっております。項目のなかには，現在の日本事情とでもいうべきものも含めてあり，それらを英語でどのように表現したらよいのか，どのようなすじみちで説明したらよいのかについて，簡潔にまとめてあります。読者が自由にバリエーションを考えられるようにと日本語であらすじをそえておきました。前著『日本文化を英語で説明する辞典』(有斐閣)は「目に見える文化」を中心とし，本書は「目に見えない文化」を主としてあつかっております。2冊合わせて，ご利用いただきたい思います。

　本書の出版にあたっては，多くの友人のお世話になりました。寄稿者のかたがたは，編者の意図をよく理解して，各人の異文化

体験を基にした有益で興味ある原稿を執筆してくださいました。鈴木紀之さんは，それ以外にも困難な編集の全領域にわたって編者を援助してくださいました。また，有斐閣編集部の酒井久雄さんは，項目の選定，記事の内容，文体の統一などについて，全面的にご協力くださいました。ここに感謝の意を表します。

1989年春

本 名 信 行

ベイツ・ホッファ

Preface
—Reporting on the American reception of the
first volume of this series—

An English Dictionary of Japanese Culture, published three
years ago, had an interesting reception in the United States.
Professor Nobuyuki Honna and I had worked on U.S.-Japan
projects together and had taught a course together at Trinity
University in 1983. The special course quickly filled with students and we knew that there was a great interest in Japan
among students as well as others in the U.S. We looked forward to the publication of the Culture Dictionary, but we
could not be sure of the reception of the book here, especially a bilingual book. In America, usually only specialists are
familiar with books printed in two languages.

The first indication of the impact of the book was a
phone call to my office from an American who worked in an
office in Cincinnati, Ohio. Only a short time after the book
was available in this country, his phone call reached me at
my office. He praised the book highly, said it was exactly
what he had been looking for, and hoped we would publish
more. He had read other books on Japan, but he felt the
format of the Culture Dictionary was perfect for him. I must
confess to amazement that a reader would take the trouble to
make such a call. After publishing many dozens of books and
articles over the past 25 years, I had never had a stranger
call about a book——and we talked for about 15 minutes or
so.

The second indication of the reception of the book occurred at a professional meeting in San Francisco. On a visit to
the large book exhibit area, I talked with the representatives
of Kinokuniya of America, the distributors of the Culture Dictionary in the U.S. The two young men told me that the
display copy of the book was the only one they had left in

v

the store. It had sold out quickly and they had several orders on hold. When I indicated that a second volume was being planned, they became rather excited and suggested that we finish "as quickly as possible." I kept in touch by phone with the California store and they continued to echo the book exhibit representatives. The American readers seemed to be eager to learn from such a volume.

After the trip to California, there was still a small concern. Americans are surely interested in Japan and Japanese culture. Perhaps, then, the book was of interest only because of the subject. In addition, the first book was written with a Japanese audience in mind. That is, it was useful for Japanese who wanted to talk about their culture in a manner best suited for English-speaking people. Would Americans, especially Japanese Americans, find the book helpful or of interest or both?

The answer to the concern came not long after the trip. A native Japanese who has lived in the U.S. for several decades and who has been teaching about Japan and the Japanese language for many years asked to visit me in my office. After we talked about the book in general, she told me that it had helped her explain to Americans some topics which she had not been able to explain well in the past. Her special example was "on." She had been talking to Americans about sense of responsibility, about returning favors, and so on. Americans could not seem to grasp the depth of meaning in the Japanese term until she saw the phrase "moral indebtedness," which begins the explanation of "on" in the book. Americans can begin to understand such concepts better when they are put in the context——as the entry indicates——of "a complicated network of mutual responsibilities and obligations."

After the discussion with a person who has been teaching about Japan for so long yet who found many entries to be what she needed for the American audience, I concluded that the work done by the several people who contributed to the volume was a worthwhile contribution to the understanding of a culture. For three years many of the students in my classes dealing with Japanese culture have used the book and have told me that it is especially useful to complement the usual textbooks. The suggestions of the many people who have discussed the first book with me have been included in the planning for this second volume, *An English Dictionary of Japanese Ways of Thinking*. Those of us who have contributed to this volume hope that it will be as useful as the first volume in helping intercultural understanding.

Spring, 1989

Bates Hoffer

執筆者一覧 （五十音順 ＊編者）

Editors and Writers

＊本 名 信 行（Nobuyuki Honna）	青山学院大学
＊ベイツ・ホッファ（Bates Hoffer）	トリニティ大学
秋 山 高 二（Kouji Akiyama）	山梨大学
小 田 三千子（Michiko Oda）	東北学院大学
近 藤 光 雄（Mitsuo Kondo）	慶応義塾大学
鈴 木 紀 之（Toshiyuki Suzuki）	金城学院大学
高 橋 一 修（Issyu Takahashi）	法政大学
高橋みな子（Minako Takahashi）	名古屋短期大学
高 原　 脩（Osamu Takahara）	神戸市外国語大学
田 辺 正 美（Masami Tanabe）	青山学院大学
中 村 良 廣（Yoshihiro Nakamura）	筑紫女学園大学
信 原　 修（Osamu Nobuhara）	同志社女子大学
平 賀 正 子（Masako Hiraga）	放送大学
矢 野 安 剛（Yasukata Yano）	早稲田大学

Simplified Pronunciation Guide

Japanese words are easy to pronounce. For the purpose of this dictionary, following rules are important.

(1) A word is composed of one or more than one syllable.

(2) A syllable is chiefly composed of either (a) a single vowel or (b) a combination of a consonant and a vowel.

(3) There are five vowels. They are always pronounced in the same way :

> **"a"** as in al<u>o</u>h<u>a</u> **"e"** as in b<u>e</u>ll **"i"** as in <u>i</u>nk
> **"o"** as in <u>o</u>il **"u"** as in f<u>u</u>ll

Note 1. When two vowels come together, read them separately :

kuiawase＝ku＋i＋a＋wa＋se

Note 2. A bar mark above a vowel shows that the vowel sound is long :

ā, ē, ī, ō, ū

(4) There are nineteen consonants. They are presented alphabetically as follows :

> **b, ch, d, f, g, h, j** (read as in Jack), **k, m, n, p, r, s, sh, t, ts, w, y, z**

Note 1. Consonants always precede vowels to form syllables :
ba, be, bo, bu

Note 2. Postvocalic "n" forms a syllable alone :
hon＝ho＋n

(5) Double consonants are of the two kinds :

1. Consonant "y" following another consonant to make up a syllable such as **kya, kyo, kyu**.

2. Two identical consonants appearing in the middle of a word such as **kappa**. In this case a slight glottal constriction constitutes the pronunciation of the first consonant.

AN ENGLISH DICTIONARY
OF
JAPANESE WAYS OF THINKING

Adolescence and youth   In present-day Japan there are two different, if contradictory, reactions toward the older generations among young people. One is the *shin-jinrui* (new human species); the other is the dropout.

The former refers to the "new generation," so entirely "new" that its members can hardly believe that Japan was once a poor country and take Japan's present prosperity for granted. Their parents' contemporaries, on the other hand, still have an undeniable pride in their strenuous efforts to have sustained it. Here arises a big generation gap. Most young people think that there is not much to say even if they sit face-to-face with their parents, and they build up thier own private world, a "capsule," in which they hole up and spend most of their time glancing through magazines and playing with thier "pet" computers.

Blessed with an overabundance of material things and information, they place a greater emphasis on leisure and pleasure than on traditional work-ethic values. However, unlike their parents' generation, young people have cultivated a keener aesthetic sense which may grow somewhat akin, if more refined, to that of "*iki*" (chic) and "*karumi*" (taste) which developed in the Edo period(1603-1867); that is, they are highly sensitive to the trendy fashionableness combined with discreet elegance and a light lifestyle. A major difference from the older generations also lies in their belief that they are world citizens and that they will be able to live

2

若者たち　　今日の日本の若者たちは，親たちの古い世代に対して，一見矛盾した2つの異なった反応を示します。ひとつは「新人類」もうひとつは落ちこぼれです。

「新人類」とよばれるタイプは，日本がかつて貧しい国だったことなど思いもよらず，現在の日本の繁栄を当り前のことと考える，全く新しい世代です。古い世代の人々は，自分たちこそ必死の努力をして，今日の繁栄を支えてきたのだという，強い自信と誇りをもっています。世代間の断絶は，まさにここに起因しています。例えば，若者たちの多くは，親と向かい合って坐っていても，あまり話すこともなく，従って自分たちだけの「カプセル」世界を作り上げ，終日こもりっきりで，雑誌や愛用のコンピューターと向き合うことになります。

また，「新人類」は溢れるばかりの物質文明と情報社会の中で，もっぱらレジャーや娯楽に関心が向かい，親の世代のもつ，勤勉という伝統的価値観を軽んじるようです。しかし，古い世代と違って，彼らのセンスのよさは，さらに磨きをかければ，あの江戸時代（1603～1867）の「粋（いき）」や「軽み」とも一脈通じるような美意識に育つ可能性もあるかもしれません。つまり，彼らは最先端の流行に極めて敏感に反応するだけでなく，雅（みや）びといったハイセンスな感覚や，スマートな生活スタイルを持ち合わせているからです。さらに彼ら「新人類」は，親の世代と大いに異なり，自分たちは世界市民であり，地球上のどこでもうまくやってゆけると信じています。

他方，十代の多くの若者たちは，丸暗記とテストで悪名の高い日本の詰め込み教育のもとで，極度の緊張を強いられています。しかも彼らの親たちの心には，この国の厳しい階級序列的なタテ社会の中で，自分たちの子供をできるだけ立派な学校に入学させ，よい会社に就職させたいという，過剰とも思われるほどの根強い願望があり，この親たちの期待に耐え切れず，落ちこぼれてゆく

peacefully with any people in any country on the earth.

On the other hand, a large number of teen-agers are straining under Japan's grinding educational system notorious for rote learning and test taking. Some drop out because of the intensive pressure from an excessively strong desire still rooted in their parents' mind to advance their children much higher up Japan's hierarchical ladder to better schools and jobs. A recent survey disclosed that the number of schoolphobic junior high students absent from school for more than 50 days in 1986 was 29,694; that is, 2.7 students per school. It also reported that there were 110 student suicides and 979 incidents of school violence.

However, the energy and flexibility of today's young people are leading them to begin to protest against the preceding generations' work-ethic and the pressure of the current educational system. They are rejecting the current tough situation positively by seeking a more diversified and judicious choice in the course of their careers and schooling. (ON)

Affluence   Japanese people have ambivalent feelings toward affluence. Few people feel that they are as rich as they are said to be. Statistically, Japan is economically ahead of the United States. Japan's per-capita GNP for 1987 was $19,200, while that of the United States was $18,200. But they find it very hard to believe that theirs is the richest country in the world. Put differently, their society has become affluent and

若者が生まれることになるのです。1986年の中学生調査によると，学校嫌いで年間50日以上の長期欠席者は29,694人にもなります。1校につき2.7人の割合です。自殺者は110人，校内暴力も979件にのぼっています。

　しかしながら，勤勉を是とする親たちのこうした厳格な価値観や，現行の教育制度の圧迫に対して，今日の若者たちは，その若いエネルギーと柔らかな感性とで，徐々に自らの活路を見出しつつあります。

　豊かさ　　日本人は豊かさについて相反する気持ちを抱いています。なるほど，1987年度の1人当り国民総生産を見ると，米国の18,200ドルに対し，日本は19,200ドルで，アメリカを抜いて世界一位になりました。しかし，実感として，自分たちが一番豊かであると感じる日本人はほとんどいないでしょう。換言すると，日本は豊かになったけれども，国民はその豊かさを享受するところまで行っていないのです。

　日本人は，昔に比べて，暮らし向きが良くなったと思ってい

the people are struggling to catch up with it.

The Japanese at large consider themselves better off than they used to be. This feeling seems to stem from the drastic changes in life style that have been under way during the last few years. People actually earn more money, nearly double the pay they got some ten years ago. They live and work surrounded with fantastic electric and electronic equipment both at their office and at home. All this leads them to feel that they are living in a more affluent, convenient society than before.

However, they are not at all satisfied with their present situation. In fact, they are having a hard time trying to keep their head above water in their daily life. A fairly large sum of money goes on housing loans, house rents, or room rents. This is particularly true of city dwellers. They also have to spend more money than before on daily necessities and comforts because the prices keep soaring.

A lot of middle-aged workers are anxious to buy a house or a condominium. They put aside part of their pay for that purpose. But the rate of the rise in the value of land far exceeds that of the wage increase. It seems as if they are crying for the moon.

Young people, particularly those who are still single, are enjoying modern living. They are more likely to use what they earn for expensive cars, videotape recorders, CD players and so on. You may sometimes see a young couple driving a large, luxurious car, while

6

す。これは一つには，ここ数年間の生活面での急激な変化に起因しているようです。給与は 10 年ほど前の 2 倍近くになりました。また，家庭の生活環境や仕事場の作業環境には，さまざまな電化製品や電子機器があふれています。こうした状況で生活しているため，暮らし向きが良くなったと思うのです。しかし，暮らし向きが実際に良くなったかは疑問の残るところです。

現状は決して満足できるものではありません。生活水準は上がり，生活は便利になったけれども，実際の生活ぶりにはかなり苦しいものがあります。たとえば，特に都市部に住んでいる人の場合，住宅ローンあるいは家賃，部屋代に相当の金額がかかります。また，生活必需品や生活便利品も，物価の値上がりで，ままになりません。何もかも家計を圧迫するものばかりです。

多くの中年労働者の夢は庭付き一戸建の家，あるいはマンションを持つことです。そのために月々の給料の一部を貯金しています。しかし，土地価格の上昇率のほうが給与の上昇率をはるかに上回っていて，現状ではまるで「ないものねだり」をしているかのようです。

そのような中年の既婚者とは対照的に，若者たちはモダンライフを満喫しています。高級車，ビデオ，CD などに，満足するまでお金をつぎ込んでいます。若いカップルが大きな高級車を乗り回し，その一方で家族連れが小さな車に肩を寄せ合うようにして乗っている光景は，何とも皮肉なものです。

豊かな社会の見返りに，日本人は深刻な社会問題に直面することになりました。中高年層の労働者の中には，急激なオフィスオートメーションに付いてゆけず，フラストレーションに陥っている人がいます。寿命が伸びて老齢者人口が増えた反面，彼らの拠り所とすべき大家族制が崩壊し，核家族化が進行して，弱い老人にとっては住みにくい世の中になってしまいました。とりわけ「ボケ老人」問題は深刻です。日本人は豊かな社会におけるこの

7

you see a family of four or five riding a small car.

Some serious social problems which seem like concomitants of an affluent society are confronting the Japanese. Office automation has begun to produce maladjustment among middle-aged and senior office workers. With the extension of a life span and the decline of the family, senile dementia is growing in incidence. Japanese people should be ready to, and, in fact, are beginning to, learn how to cope with these problems in an affluent society. (MAT)

Aging   Recently the number of elderly people in the world is growing at an unprecedented rate, and the speed of Japan's aging is the world's highest as the natural result of fewer births and fewer deaths. The proportion of those aged 65 and over in the total Japanese population was seven percent in 1960. It will take only 26 years for Japan to double its percentage of the aged from 7% to 14%, as compared with 66 years for the United States, 85 years for Sweden and 115 years for France.

Japan is now proud of its average life expectancy being the longest in the world, reaching 75.61 years for men and 81.39 years for women in 1987. Traditionally, the continuity of families is highly valued and respect for old age is reflected in numerous customs and institutions. A typical example is the seniority system in companies, though it has come to be replaced by the merit system in varying degrees.

ような問題に対処する方法を真剣に模索する必要に迫られ，その解決に向けて今歩み始めたところです。

　老　い　　このところ，世界的に老人の数が空前の速さで増えていますが，中でも日本の高齢化は，出生数と死亡者数の減少にともない，世界一の速さで進んでいます。65歳以上の高齢者が全人口に占める割合は，日本では1960年には7％でした。その割合が倍増するのに，アメリカが66年，スウェーデンが85年，フランスが115年かかるのに対し，日本はわずか26年ということとです。

　日本人の平均寿命は1987年現在，男75.61歳，女81.39歳に達し，世界一の長寿国です。伝統的に，家の継続が重んじられ，高齢が尊ばれていますが，それはいろいろな慣行や制度に反映しています。典型的な例は，企業における年功序列制です。もっとも，部分的に能力主義がこれにとって代わるようになってきました。

　長寿は確かに慶賀すべきことですが，一方では急速な高齢化のために個人も政府も共に取り組まなければならない深刻な問題が生じています。1人の老人を支える生産年齢人口は現在7人ですが，2000年には4人になり，2020年には2.5人に減ると推計されています。経済大国にはなりましたが，日本人の大多数は自分

Longevity is indeed a matter for congratulation. However, rapid aging is posing serious problems with which both the individual and the government have to cope. It is estimated that the number of workers supporting one aged person will decrease from the present 7 to 4 in the year 2000 and to 2.5 in 2020. Despite their economic success, a majority of Japanese are worried about health and financial prospects for their old age. They feel the government should take urgent steps toward more employment opportunities for healthy old people, care for people confined to bed or suffering from senile dementia, a sufficient old-age pension, and support for families tending elderly patients at home. At any rate, the whole nation will have to shoulder an increasing welfare burden in the future. (MT)

Ainu   The origin of the present-day Ainu is still difficult to determine with certainty. Their language, for example, is unrelated to any other known language of the world. However, archeological and anthropological evidence indicates that they were the aboriginal settlers of the northeastern part of the Japanese islands. Their presence there was recorded as early as the seventh century by Japanese court historians. Their highest estimated population was 25,000 in the early nineteenth century.

In the late nineteenth century, partly threatened by the Russians who were escalating their activities in the south, the Japanese Government began intensive maneu-

の老後の健康や経済的見通しについて不安に思っています。そして，政府に対して，健康な老人の雇用の拡大，寝たきり老人やボケ老人の養護，老齢年金の充実，老人介護家庭への援助など早急に対策をたてるように求めています。とにかく，国民全体が，将来，いっそうの福祉の負担をになわなければならないでしょう。

　　アイヌ　　アイヌ民族のルーツは依然として謎につつまれています。たとえば，アイヌ語は世界の他の言語と，どのようにつながっているのかがはっきりしません。しかし，考古学や民族学の研究により，アイヌ民族が日本列島北東部の先住民族であることはあきらかです。その存在はすでに7世紀に，大和朝廷の歴史家によって記録されています。人口は19世紀前半がピークで，2万5千人と推定されています。

　日本政府はロシアの南下政策に脅威を感じたこともあって，19世紀の後半に北海道の開拓と入植に力を注ぎました。アイヌ民族は狩猟と漁業を中心とした経済を営み，統一組織が弱かったため，日本人の侵入に十分な抵抗力を発揮することができませんでした。

　日本政府は北海道開拓に続いて対アイヌ政策を立案し，アイヌ民族を日本社会に同化させることを基本方針としました。そして，

vers to explore and colonize the northern part of Japan. Due to the loose-knit nature of their traditional social structure, common to their hunting and fishing economy, the Ainu could not put up successful resistance to the invading Japanese.

Soon, assimilation of the Ainu into the formal structure of Japanese society became a principal object of national policy. In mapping out the strategy, the Japanese Government sought the assistance of other countries which had similar experiences with minority groups. Thus, the United States sent consultants to explain their experiences with the American Indians. In the end, the Japanese Government rejected the reservation policy, choosing instead the complete detribalization and assimilation under the principle of civil equality.

What actually happened, however, is the history of Ainu subjugation to a colonial power. The experience of the Ainu was exactly the same as that of any people overwhelmed by a technically advanced and territorially expanding power. In spite of *de jure* equality as Japanese citizens, most of the Ainu are still suffering from poverty, lack of education, and various forms of social injustice such as job discrimination.

The current upsurge of their ethnic assertiveness is an indication that the Ainu wish to reestablish the Ainu world by restoring and maintaining their language and culture. Their restoration and maintenance programs are now at an incipient stage. The Japanese general public apparently is beginning to acknowledge that the Ainu

この政策を実行するにあたって、同じような少数民族問題の経験をもつ外国の援助をあおいだりもしました。アメリカはこれを受けて、アメリカインディアン政策の専門家を派遣してきました。政府は検討のすえ、アメリカのような居留地政策をとりませんでした。そのかわりに、平等の公民権を原則として、アイヌ人をアイヌ人としてではなく、日本人としてあつかう完全な同化政策を進めることにしたのです。

しかし、その後のできごとは、アイヌ民族の入植勢力に対する服従の歴史といえましょう。彼らの歩んだ道は、高度の先進技術をもち領土を拡張しようとする勢力を目前に、服従を余儀なくされた民族の歴史であります。法律上は日本人として平等の権利をもつとはいえ、多くのアイヌ人は、現在も、貧困に苦しんでいます。教育も十分ではありません。また、就職のさいにみられるように、社会生活のさまざまな分野で、不当な差別を受けています。

彼らは最近、民族の意思を強く表明しています。それは民族の言語と文化を回復し、あるいは維持することによって、アイヌの世界を再現しようという声に聞こえます。その具体的な形態はまだはっきりしていません。多くの日本人は、日本社会の全体的な枠の中であるかぎり、アイヌ人がアイヌ人であることを主張する権利を当然のことと考えているようです。日本人が日本社会で民族と文化の違いをどの程度認めるつもりなのかは、アイヌ人の計画がはっきりとした形で示されるときに、テストされることになるでしょう。

have a right to be Ainu, although within the framework of overall Japanese society. How far Japanese are willing to accept ethnic and cultural differences in their society will be really tested when actual programs are proposed. (NH)

Ancestor worship   There are various religions in Japan—Shinto, Buddhism, Christianity, Confucianism and many others. Ancestor worship can also be regarded as a religion, in which ancestors are objects of profound veneration and are believed to have a supernatural power over the living. Buddhism, a dominant religion in Japan, has taken a firm hold on the people mainly in the form of ancestor worship.

To most Japanese no religion is exclusive. It is quite common that the same person, without any feeling of conflict, holds or attends rituals of different religions. For example, a Japanese might visit a Shinto shrine for the New Year's prayer, have a wedding in a Christian church, and organize a funeral according to Buddhist rites. Weddings, funerals and a variety of festivals such as *O-bon* (Buddhist Festival of the Dead)—all these observances provide an opportunity for the relatives to gather, thus strengthening their sense of unity and emotional ties with their ancestors.

The spirits of the dead relatives are believed to give moral guidance and protection to the living, who pray to them for spiritual support when faced with difficulties. Families try not to bring disgrace on their

14

祖先崇拝　　日本には，神道，仏教，キリスト教，儒教などさまざまな宗教があります。祖先崇拝も一種の宗教とみなすことができます。祖先は深い崇拝の対象となり，生きている者に影響を及ぼす超自然的な力を持つと信じられています。日本の主要な宗教である仏教も，主に祖先崇拝の形で人々の心に定着しました。

　たいていの日本人にとって，宗教は排他的なものではありません。同じ1人が何の矛盾を感じることもなく，いろいろ違った宗教の儀式を行うことはごく普通です。例えば，初詣に神社へ行き，結婚式をキリスト教の教会であげ，葬儀は仏式ですることもあります。結婚式や葬式，またお盆などの祭事は，親戚一同が集まるよい機会になります。これによってお互いの一体感と祖先との精神的絆が強まります。

　祖先の霊は生きている者が道を踏み外さないように導き，守ってくれます。困難に直面した時，人々は祖先に対し精神的な支えになってくれるよう祈り，祖先に恥をかかせることがないように努めます。もし一家の中に悪事を働くような者が出ると，家族の者はまず「ご先祖様にお詫びのしようがない」と言うでしょう。

　祖先の墓にお参りに行くだけでなく，多くの家庭には仏壇が置かれ，亡き縁者を拝みます。これは祖先崇拝の具体的な表現であり，生きている者に祖先の恩を忘れないようにさせるものです。日本では，第2次大戦後古い家族制度が廃止され，核家族が増加し，一般に信仰心が薄れました。そのため祖先と子孫との親密な関係は，以前よりは弱くなりましたが，基本的には今も変わって

ancestry. If anyone in a family should be involved in wrongdoing, it is most likely that the rest of the family will first say, "We don't know how to apologize to our ancestors."

Many families pay respect to deceased relatives not only at the graveyard but at a Buddhist altar placed in the home. This is a concrete expression of ancestor worship and a reminder of a debt of gratitude on the part of the living. Such close ancestry-posterity relationships still remain basically unchanged in Japan, though weakened by the postwar abolition of the old family system, a steady increase of nuclear families and the general decline in religious faith. (MT)

Appreciation of seasonal changes *Me ni wa aoba, yama hototogisu, hatsu-gatsuo* (Fresh green for the eye, a cuckoo's singing for the ear, and the first bonitos for the mouth). Almost all Japanese are familiar with this *haiku* composed by Yamaguchi Sodō (1642-1716), a poet contemporary with Bashō. This is mainly because they can share the poet's appreciation and joy of the coming of early summer. Fresh green, a cuckoo's singing, and the first bonitos are all employed for this seasonal reference. In fact, the people of the Edo period (1603-1867) usually sensed the coming of early summer by tasting bonitos which come in this season every year on the warm ocean current along Japan's islands and are first caught off Kamakura and Odawara. Minimally required for *haiku*-making is thus

いません。

　季節感　「目には青葉　山ほととぎす　初鰹」　芭蕉と同時代の詩人山口素堂（1642～1716）のこの一句は，日本人の間であまりにも有名です。青葉，ほととぎす，初鰹，これらすべてが季語として用いられ，初夏の訪れを喜ぶ詩人の心が共感できるからでしょう。事実，江戸時代（1603～1867）の人々は，この時期黒潮に乗って日本列島に回遊し，鎌倉や小田原の沖合いで初めて獲れる鰹に舌鼓を打ちながら，初夏の訪れをしみじみと感じたのです。俳句を作るには，季語を少なくとも1つは入れることが最小限必要なのですが，俳句の心とは，まさに季節の移り変わりによって喚起される微妙な感覚を，このように言葉の上に結晶させることなのです。
　料理も同様で，日本は海の幸，山の幸に恵まれているために，人々は初物や旬の物を好み，その風味や色合いを大事にしてきました。生魚を醤油につけて食べるだけの刺身はその典型です。視覚に訴える盛りつけもまた大切です。季節感をそそるように，夏

the inclusion of at least one *kigo*, a seasonal word or expression related to or reminiscent of each of the four seasons. Hence the verbal crystallization of subtle sensations evoked by seasonal changes is the soul of *haiku*.

The same is also the case with Japanese cooking. Since Japan is blessed with an abundance of seafood, vegetables, rice, and many other natural foodstuffs, people have highly valued the first products of the season and tried to preserve their original flavors and colors. The consumption of raw fish (*sashimi*) with only a dip of soy sauce (*shōyu*) is a beautiful example. Equally important is the visual effect of serving food and receptacles have to be carefully chosen—glass or bamboo-made dishes for summer and thick earthenware for winter. The food is all beautifully arranged on these receptacles so as to arouse the diner's sense of the season. All this is nothing other than the Japanese appreciation of the blessings of nature.

The openness of Japanese-style wooden houses with tile roofs and sliding-door partitions like *shōji* and *fusuma* suited to Japan's hot and humid summer is another example of the Japanese wisdom of coexisting with the severity of the climate. The light passing through *shōji* is softened and tender to the eye. For this reason, even today more and more reinforced concrete condominiums tend to incorporate into them those typical Japanese-style rooms with *shōji*, *tatami* (straw mats), and *tokonoma* (alcoves).

は涼しげなガラスや竹の器に，冬は厚手の焼物の器に，実にきれいに盛りつけされます。これこそ日本人の自然の恵みに対する感謝と喜びの表現なのです。

　日本の蒸し暑い夏に見合った，障子や襖で部屋を仕切り，屋根には瓦をのせた開放的な日本の木造家屋も，厳しい気候の中で自然と共に生きようとする日本人の知恵です。障子越しの光は目にやさしく，しだいに数を増してきた鉄筋コンクリートのマンションにすら，障子や畳や床の間のあるこうした和室がとり入れられています。

　日本人の季節に対する感受性といった面で，もっと注目されてよいのは，「歳時記」です。これは美しい写真や挿絵入りの季語集で，日本の伝統の年中行事や，動植物，自然現象などの百般について解説したものです。季語はすべて四季順に配列され，俳句による例証があります。従って，「歳時記」は，日本の自然や文学に関心を寄せる人にとっては必須の本なのです。

With regard to the Japanese sensitivity to the season, a much greater attention should be paid to *Saijiki*. It is a beautifully illustrated glossary of words with seasonal connotations regarding Japan's traditions, annual events, animals, plants, natural phenomena, and so on. All the words and phrases are exemplified by sample *haiku* poems and arranged according to these well-defined four seasons. Therefore, *Saijiki* is regarded as one of the "must" books for people interested in Japan's nature and literature. (ON)

Artisan spirit   Even today there are many sayings describing artisan (*shokunin*) spirit, although artisans themselves have been declining in type and number since the Meiji Restoration in 1868 with the rapid development of mechanized factory production. Examples of such sayings include the following: for the potter, "3 years for compounding potter's clay; another 10 years for potter's wheel"; for the cook, "10 years for learning how to use kitchen knives; another 10 years for the acquisition of seasoning"; for the Japanese-style confectioner, "3 years for building fire in the kitchen oven, another 10 years for making bean jam"; and for the sculptor of Buddhist images, "3 low bows before a stroke of the chisel."

Consequently, artisans are now regarded not only as experts who have obtained something true in life through their own careers but also as an incarnation of honesty, stubbornness, bluntness, and human warmth.

職人気質　　1868 年の明治維新以来，急激な機械化による工場生産のお蔭で，いわゆる「職人」とよばれる人たちの数も種類も減ってきていますが，それでも今日なお，これら職人の気質を物語る，数多くの諺が残されています。例えば，陶工には「土もみ 3 年，ろくろ 10 年」，板前には「庖丁 10 年，塩味 10 年」，和菓子作りには「火床 3 年，あん炊き 10 年」，また仏師には「一刀三礼」といった類です。

　従って今では，こうした職人たちはその専門職を通して，何か人生の蘊奥を極めた熟達者だと一般にみなされ，さらに，正直，一徹，ぶっきら棒，温かい人間味などの代名詞とさえなっています。こうした職人気質は，昔も今も，伝統的な厳しい徒弟制度によって培われるものです。この徒弟制は，江戸時代（1603 〜 1867）の株仲間の成立と前後して確立された制度で，当時の丁稚奉公制とも極めてよく似ているものです。

　例えば，大工職人の場合，12 〜 13 歳になると，奉公に先立ってまず親方のもとに連れてゆかれました。この親方との初顔合わせを目見得とよびますが，その場で親方と食事を共にすると，それで年季奉公の約束が整ったことになり，支度金として，その両

These characteristics were and still are cultivated and developed through the tough traditional apprentice (*totei*) system, which became firmly established with the formation of merchant guilds (*kabunakama*) in the Edo period (1603-1867). This was quite similar to that of merchant-training system of that time.

As to carpenter-training, for example, a 12- or 13-year-old boy would be first taken to his master (*oyakata*) as a formal visit (*memie*) before being apprenticed. If he was allowed to dine with his master, that meant a promise of apprenticeship being arranged, with advance money (*tetsuke*) paid to his parents for his preparation. The term of service was usually 7 to 10 years. And during this period he was never allowed to return to his parents except for the New Year and mid-summer holidays, called *yabuiri*, even if he happened to be in the neighborhood of his home on an errand. He worked under his master's supervision with no financial compensation, living together with his master's family.

When his term of service was over, he was given a set of tools by his master, but he had to work for another year to show his gratitude to the master. After that he became independent and could set up his own shop. Hardship of the training is expressed by such a saying as "Sweep out tears under the eaves, and swallows will be your friends." Some of these skilled carpenters, handicraftsmen, and performers like *kabuki* actors have been designated as Living National Treasures

親に手付けが支払われます。年季は普通7年から10年で、この間、藪入りとよばれる正月とお盆の休み以外は、たとえ自分の家の前を使いで通っても、立寄ることさえ許されませんでした。こうして奉公人は親方のもとで生活し、その監督を受けて無給で働いたのです。

　年季が終わると、親方は道具一式をその奉公人に与えますが、さらに1年の礼奉公（恩返し奉公）が待っていました。この礼奉公が終わって初めて一人前の職人として認められ、自分の店を持って自立できたのです。この大工職人の苦しい修業は、「大工と燕は軒で泣け」という諺によく表されています。

　1950年以来、日本の伝統工芸の技術を保存継承するために、政府は人間国宝を指定し、建築、手工芸、歌舞伎などの分野で、こうした優れた職人芸の名人たちが顕彰されています。

(*ningen kokuhō*) by the government since 1950 for the preservation and transmission of valuable cultural skills necessary for Japan's traditional arts. (ON)

Bodily contact and eye contact   Japanese are used to small personal space in public transportation, offices, and homes. But they normally are not inclined to intensive tactile and visual contact.

Most people still prefer bowing to handshaking. Actually bowing is considered more polite and formal than handshaking. Although some people shake hands with casual friends, they do so in their traditional cultural contexts. While they shake hands, they may bow and even salute with the other hand at the same time.

In business interaction, many Japanese shake hands with Americans in an effort to accommodate themselves to the Western greeting manner. Yet they do not grip as firmly as Americans are expected to do. They may also give a "finger shake" or a "dead fish."

Of course, by doing so, Japanese do not intend to signal a message, as Americans might, that they are not interested in the relationship. It is simply that Japanese have adopted this greeting ritual in accordance with their traditional norm of body contact behavior.

When Japanese talk face to face, they do not exchange eye-to-eye contacts. They tend to glance at each other somewhere from under the eyes to around the mouth tenderly or vaguely. Although direct eye contact may occur occasionally, it never is intense and prolong-

24

身体接触と視線　乗り物，職場，家庭などで，日本人は狭い個人空間になれています。しかし，身体を触り合ったり，目を見つめ合うことはあまりしません。

　たとえば，人々は握手をするよりも，おじぎをするほうを好みます。握手よりも，おじぎのほうが礼儀にかなった，正式の作法とされています。気さくなあいだがらでは握手をすることもありますが，その場合には，日本式のやり方になります。おたがいに一方の手を握りながら，おじぎをしたり，別の手で敬礼したりするのです。

　ビジネスの世界などでは，日本人はアメリカ人と握手をしますが，これはアメリカ人のマナーに合わせているのです。しかし，日本人の握り方はアメリカ人のよりも弱く，ときには手の平を開かずに指先を差し出したり，力の抜けた手を差し出し相手が握っても握り返さないこともあります。アメリカ人ならこれを関係の拒絶ととるかもしれませんが，日本人にはもちろんそのような意図はありません。日本人は握手の習慣を，日本人の身体接触の方法に合わせて採用しているにすぎません。

　日本人は向かい合って話すときに，目と目を見つめ合うことはあまりしません。日本人は目もとから口のあたりを，柔らかくぼんやりと見ます。目と目を合わせることがあっても，弱い視線で，しかも一瞬のことです。相手の目を強くじっと見つめることは，礼儀に反しますし，攻撃的で挑戦的な行為となります。このことは，討論，相談，説得，交渉の場面であっても，あてはまります。

　アメリカ人は日本人のこのような視線に当惑を感じるようです。正直さと誠実さに欠けると解釈することもあります。ぎゃくに，

ed. Intensified and protracted eye contact is considered rude and impolite or aggressive and challenging even in discussion, consultation, persuation, or negotiation.

Americans find Japanese gaze behavior embarrassing and discouraging. They may interpret it as dishonest or insincere. On the other hand, Japanese feel uneasy about the way Americans stare. To them, it is too offensive and intimidating. Japanese feel defeated, because they cannot endure it or deal with "an eye for an eye." (NH)

Bushidō as reflected in business   Formulated in the 17th century with some Confucian ideas as its philosophical foundation, *bushidō* or the feudal-military Japanese code of behavior puts special emphasis on a *samurai*'s (warrior's) loyalty to his lord. It maintained among other things that a *samurai* must serve his lord and his country at the risk of his life. As a famous book of quotations from an advocate of *bushidō* puts it, "The business of *samurai* is to die." *Bushidō* as behavioral aesthetics and as practical morality flourished among military men until the end of World War Ⅱ.

People today are well aware of the past tragedies brought by fanatic believers in *bushidō*, but the spirit it fostered somehow survives in the business world to the present day. A company adopting a life-employment system is often compared to a feudal clan. For loyalty to business organizations and total involvement in work are highly valued, and the *bushidō* principles of resolu-

日本人はアメリカ人に見つめられると，不安になります。あまりにも強く，攻撃的ですらあるからです。それに耐えられなかったり，同じように見返すことができないと，敗北感を味わってしまいます。

仕事と武士道精神　　武士道は 17 世紀に儒教的理念を基礎に形成された封建武士の行動規範ですが，特に主君に対する臣下の武士の忠義を強調していました。とりわけ，主君と郷土に仕えるために，武士は生命の危険も冒さなければならないとされました。武士道の唱道者の有名な聞き書き（『葉隠聞書』）によれば，「武士道というは死ぬことと見つけたり」ということになります。行動美学としての，また実践道徳としての武士道は，第 2 次大戦の終わりまで軍人のあいだで，もてはやされました。

武士道の狂信的信奉者がもたらした過去の悲劇についてはだれもがよく認識していますが，武士道精神は今でもビジネスの世界にどうやら生き残っています。終身雇用制度の会社はよく封建時代の藩に比べられます。企業組織に対する忠誠や仕事一筋の態度は高く評価されています。また，決意，勇気，知恵といった武士道の理念が，社員の士気を高めるために引き合いに出されます。多くの会社員が，意識的，無意識的にこうした考えを受け入れ，義務を果たすために相当な努力をし，自発的に残業をします。仕事のために私生活を犠牲にすることも厭わず，遠隔地に転勤になれば家族と離れて働くこともします。昔の武士と同じように，面

tion, courage, and wisdom are referred to in boosting employee morale. Many businessmen, consciously or unconsciously accepting these ideas, make strenuous efforts to fulfill their duty and work overtime on their own accord. Always ready to sacrifice their private life for business, they are willing to work apart from their family when transferred to a post in a distant place. They worry about losing face just as ancient warriors did, try their best to save their reputation, and rarely show weakness in a moment of crisis.

Figurative use of the *bushidō* language is not uncommon among the average businessmen. To cite a few examples: "to commit *harakiri*" (literally "to commit suicide", but in this context it means to bear the whole responsibility for any loss the company may sustain); "to show a *samurai*'s mercy" (to overlook someone's error); "A *samurai*'s word is as good as a bond" (A sincere businessman would never break his word; hence the attachment of importance to a verbal agreement in business transactions). (TS)

Business management Even in modern firms there are still some features of traditional business management as represented by such sayings as *Noren ni kizu ga tsuku* (The company's reputation will suffer) or *Soroban ga awa-nai* (It doesn't pay). These suggest how persistently what is symbolized by *noren* (split curtains hung in the entryway to shops) and *soroban* (abacuses) is entrenched and still alive in everyday life. The for-

目を失うことを恐れ，自分の評判を保つためには最善を尽くし，危機に陥ってもめったに弱味を見せません。

　武士道に関係する言葉も，会社員の間で比喩的によく使われています。いくつか例をあげましょう。「腹を切る」（会社に迷惑が及べば，その全責任を負う），「武士の情け」（だれかの過ちを大目に見る），「武士に二言はない」（真面目なビジネスマンは約束を破らない。商取引で口約束が重要なのはここからきています），などです。

　商　い　　近代的な会社でも，今なお「ノレンに傷がつく」とか「ソロバンが合わない」といった言い方をするように，伝統的商取引きの名残りがみられます。このことは，ノレンやソロバンの象徴する慣習が，どれほど深く日常生活の中に根づいて今もなお生きているかを物語っています。ノレンは信用，名声といった商人の顔を，ソロバンは計算高い商人の抜け目のなさを指しているのです。

　昔は丁稚奉公の制度があって，10歳にもなると主人のところ

mer refers to a merchant's face, i.e. trust and reputation, and the latter to a merchant's soul and shrewdness, i.e. calculation.

In the first place, there used to be the apprentice (*decchi*) system. An apprentice was usually indentured to his master at about the age of 10, and acquired not only his trade but also manners and customs by living together with his master's family and doing their household chores everyday, wearing an apron dyed with the shop's insignia. When his term of service, nearly 20 years, was over, he was promoted to the position of a senior clerk (*bantō*) and in some cases allowed to open his own shop where he could use his master's *noren*. Some features of company management in Japan today, such as seniority-based wages and lifetime employment—though now gradually declining—along with workers' loyalty to their companies, strong group mentality, and seemingly vague delineation of responsibility, may well be said to have all stemmed from this apprentice system.

In the second place, the adoption of an heir from outside the family used to be common. And the master did not hesitate to adopt an able heir if he judged his legitimate son to be unfit as a successor to his business or if he had no heir. He would place a greater emphasis upon the proper transmission of his business to the next generation and the social responsibility of his commercial activities than upon genealogical succession. He would highly value the commercial ethic, espe-

に丁稚入りをしました。丁稚は主人一家と起居を共にし，屋号を染め抜いた前垂れをして，毎日家事万端を手伝いながら商売だけでなく，行儀作法や商習慣を身につけたのです。そして，約20年に及ぶ年季奉公ののち，番頭に昇格しました。主人からノレン分けをしてもらって，自分の店を持って自立する場合もありました。今も残る年功序列型の給与体系や終身雇用制は，徐々に少なくなってはいるものの，皆この丁稚奉公制に由来していると言っても言い過ぎではありません。会社員の自社への忠誠心や根強い集団意識，また一見不明確な責任体制のあり方なども同様です。

　また，よく跡取りという制度も利用されました。たとえ実子であっても，家業を継ぐに不適格であるとみなされたり，また家督相続者のない場合は，主人は積極的に外部から有能な血を入れました。世襲以上に，能力のある者に家業を継がせることを重んじたからです。こうして，商家の主人は自らの経験や，心学の祖，石田梅巌（1685〜1744）の実践的で倫理的な教えに基づいて，商業道徳，中でも倹約と信用を旨とし，後継者にもこの商業道徳を守って生きてゆくことを求めたのです。

cially thrift and trust, which was based both on his own experience and on the pragmatic ethical teachings by Ishida Baigan (1685-1744). He would also expect his successor to live up to this ethical system. (ON)

Centralization of power It may not be an exaggeration to say that Tokyo has everything—facilities, information, and opportunities. Every major campany wants to have an office in Tokyo. Almost all the head offices of large companies are actually located in Tokyo. It may be a status symbol for a company to have its head office in Tokyo. Likewise, all the government ministries and agencies center in Tokyo.

Historically speaking, modern centralization of power began after the Meiji Restoration, which took place in 1868. Before then, centralization had never been complete in Japan. During the feudal age which preceded the Meiji Era, feudal lords had enjoyed autonomy to a certain extent, and the Tokugawas had to keep an ear to the ground, since ambitious lords were always jockeying for power.

Since the end of World War Ⅱ, Japan's administrative system has been shifting from centralization of power to decentralization of power as a result of the establishment of the Local Government Act. For example, the governor used to be an appointive office, whereas it is now an elective one. Mail service used to be a monopoly of the Ministry of Posts and Telecommunications, whereas today door-to-door service companies abound and

中央集権　東京にはすべてが揃っていると言っても過言ではありません。そこにはさまざまな施設，情報，機会があります。会社が大きくなれば，東京に社屋を持ちたくなります。大会社と呼ばれるもののほとんどは，現に東京に本社があります。同様に官庁のすべてが東京に集中しています。

　歴史的には，日本の近代的中央集権は，1868 年の明治維新以降に始まりました。それ以前の日本は完全な中央集権国家と言えるものではありませんでした。封建時代には，封建君主がある程度独立した自治権を持っており，野心的な大名は絶えず政権奪取を画策していました。そのため，徳川幕府は謀反の動きに目を光らせ，参謹交代などの義務を押し付けたりしたのでした。

　明治時代の中央集権化も第二次大戦で終わりを告げ，戦後は地方自治法の制定を機に，行政制度は中央集権から地方分権へと移っていきます。任命職であった知事は，公選職に変わりました。郵便業務は郵政省が独占していましたが，今では郵便小包は宅配便にすっかり押された格好になっています。こうして風潮としては，地方分権化が広まっているものの，地方自治体の受け持つ事務とそれを行う上で不可欠の権限の再配分の問題，そして，「三割自治」に象徴される財源の再配分の問題など，今後に待たねばならない問題もたくさんあります。

are prospering. But as things stand, local governments are still inescapably tied to, or dependent on, the central government for administration and finance. (MAT)

Child-rearing   Child-rearing is closely associated with the nature of the home. It is customary in Japan for the father to work outside of the home and for the mother to devote herself to household chores. The mother-child relationship is characterized by emotional as well as physical closeness. The mother is supposed to be available to her family 24 hours a day, especially while the child is young. The mother and the infant often sleep in the same *futon* (or bedding) and bathe together. She carries her baby on her back while shopping or attending to the household chores. Her constant attention results in her child being relatively docile and well-behaved. Even in later years, the mother-child relationship continues to be the closest within the family, and some mothers even address their grown-up sons as *boku*, which is a first-person pronoun used by men. As for the father, who is away to work most of the time, he is supposed to represent a model of proper behavior and he commands or punishes the child when necessary.

This traditional outlook on child-rearing is changing due to the shrinking family size, the increasing number of mothers with jobs, and the higher divorce rate, among other reasons. Fewer children and more nuclear families deprive prospective parents of the opportunity

子育て　　子育ては家庭の特徴と密接に関係しています。日本では伝統的に，父親は外で働き，母親は家事に専念することになっています。母親と子供は，物理的にも，気持ちの上でも密接な関係にあって，ことに子供が幼いうちは，母親は四六時中家族のために尽くすものとされています。母親は子供と1枚の布団に眠り，一緒に風呂に入り，背におぶって家事や買物をすることがよくあります。このように常に注意深く育てられると，割合おとなしくて行儀の良い子に育ちます。子供が大きくなってからも，家庭において母親と子供は一番近い関係にあり，母親の中には，大きな息子に"ボク"と呼びかける者もいます。"ボク"は，男性が使う1人称の代名詞です。仕事で留守がちな父親に期待されるのは，子供の行儀の手本になったり，必要に応じて子供に命令したり，罰したりすることです。

　このような従来の育児観にも変化が見られます。家族の人数の減少，働く母親の増加，離婚率の上昇などが，変化の理由です。子供の数が減少し，核家族が増加すると，親になる前の育児体験の機会が少なくなります。1987年度版の『国民生活白書』（経済企画庁編）によりますと，1982年に，家庭での幼児のしつけと教育に自信のある者が17%，自信のない者が51%となっています。また，1986年の総理府調査によりますと，「子供のしつけは妻の義務」とする回答者が49.2%，「夫婦両方の義務」とする者が42.6%となっています。家庭の特徴の変化に応じた，新しい育児法が必要になっています。

to learn how to nurture their children. According to the 1987 White Paper on People's Livelihood released by the Economic Planning Agency, in 1982 17% of the respondents thought that the current way of disciplining and educating young children at home was satisfactory, and 51% thought it unsatisfactory. A 1986 survey by the Prime Minister's Office, furthermore, reports that 49.2% of the respondents thought child-discipline was the wife's duty, and 42.6% the duty of husband and wife together. (MO)

Children's social environment   Japanese children start first grade at the age of 6. Compulsory education consists of six years of primary school and three years of junior high, but almost all graduates continue their studies for the three years of high school. They have classes six days a week for forty weeks a year. During the summer break, they also have to do their homework. In addition to regular school, some students attend "cram" schools (called *juku*) after school, on weekdays and weekends or even during school holidays. There they review schoolwork or get extra preparation for the entrance examinations to upper schools.

Since Japanese children have relatively little time at home and since many Japanese fathers work till late in the evening, the children's home life often centers around the mother. The children can usually find little time to play outside with their friends. The most popular games among school children today, especially

子供をとりまく環境　　　日本では6歳になると小学校に入学します。義務教育は，小学校6年，中学校3年ですが，ほとんど全ての生徒が高校へ進学し，3年間勉強します。1週間に6日，年間40週授業があります。夏休みでさえ，宿題が出されます。学校の勉強に加えて，放課後や日曜日や夏休み，冬休み，春休みの時でさえ，塾に通う生徒もいます。塾では，学校の勉強の復習をしたり，入学試験の受験勉強をしたりします。

　日本の子供たちは家庭で過ごす時間が比較的短く，また多くの父親は夜遅くまで働いているので，家庭では母親中心に生活することになります。友達と外で遊ぶ時間がほとんどない子供もいるほどです。学齢期の子供たちの間で最も人気のある遊びはコンピューター・ゲームです。

　日本の親たちは自分の子供たちの教育に対してとても熱心です。「子供のために」自分たちの生活を犠牲にすることも厭いません。例えば，父親が遠くに転勤になり，そこによい学校がない場合には，子供をよい学校へやるために別居生活をする親もいます。こういう理由で単身赴任をしている家庭が日本にはたくさんあるのです。

among boys, are computer games.

Japanese parents are very keen about their children's education. They are willing to sacrifice their lives "for the good of the children." For example, if the father is transferred to a distant office where no desirable school is available, he may live alone away from his home to keep the child in a good school. There are many temporary single-parent families in Japan for this reason.

Bullying is one of the more serious types of problems in the children's social environment at school. Schools are having difficulties with students who tease and bully others. These students are usually so upset or frustrated by their scholastic, social, or family circumstances that they tend to resolve their anxiety, fear, and uneasiness by bullying. Their targets are weaker and smaller students, or those who are different in some way, often including those who have just returned from abroad. (MH)

Clothing　For the Japanese, clothing is worn not so much to express their individuality as to identify themselves with a group to which they belong, whether it is a school, a company or a community. In other words, the Japanese avoid being singled out by dressing like others in the same group. Furthermore, looking neat and appropriate is important since one's group is likely to be judged by the members' appearance.

Different groups have different dress codes which are more often than not unwritten but socially understood.

子供をとりまく環境，とりわけ学校において重大な問題となっ
ていることの1つにいじめがあります。他の生徒をからかったり
いじめたりする生徒に頭を悩ませている学校があります。いじめ
をする生徒は，学校の成績，友達づきあい，家庭環境などに悩ん
でいたり不満をもっていたりすることが多く，そういう不安や不
満などをいじめによって発散しようとします。いじめられるのは，
弱い生徒や小柄な生徒であったり，またどこか他の子供とは違っ
ている生徒だったりします。そのため，海外帰国子女がいじめら
れることも多いそうです。

　衣　服　　日本人にとって，衣服は，自己表現のためというよ
り，むしろ学校・会社・コミュニティーといった所属団体との連
帯性を明確にするためのものです。ですから，日本人は，グルー
プのみんなと同じ恰好をすることで，1人だけ目立つことがない
ように気を配ります。それに，仲間1人の外見でグループ全体が
判断されることがよくあるので，きちんとした身なりをすること
が大切になります。
　グループには，それぞれ服装に関するきまりといったものがあ
ります。通常，明文化されたものではなく，こういうものだと世
間で考えられているものです。例えば，日本のビジネスマンの多

Most Japanese businessmen, for instance, dress conservatively in both style and color. Solid business suits in subdued blue or gray are generally considered to be proper for businessmen. Older people, men and women alike, are expected to wear plain clothes and they refrain from harsh or bright colors usually worn by children and young women.

Nothing illustrates more clearly the importance of group affiliation than uniforms. In Japan, not only military personnel, policemen, and mail carriers but also clerks, taxi drivers, and students wear uniforms. Dressed in the same uniform, no one stands out, and a feeling of belongingness develops among those wearing the uniform of the same company. In fact, Japanese people take pride in their uniforms especially if they work for first-rate companies or study at outstanding schools. Most Japanese do not like to express themselves by way of clothing at the risk of being excluded from their groups, and they are ready to suppress their individual uniqueness under uniforms. (YN)

Colleague relation One's human relations within his/her business company are considered no less important than his/her kinship and neighborly relations. In fact, the former is often assimilated to the latter in most Japanese companies, where family-like harmony is more highly valued than open competition among workers. Colleagues are, therefore, regarded basically as teammates who are to cooperate with one another in

くは，スタイルや色などの控え目なものを身につけます。一般的に，無地で落ちついたブルーやグレー系統のスーツがビジネスマンにはふさわしいとされています。男女を問わず，年輩者は，若い女性や子供のためとされている派手な色や明るい色を避け，地味な服装をするものと期待されます。

　ユニフォームほどグループとの連帯をはっきり示すものはありません。日本では，軍人・警察・郵便配達人ばかりでなく，店員・タクシーの運転手・学生などもユニフォームを着用します。同じユニフォームであれば，1人だけ目立つこともないし，それを着ることでグループとの一体感が生まれます。実際，日本人はユニフォームに誇りを感じています。一流会社に勤めていたり，一流校に通っていたりすればなおさらです。多くの日本人にとって，個性とは，仲間はずれにされる危険を冒してまで表現しなければならないものではないのです。むしろ必要とあれば，進んでユニフォームの下に個性を隠します。

　同僚関係　　会社での人間関係は肉親関係や近隣関係に劣らず重要なものとされています。実際，日本の会社では会社員の間での競争よりも家族的な調和が大切とされますから，人間関係も肉親関係のようにとらえられます。したがって，同僚はより高い給料と地位をめぐっての競争相手ではなく，会社の利益のために互いに協力し合うチームメイトであるとみなされます。たいていは，互いに仕事を手伝ったり，会社が終わってから一緒に一杯やったりして，和気あいあいの関係が保たれます。日本で一般的な年功

the interest of the company, and not as competitors for better wages and higher positions. Generally, they maintain friendly or harmonious relations among themselves, helping one another with their work and occasionally having meals or drinks together after work. Life-employment and seniority systems prevalent in Japanese companies are probably what make this possible, for they both serve for elimination of excessive competition among individuals.

One characteristic of the colleague relation in Japanese companies is the feeling of closeness cultivated among *dōki* or contemporaries who enter a company at the same time. Every spring a number of new workers of about the same age and similar backgrounds join the company right after their graduation from universities and high schools and undergo on-the-job training together. They work in low positions with no title and under the pressure from unaccustomed jobs, so they tend to feel strong affinities with one another. They sometimes form a social group, which can develop into a faction intending to undertake a significant role in the company. This consciousness of being equally ranked and working in the same situation is figuratively expressed as "eating boiled rice cooked in the same iron pot."

However, differences in competence and enthusiasm will sooner or later be disclosed through everyday work to all the staff. Those who distinguish themselves by their competence, reliability, kindness to others, and modest behavior are sure to gain the popularity among

序列制度と終身雇用制度がこれに一役買っているのでしょう。これらの制度は両方とも個人間の過度の競争をなくすのに役立っているからです。

　日本の会社の同僚関係についての特徴は，同時に入社した同期社員の間に親近感が生まれることです。毎年春に，同じ年齢で同じような経歴を持った大学，高校の新卒者が大量に入社し，一緒に研修を受けます。彼らはヒラ社員として慣れない仕事の重圧を感じながら働いていますから，自然とお互いに親しみを感じるようになります。そのうち，彼らはグループを作ってつきあうようになり，時にはそれが会社内での派閥にまで発展することがあります。同じ地位，同じ状況で働いているというこの意識のことを「同じ釜の飯を食う」といいます。

　しかし，仕事に対する熱意や能力は，日常の働きぶりを通して遅かれ早かれ他の仲間に明らかになるものです。能力があり，信頼でき，仲間に親切で，態度が謙虚な人は同僚の人気も集まります。そして，結局，このような同僚の人気は昇進に必要不可欠なものなのです。

their colleagues, which is one of the essentials to promotion. (OT/TS)

Coming of age In Japan a person legally becomes an adult at the age of 20, when he or she gains the right to vote, the power to take legal action, and the freedom to marry without parental consent. Even minors, if males are at least 18 years old and females at least 16, are regarded in some respects as adults when they are married lawfully with parental approval.

In premodern Japan, coming of age was celebrated in various ways. Though they differed with the era, class, sex, locality, and so on, the ceremonies were usually observed at a certain point between the ages of 13 and 17. They involved changes in clothing and hairstyle, which indicated the transition to marriageable age. Today the concept of such rites of passage survives in the national holiday called Coming-of-Age Day. On January 15 each local government holds a congratulatory ceremony for its new citizens who have attained their legal maturity during the preceding year. They attend the ceremony in their Sunday best, many females in their beautiful formal *kimono*.

In present-day Japan, over 90% of the students who finish nine years of compulsory education go on to senior high schools and are encouraged to study hard to enter prestigious universities. Those who have fortunately overcome the hurdle of difficult entrance examinations feel quite relaxed and enjoy college life.

成　人　　日本では，満20歳になると法律上，成人になります。成人になると，選挙権が与えられ，法律行為を行うことや，親の同意がなくても結婚することができるようになります。未成年であっても，18歳以上の男子，16歳以上の女子が親の同意を得て法的に結婚しているならば，成人とみなされる場合があります。

　近代以前の日本では，成年の儀礼はさまざまなやり方で行われました。そのやり方は，時代，階級，性，地域などによって違っていましたが，普通13歳から17歳の間の一定の時期に行われました。成年をむかえると，髪型や服装も変化し，婚姻が許されました。このような通過儀礼の概念は，今は国民の祝日である「成人の日」に引き継がれています。1月15日には，各市町村がその前年に成年に達した住民のために，祝賀式を催します。新成人は晴着で，特に女性の多くは美しい正装の和服を着て成人式に出席します。

　現在日本では，9年間の義務教育を修了した生徒の90％以上が高等学校へ進み，有名大学入学を目指して勉強に励むことになっています。幸いにも難しい入学試験に合格した者は，大学に入ると緊張感から解放され，学生生活を楽しみます。アメリカの大学生と違って，日本の大学生のほとんどが授業料や生活費は親に依存し，自分がアルバイトをして稼ぐお金は，ドライブや旅行などのレジャーに使います。学生たちはあまり早く大人になりたくないと思っているようです。そのため，法律上は成人であっても，定職に就き，結婚して落ち着くまでは一人前ではないというのが一般的な考えです。

Most of them, unlike their American counterparts, are entirely dependent on their parents for tuition and living expenses, while spending the money they earn by part-time jobs for leisure activities such as motor rides and trips. They seem reluctant to grow into adulthood so soon. Thus the popular opinion is that, despite legal maturity, college-age people are not at all *ichininmae* (full-fledged responsible persons) until they settle down to steady work and married life. (MT)

Community　The proverb goes that a neighbor at hand is better than a brother far away, and in fact, neighborly relations are considered very important in the Japanese society. However, human relations and social obligations greatly differ between rural and urban communities.

In rural districts, particularly in geographically secluded regions, an old type of communal life survives to a certain degree. The inhabitants in such a community are all parishioners of the same shrine enshrining their tribal guardian god. Observing autonomous order and sharing traditional values and beliefs maintained for generations, they often proudly identify themselves with the community. Having very close relations among themselves, they provide mutual help in farming, fishing, or performing ceremonies. Punishment for negligence of obligations and for disturbance of social order used to be *mura-hachibu* (ostracization) or discontinuation of all relations with the offender. Recently, de-

地域社会　「遠い親戚よりも近い他人」という諺があります
が，実際に日本の社会では近隣関係が大変重要です。しかし，田
舎と都会では人間関係や近所づきあいは非常に違っています。

　田舎では，特に地理的にへんぴなところでは，昔の共同体的生
活がある程度残っています。そうした地域社会の住民は同じ氏神
を祭った神社の氏子で，代々伝わった価値観や信条を共有し，そ
の地域との一体感を持ち，それを誇りに思うこともあります。住
民同士の関係は緊密で，農業や漁業の仕事をしたりさまざまな儀
式をするときには，お互いに手伝います。昔は近所づきあいをな
いがしろにしたり，社会秩序を乱したりした場合，いっさいの関
係を断つ村八分という制裁が違反者に加えられたものです。最近
は地方の村の人口が減少し，生活も現代化してきたので，この種
の地域社会は少なくなっています。

　都市や近郊の団地には，さまざまな文化的背景の人が住んでい
ますが，そうした社会では住民同士の関係がよそよそしくなりが
ちです。都会の地域社会の特徴は，さまざまな規模の町内会また
は自治会が結成されていて，メンバーの福祉に努めていることで
す。この組織は居住環境の保全や改善のために働きます。また，
祭りやスポーツやさまざまな文化的活動も企画実行しますが，こ

population of local villages and modernization of life have brought about a decline in this type of community.

In cities and housing projects, where people with different cultural backgrounds live, one's relations with other members of the community tend to be estranged. Characteristic of urban-type communities are self-governing neighborhood associations (*chōnaikai* or *jichikai*) of various sizes formed to ensure the welfare of its members. These organizations work for a favorable living environment. They coordinate festivals, sports, and various kinds of cultural activities, which may be, in effect, attempts at the retrieval of a community spirit now lost. Generally, they are not politically motivated, but they can form the basis of citizen movements when a local government decides on issues to the members' disadvantage. (TS)

Company　Japanese companies look like a big family. A company takes care of the workers and their dependents as the head of a family does. Life-long employment is pervasive. Pay and promotion systems are based on seniority rather than ability. Management-labor conciliation, cooperation among workers, group solidarity, group approaches to decision-making, sense of job security and economic stability, and perhaps rewards for excellence are other characteristics which are believed to have led the Japanese companies to success. Most of this has been attained by the continuous effort made on

れは今では失われた共同体意識を回復する試みともいえるでしょう。一般に町内会は政治的ではありませんが，地方行政府が住民にとって不利になるような決定をしたときには，市民運動の基盤となることもあります。

　会　社　　日本の会社は大きな家族に似ています。ちょうど一家のあるじが家族の面倒を見るように，会社は従業員とその家族の面倒を見るのです。終身雇用が広く採用されていて，昇進や給与のシステムも能力というよりはむしろ年功序列に従います。これに加えて，協調的労使関係，労働者間の協力，連帯意識，グループ・コンセンサスにもとづく意志決定，雇用保証，経済的安定指向，そして特別賞与などが日本企業を成功に導いた鍵だと信じられています。このような日本企業の特性は，会社全体の利益と個々の労働者の利益とを同一のものとしてとらえようとする企業努力によって達成されてきました。

　日本で職業を変わる人が比較的少なく，また他社による引きぬ

the part of the company to identify the interests of the individual workers with those of the company.

Probably this is why there have been comparatively little job migration and corporative head hunting in Japan, though the situation is changing gradually and at an accelerated pace with the development of international markets. Normally one enters a company for life, he and his family sharing the fate of the company.

However, both the companies and the workers seem to have gone too far. Once a man joins a company, he belongs to the company heart and soul. His job comes before his family, since a high level of worker commitment is expected by management. He devotes a major part of his life to the company, working overtime, attending clients and business affiliates at restaurants, bars, mahjong parlors after office hours, or at the golf course on weekends. He even dares to sacrifice his family life by accepting a position at a distant branch, where he works apart from his family.

Women workers have been an exception to the rule. Particularly in large traditional companies, women work for only a few years as office ladies, secretaries, receptionists, and so on. They usually retire when they marry or when they have their first child. They have been also very poorly represented in upper management in Japan, which, however, appears to be improving thanks to the enactment of the Equal Employment Opportunity Law in 1986. (MH/TS)

きもほとんど行われていないのは，恐らく会社への帰属意識が強いためだと思われています。もちろん，国際市場への発展にともなって，状況は徐々に変化しつつあります。とはいえ，一生勤めるつもりで入社し，家族も含めて会社と運命を共にするというのが普通です。

　しかしながら，会社にしても労働者にしてもいささか度を過ぎている傾向があります。一旦会社に入ると，身も心も会社に捧げて働くことになります。経営陣からは労働者の愛社精神が強く求められているので，家庭より仕事が優先します。残業にはじまって飲食，マージャン，ゴルフの接待というようにサラリーマンは生活の大部分を会社のために捧げます。単身赴任のために家庭生活を犠牲にすることすら厭いません。

　女性労働者はこうした仕組の例外としてあつかわれてきています。特に伝統的な会社では，女性はOL，秘書，受付嬢などとして数年間だけ勤務するものだとされています。女性は結婚や出産を機に退職するのが普通なのです。ですから，会社の管理職にまで出世する女性は非常にまれです。しかし，男女雇用機会均等法の施行にともなって，女性の労働環境が改善されることが期待されます。

Competition The Japanese are said to be extremely status conscious. The use of *meishi* or business cards in conducting introductions, especially in the business world, exemplifies this very clearly. By exchanging *meishi* at their first meeting, the Japanese invariably draw attention to their institutional affiliation and position. Because one's social rank and role are judged chiefly by the institution to which one belongs and the position that one holds, the information provided by the *meishi* is of vital importance to the Japanese.

Japanese people take pride in being a member of a prestigious group. Such a group may be a school, a business firm or a social club. It is this desire for social elevation that involves the Japanese in fierce competition. Social status is achieved primarily through education and occupation. In order to secure a job at a top-ranking business establishment, one must graduate from a first-rate university. Prior to admission to such a university, one is likely to have to graduate from an outstanding high school. Academic competition is so fierce that students need to go to cram schools after their regular school schedule to prepare for the university entrance examinations.

It is often said that competition in Japan takes place between groups of the same kind. For instance, a university competes against other universities and a company engages in constant competition with other companies. Competition is also likely to take place among peers or colleagues since one's elevation to a

競　争　　日本人は身分・地位にすこぶる敏感だと言われます。このことは、お互いを紹介するときの名刺交換によく表れています。特にビジネスの世界ではそうですが、初対面での名刺交換の際、日本人は必ず相手の勤務先・役職名に目をやります。個人の社会的地位は、主としてその人がどこに勤め、どんな役職に就いているかで判断されるので、名刺に記されたインフォメーションは日本人にとって非常に大切です。

　日本人は、学校であろうと、企業あるいは社交クラブであろうと、およそ一流と言われるグループのメンバーであることに誇りを持ちます。日本人を激しい競争へと駆り立てるのは、まさにこの社会的地位の上昇志向です。社会的地位は、特に学歴と職歴に左右されます。一流企業で働くには一流大学を卒業することが必要ですし、一流の大学へ入るためには、名門高校を卒業することが前提になります。受験競争は非常に厳しく、生徒たちは放課後、進学塾へ通います。

　よく言われるように、日本における競争は同業者間で行われます。大学は大学同士、企業は企業同士で絶えず競合するといったぐあいです。普通、昇進は同じグループの仲間の犠牲の上に成り立つので、個人間の競争は仲間や同僚のあいだで行われる傾向にあります。このような形での競争は、同僚間の嫉妬や恨みの原因になることがよくあります。しかし、まさにこうしたタイプの競争が日本経済・産業の成功に寄与したことを忘れるわけにはいきません。

53

higher rank precludes another's in the same group. Such competition often raises jealous and resentful feelings among colleagues. However, it should be noted that it is this type of competitiveness that has contributed to Japanese success in business and industry. (YN)

Compliment In the vertical (hierarchical) society of Japan, complimenting is seen as one of the arts of social interaction between people, and compliments are passed especially to people of superior rank. Compliments are often exchanged among housewives in their neighborhoods, among workers on the job, and even among relatives. One can compliment others on anything, ranging from their friends to their family members or their achievements. Housewives praise each other, each other's husband, children, clothing, housing, tastes, and so on. For instance, they say, "What a beautiful girl your daughter has become!", "Your children have all become great," "Your son is so smart that he will be sure to enter the best college. I envy you." These expressions are usually based on actual facts, but they are rarely taken at face value, even though the person receiving the compliment feels flattered. Knowing that is a kind of social etiquette, the person given a compliment usually responds to the praise by speaking slightly or modestly of his/her merits, even though he/she perfectly deserves it. This reserved attitude is highly valued. After talking in a modest

54

お世辞　　タテ社会の構造をもつ日本では，人を巧妙にほめることは，社会的な付き合いにおいて1つのこつと見なされますが，特に自分より目上の人に対して，よくお世辞が使われます。またしばしば隣近所の奥さん方，仕事仲間，そして親戚の間でもお世辞は交わされます。お世辞の中身は，相手の家族のことであったり，相手の業績であったりさまざまです。奥さん方は，おたがいを，またおたがいの夫や子供たちを，あるいはおたがいの服装，住い，趣味などをあいそのよい言葉でほめあいます。例えば，「お宅のお嬢さんは何てお美しくなったんでしょう」とか「お子さん方が立派になられましたね」「息子さんはよくおできになるんですってね。きっと一流大学に入学できますことよ。うらやましいわ」などと言います。もちろんこのような言葉は普通真顔で述べられますが，言われた人は内心嬉しく思っても，これを額面通りに受け取るようなことは滅多にしません。世渡りのための作法の1つだということを知っているので，述べられたことに価すると思っても，謙遜するのが普通です。この控目な態度は大切なことです。控目な対応をしたあと，今度は相手に対して同じ話題を別の面から言及することによって，しばしばほめ言葉を返します。このようなお世辞の交換は，イギリスの文化人類学者マリノウスキーが「言葉交し」と呼んだように相互の人間関係を維持し，また確かめるための手段の1つなのです。

way, the person often returns the praise to his/her companion by referring to other aspects of the same topic. This kind of exchange of compliments, practiced for the purpose of maintaining or reconfirming a relationship, is part of what Malinowski, an English anthropologist, called "phatic communion."

In a company or business situation, compliments are often paid to gain favor or an advantageous ground in one's position or in a business negotiation. In its extreme case complimenting is often considered apple polishing and can be despised, if the compliment sounds too coarse and obvious and more like flattery.

Japanese have a phrase, *aiso ga ii* (to be clever at flattering), which refers to a person who sprinkles compliments, always smiling and easily accepting people and never interrupting them by saying something contrary. Such a person is usually accepted favorably, but not always highly valued because a person good at making compliment can be very simple-minded or two-faced. (KA)

Compromise　Since a conciliatory attitude is more highly valued in Japanese society than an unyielding spirit, a compromise is very often sought when a dispute arises. In a labor situation, people concerned sooner or later abandon their initial "all-or-nothing" policy and start to grope for a satisfactory settlement by arbitration or by mutual concessions to avoid a breakdown or a deadlock in negotiation. This is why

仕事の面では，自分の立場や取引きに目を掛けてもらったり，その仕事を有利に展開させたりするため，相手にお世辞を使うことがよくあります。しかし，これが極端になり，その言葉がうわべだけを飾るもので，その意図が見え透いてしまうと，ごますりやおべっかと取られ，その好意自体が蔑まれてしまうこともあります。

　「お世辞」と同じような意味を表す「お愛想」という言葉があります。これから派生した「愛想がいい」という表現は，相手の言ったことに反対せず，いつも微笑みながらそれを全て受け入れてしまう一方で，相手を立てるようなほめ言葉をいつも言っているような人を形容します。このような人は，普通好意的に受け入れられはしますが，子供のようにきわめて単純だとか，あるいは時には逆に心の中に「ウラ」と「オモテ」があるのではないかと勘ぐられ，あまり高い評価は受けないこともあります。

妥　協　　日本では自分の主張を曲げない精神よりも協調的な態度が高く評価されるので，紛争が起こると多くの場合，妥協が計られます。例えば，労使紛争の場合，交渉の行き詰まりを避けるために当事者は遅かれ早かれ最初の「オール・オア・ナッシング」の方針を捨てて，調停や譲歩によって解決の道を探り始めます。ですから，よく西欧諸国でみられるような長期の泥沼の労使紛争はめったに起こりません。日本のたいていの労働組合は企業別組合で，労働者にとっても雇用者にとっても会社の繁栄が優先

there scarcely have occurred quicksand employer-striker struggles of long duration as are often seen in Western countries. Since most of Japanese labor unions are company unions and companies' prosperity comes first in the priority for both the employers and employees, the conciliatory mood can easily be fostered on both sides.

Although negotiations may start with debates giving opposing opinions backed up by facts and statistics, the final stage involves a reciprocal abatement of extreme demands or rights and recalculation of supposed gains and losses resulting from concessions. This is where the "soft sell" approach through a strong appeal to human feelings replaces the "hard sell" approach based on logical and rational persuasion. A most usual clincher (or rather a cliche) that wraps up a struggle would be "For the general good of the company and its workers."

On the other hand, when it comes to a matter of an individual's (or individual group's) principle, cases are more varied and complicated. The Japanese used to have a belief in dying for the cause as was seen in ancient warriors' *harakiri* (suicide). To live up to one's principle meant to allow no compromise that was likely to jeopardize the principle . Though this kind of uncompromising attitude has been inherited by some hard-shell radicals, people in general seem to have learned a more realistic way of settling disputes by coming to terms with their opponents. There usually is a tacit understanding between the opposing parties that

します。そのために，両方の側から協調的ムードが容易に醸し出されるのです。

　交渉は事実や統計に基づく議論で始まっても，最終段階では極端な要求や権利の主張は和らげられ，譲歩によって生じる得失の検討がされます。ここでものをいうのは人情に訴える「ソフトセル」方式で，これが論理によって説得する「ハードセル」方式にとって代わります。紛争を終結するいつものとどめの文句（あるいは決まり文句）は「会社とその社員の全体的利益のために」というものです。

　他方で，個人または集団の理念にかかわる場合には，問題は多様で複雑になります。昔の武士の切腹の例にみられるように，日本人はかつて大義のために死ぬことを潔いことと信じていました。自分の理念にしたがって生きるということは，その理念を脅かすような妥協は許されないということだったのです。こうした非妥協的な態度は頭の固い急進的な人たちに今もみられますが，相手と妥協して争いを解決するという現実的なやり方が一般的になっています。妥協をしたからといって，掲げていた理念を捨てたわけではないということが対立する両方の側に暗黙のうちに了解されているのです。妥協は単に調整に過ぎないとみなされます。したがって，理念を放棄しないで妥協をすることができるのです。

making a compromise by no means implies abandonment of the principles they are upholding. They believe that a compromise is merely a means of adjustment. It is not impossible for them, therefore, to make a compromise without abandoning their principles. (OT/TS)

Computer and computerization   Computers have long been used in Japanese business and industrial world, and further computerization is being vigorously pushed forward throughout the country. Small business computers in offices, CAD (Computer-Aided Designing) and CIM (Computer-Integrated Manufacturing) in factories, CTS (Computerized Typesetting) in printing shops, CDs (Cash Dispensers) in banks, CAT (Computerized Axial Tomography) scanners in hospitals, and CAI (Computer-Aided Instruction) in schools have all lost their novelty during the past few years. Actuated perhaps by the very Japanese desire for convenience and efficiency, experts are now developing computers with AI (Artificial Intelligence) and super-computers.

Computers are also very popular among the general public. Many new models of computers for personal use appear on the market every year and are appealing to a large number of families. Housewives use them for keeping household accounts and children for playing various kinds of computer games. To save commuting, some companies are planning local or satellite offices furnished with computer work stations and new mass-communication media devices—a situation akin to what

コンピューターとコンピューター化　　日本の会社や工場では
コンピューターはかなり前から使われていますが，さらに国をあ
げてコンピューター化が強力に進められています。会社でのオフコン，工場での **CAD**（コンピューター援用設計）や **CIM**（コンピューター使用統合生産），印刷所での **CTS**（コンピューター使用組版方式），銀行での **CD**（現金自動支払い機），病院での **CAT**（コンピューター化体軸断層写真），学校での **CAI**（コンピューター援用独習）などは，どれもここ数年のうちに珍しくなくなってしまいました。
便利さと能率の良さを求める日本人の国民性からか，専門家は今
や人口知能を備えたコンピューターや，スーパーコンピューター
を開発しています。

　一般大衆にもコンピューターは普及しています。毎年，個人用
のパソコンの新しいモデルが多く発売され，家庭向けに宣伝され
ています。この種のものは主婦が家計簿をつけたり，子供がいろ
いろなゲームで遊ぶのに使われています。通勤をなくすために，
ワークステーションとニューメディアの機能を持ったサテライト
オフィスを計画している会社もあります。これはもうアービン・
トフラーが『第三の波』で描いた世界です。

　コンピューター企業は「コンピュートピア」という理想を宣伝
していますが，コンピューター時代についてあまり楽観的になる
のは危険だという警告の声も出ています。コンピューター犯罪は
別にしても，新しい社会問題が発生しています。コンピューター
化によって事務的な仕事はずっと容易になりましたが，機械的な

Alvin Toffler described in *The Third Wave* (1980).

Though the computer industry advertises the idea of "Computopia," warnings are raised against unqualified optimism about the computer age. Apart from computer abuses and crimes, there have arisen new types of social problems. While computerization has much facilitated office work, it has become a threat to those workers who do more or less automatic kinds of jobs. Quite a few computer operators are suffering from mental and physical disorders generally called "techno-stress" caused by watching video display terminals for long periods of time. Many senior citizens find it very hard to keep pace with the fast tempo of modern life accelerated by computerization. Coexistence with computers is a problem that remains to be solved. (TS)

Constitution, the Japanese Promulgated November 3, 1946 and taking effect May 3, 1947, the Constitution of Japan was politically and socially revolutionary compared to Imperial Japan's old Constitution. First, the new Constitution declared popular sovereignty, removing the Emperor from the position of a living God to the mere "symbol of the unity" of Japan. Second, it set the separation of powers on a more democratic foundation. Notably it gave the judiciary the power to strike down unconstitutional legislative and administrative acts, an authority which was unknown to the old constitutional system. Third, the Constitution guaranteed people wider freedoms and fundamental human rights. Among

仕事をしている人は失業の脅威を感じるようになりました。コンピューターを操作するかなりの人が「テクノストレス」と呼ばれる身体的，精神的障害を訴えています。これは長時間ディスプレイの画面を見続けることから起こる障害です。老人はコンピューター化で拍車がかかった現代生活の速いテンポについていくのが困難だと感じています。人間とコンピューターとの共存の問題はまだ解決されていません。

　　日本国憲法　　1946 年 11 月 3 日に発布され，翌 47 年 5 月 3 日に施行された日本国憲法は，帝国日本の旧憲法と比較して，政治的にも社会的にも革命的でありました。新憲法は第 1 に，国民主権を宣言し，天皇を現人神の地位から単なる日本の「統合の象徴」にひきずり降ろしました。第 2 に，新憲法は三権分立をより民主的な土台の上に定めました。とりわけ司法部は，憲法に違反する立法部・行政部の行為を無効にする権限を与えられましたが，この権限は旧憲法体制下では認められていなかったものです。第 3 に，新憲法は国民に，より広範な自由と基本的人権を保障しました。なかでも，表現の自由，宗教の自由，労働者の団結・団体交渉の権利，刑事被告人の手続的保護などは，戦前はすべて無視または抑圧されてきたものですが，戦後の日本に，より自由な社会を樹立するために新たに，あるいはより強固に保障されることに

others, the freedoms of expression and religion, workers' rights to organize and bargain collectively, and procedural protections for the accused, all of which were ignored or oppressed in the pre-war era, were guaranteed anew or more firmly, to develop a freer society in post-war Japan. The Constitution also provided equality of the sexes, eliminating at least in principle, the legally enforced inferior status of women in public and privete life. Fourth and most importantly, the renowned Article 9 of the Constitution renounced war as a sovereign right of the nation and declared "land, sea, and air forces, as well as other war potential, will never be maintained."

Since its inception, the Constitution has been criticized by the conservatives as being "forced on Japan by the Occupation Forces (which ruled from 1945 to 1952)" and "repugnant to the customs of Japan." However, subsequent history has resolved any doubt about its birth. The economic growth of the country unfetterd by military spending, and the stability of people's life secured by various measures under the Constitution, such as farmers' better living conditions made possible by the agricultural land reform and workers' improved working conditions attained by labor unions, have provided people with ample reason for disfavoring any attempt of constitutional revision. Today, more than 80 percent of the Japanese population supports the Constitution, opposes militarism (but at the same time approves of the Self-Defence Forces), and supports the

なりました。新憲法はまた，両性の平等を定めました。これにより，少なくとも原則的には，公的・私的生活において法が強制していた女性の劣等の身分を解消しました。第4に，最も重要な点ですが，有名な憲法第9条は，国権の発動である戦争を放棄し，「陸海空軍その他の戦力は，これを保持しない」と宣言しました。

その当初より，新憲法は保守派の人々から，「占領軍（1945年から52年まで日本を支配していた）によって押し付けられた」とか，「日本の実情にそぐわない」として批判されてきました。しかし，その後の歴史が，その誕生にまつわる疑問をすべて解決しました。軍事費によって足かせをはめられない国家の経済的発展，新憲法下のさまざまな措置によってもたらされた国民生活の安定，たとえば，農地改革によって実現された農民の生活状況の改善，あるいは労働組合によって達成された勤労者の労働条件の改善などは，いかなる憲法改正の試みにも賛成しかねる十分な理由を国民に与えたのです。今日，日本国民の80パーセント以上の者が憲法を支持し，軍備に反対であり（もっとも同時に自衛隊は是認しています），「統合の象徴」という天皇の現在の地位を支持しています。このように，どのような憲法体制についても言えることですが，日本国憲法の生命も，論理ではなく，経験によって決まったといえるのです。

current status of the Emperor as the "symbol of the unity." Thus, as with any constitutional system, experience rather than logic has determined the life of the Japanese Constitution. (IT)

Deaf persons and their sign language   There are reportedly 320,000 deaf and hearing-impaired persons in Japan out of a total population of 120 million. This amounts to a deaf-hearing ratio of 1 to 430, which is a slightly high proportion in view of the statistic estimate that every one out of a thousand in the world's population is said to be born a deaf person.

The current popularity of the learning of the sign language of the deaf in Japan started with the publication in 1969 by the Japanese Federation of the Deaf of the first volume of the textbook series called *Our Signs*. The book, which contained 540 basic signs in a dictionary style, was enthusiastically received by both deaf and hearing communities.

The success of the first volume was so remarkable that it was soon followed by an additional nine volumes. The ten-volume series now lists around 4,500 entries for various words, phrases, and expressions covering all aspects of social life including business, law, politics, education, and medicine.

The spread of these resources prompted the formation of many sign language study groups organized and joined by students, housewives, or office workers interested in the message deaf people bring from the world of

ろう者と手話　　日本には32万人ほどのろう者と聴覚障害者がいます。日本の人口は1億2千万人ですから，ろう者と健聴者の割り合いは1対430になります。これはけっこう高い率といえるでしょう。現在の推計では，世界の人口のうち，千人に1人がろう者であるといわれています。

　最近，健聴者のあいだで，ろう者の手話を学ぼうとする人が増えています。それは日本ろうあ連盟が1969年に『私たちの手話』というシリーズの第1巻を発行したことから始まります。この本は辞書として540種ほどの基本的な語彙を収録したものですが，ろう者からも健聴者からも大歓迎を受けました。

　第1巻が成功をおさめたことに勢いをえて，その後9巻が続々と出版されました。全10巻には，4,500の語句や表現がおさめられています。それは仕事，法律，政治，教育，医療などの社会生活全般にわたっています。

　このような教材が広まるにつれ，手話サークルが各地に誕生しました。メンバーは学生や主婦や会社員が中心で，静寂の世界に生きるろう者の心にふれたいと願う人たちです。行政の方でも，このような市民グループの活動には援助をするようになっています。

　こういったサークルでは，グループのリーダーがろう者と一緒になって，入門者に手話を教えます。たいがいは，地方独特の手話方言をまじえた自作のテキストを使用します。交流や文化活動もさかんで，コミュニティのろう者と健聴者との話し合いの機会をつくっています。

silence. Many local and national government organizations often lend assistance to these civil group efforts.

Working together with deaf participants, group leaders give sign language lessons to their beginning members based on their own textbooks including local dialects. They also sponsor social and cultural activities designed to encourage interaction and communication between deaf and hearing members of the society.

Learning sign language, hearing persons have recognized how ignorant they were of the language system that the deaf communities have developed over the centuries. They have developed by themselves an effective system of thinking and communication which is natural to their physical conditions. The deaf people are living a complex life without the use of speech and hearing, but with the use of sign language. Treating the use of sign language as some form of deficiency or pathology stemmed from an ignorance of the nature of sign language on the part of the hearing. As hearing persons experience increased contact with deaf persons, they come to understand their earlier misconception. (NH)

Death　According to the traditional Japanese view of life and death, death is not the opposite of life, but part of it, and the dead and the living are inseparably linked. A Buddhist interpretation tells Japanese people that their lives have been passed on from their ances-

健聴者は手話を学ぶことによって，自分たちが今までろう者のことばについて，いかに無知であったかを知るようになります。ろう者は長い間にわたって，自身の身体的条件にかなった思考と伝達のシステムを発達させてきました。彼らは音声と聴覚を使うことはなくても，手話を使うことによって，多様な生活を営んでいます。手話を欠陥と考えたり，異常と考えるのは，手話を知らない人の無知のなすわざです。健聴者はろう者と交流を深めるにつれ，このような意見をもつようになっています。

　死　日本人の伝統的な死生観によれば，死は生と対立するものではなく，生の一部であり，死者と生者は分から難く結ばれています。仏教には，人の生命は先祖から受け継いだものであり，今度はそれが子孫へと引き継がれていく結果，一族と共同体の命が永遠に続く鎖となって連なるという解釈があります。死者の肉

tors and will in turn be passed on to their descendants, thus continuing in the everlasting chain of the life of the family and the community. It is believed that the spirit of a deceased relative wanders in space not far from the home for a certain period of time, usually 33 years, even after the body ceases to exist, and comes back once a year during the *Bon* Festival (a traditional Buddhist festival) season. In short, the spirit belongs to the same community both before and after death.

The Japanese do not regard death as an enemy to fight against, but rather as an inevitable destiny they must accept quietly. Their concern is how to die a decent death. To some people, an ideal way of dying is a glorious and honorable death often symbolized by cherry blossoms falling after only a few days' full bloom. Undoubtedly, longevity is respectfully esteemed, but at the same time many elderly people visit the so-called *pokkuri-dera*, or Buddhist temples which are reputed to answer their prayer for a sudden painless death.

In Japan suicide is not always condemned, but is often looked on as an acceptable way of apologizing for one's grave error, shouldering full responsibility or showing one's loyalty, for example. The most striking characteristic of suicides in Japan is the prevalence of plural suicides. Even family suicides are likely to be reported with sympathetic words. In most cases the mother kills her small child(ren) and herself because she thinks it more considerate to take them along than

体は消滅しても，霊は生前の家からそれほど遠くない空間に一定期間（通常は33年）留まり，1年に1度お盆に戻って来ます。つまり，霊は生前も死後も同じ共同体に属するのです。

　日本人は死を敵対する相手というより，運命として静かに受け入れるものとみなします。関心を持つことは，死そのものよりも，見苦しくない死に方です。理想的な死に方とは，わずか数日の満開の後に散ってしまう桜の花に象徴されるような，栄光に輝く死に方だと考える人がいます。長命が敬われることは言うまでもありませんが，それとともに多くの老人が俗にポックリ寺と呼ばれる寺へお参りに行きます。ポックリ寺は，長患いせずに安楽に死にたいという願いを，かなえてくれると言われているのです。

　日本では自殺が必ずしも非難されません。例えば，重大な誤りを犯した時の謝罪のためとか，全責任を負い，忠誠心を示すために死を選ぶことが容認されることはよくあります。日本人の自殺で最も特徴的なことは，心中がまれではないということです。一家心中とか，その中でも多い母子心中は，親が幼い子供をあとに残して死ぬよりは道連れにするほうが思いやりがあることだと考えて，まずわが子を殺してから自殺するケースです。これらは，とかく同情的な表現で報道されます。

to leave them behind. (MT)

Desirable and undesirable psychological states

Japanese often speak of the looks of the sky, of rain, or of thunder, referring not to the weather but to someone's temper, tears, and sudden anger. Such meteorological metaphors to denote one's emotions may not be peculiar to the Japanese language, but there are a number of words used both for describing atmospheric phenomena and for expressing one's psychological states. For example, *sugasugashii* (refreshing), a most frequent epithet applied to cool and clear days in May, is also used for qualifying a personally pleasant sensation characteristically caused by such agreeable weather. The antonym *uttōshii* (gloomy, depressing, or annoying), a usual adjective used for the hot and humid rainy season in June and July, is very often used for describing an unpleasant sensation or undesirable psychological state.

This seems to suggest that one's skin sensation is closely related with one's psychological state. However, the use of these two words extends beyond weather and its effect on the skin. Also used in connection with people's appearance, clothing, character, and behavior, they simultaneously express the state of an object and the impression it gives to the observer.

Another group of words describing psychological states has more of this aesthetic quality, and oddly, many of the forms are either onomatopoeic as in *sukkiri* (neat,

心理状態　日本人はよく，人の機嫌や涙や激怒を，空模様や雨や雷にたとえます。このように感情を気象の比喩で表すことは日本語に特有というわけではないでしょうが，心理状態と気象現象に共通に用いられる語句はたくさんあります。例えば，「すがすがしい」という言葉は5月のさわやかな気候を指すのによくつかわれる形容詞ですが，そのような好ましい天候から感じる壮快感も指します。反意語の「うっとうしい」は梅雨時の蒸し暑くて湿っぽい気候を指す常套句ですが，不快感や嫌な心理状態を指すのにもよくつかわれます。

　このことから，人の皮膚感覚と心理状態には密接な関係があるように思われます。しかし，これらの言葉がつかわれる範囲は天候とそれが皮膚に与える効果だけではありません。人の外見や衣服や性格や行動に関しても用いられ，対象の状態と観察者の印象を同時に表現します。

　心理状態を描写する言葉のうち，あるものはこの審美的な側面がより強く，面白いことにその多くは「すっきり」や「べったり」のように擬声語的であるか，または「はればれ」，「じめじめ」「ほのぼの」，「ひえびえ」のように反復リズムのあるものです。これらの語は自然現象が出しているように思われる音，またはそれに反応して人間の感覚が出しているように思われる想像上の音を写したものです。やはりこれも，少なくとも日本人にとっては，心理的な快・不快が環境に対する肉体的，生理的な反応に基づいていることを示すものでしょう。

refreshing) and *bettari* (close, sticky) or reduplicative as in *harebare* (clear, fine), *jimejime* (damp, gloomy), *honobono* (heartwarming), and *hiebie* (chilly). These words reproduce the imaginary sounds supposed to be emitted by natural phenomena or by physical sensations in response to them. Again, this may show that, at least for Japanese people, psychological comfort and discomfort are based on their physical or physiological reaction to the environment. (TS)

Display of self pride　In Japan social pride is often considered as a less virtuous trait because of the general attitude toward modesty. People who are seen to be proud of themselves, their family members, relatives, their breeding, or, in general, their private world, are likely to be regarded as boastful or arrogant. So when one is given praise by someone, he is expected to reply, "It's not worth your praise," "It's merely because of good luck," and so on. In formal situations, one is often expected to refer to his family, private property and achievements by rather derogatory terms like *gusai* (my odd wife), *tonji* (my odd son), *settaku* (my humble house), *seccho* (my humble book), and so on.

Even when he has to or wants to express his praise for persons within his circle, he often begins with a phrase such as "I don't really mean to praise..." or "I know it is too presumptuous to praise...". By so doing he tries to give the impression that he is not really

74

自慢する　「謙譲」の態度が重んじられている日本社会では，自慢することは徳の低いことだと考えられています。自分や家族，親戚，そして家柄など，一般に私的な面を自慢する人は横柄だとか傲慢だとかみなされがちです。そこで，人にほめられた時は，「いや，とんでもない」とか「運が良かっただけですよ」などと答えます。形式ばった場面では，自分の家族，所有物，業績などに触れる時，「愚妻」「豚児」「拙宅」「拙著」などのへりくだった言葉が，しばしばつかわれます。

　自分の身内のものをほめなければならない時，あるいはそうしたい時には，「自慢じゃあないが」とか「自分でそういうのも何だが」というような前置きで始めることがよくあります。そうすることによって，自分が実際には横柄な人間ではないという印象を与えようとするのです。自分の家族をほめることも，滑稽なこと未熟なことだと考えられているので，父親は自分の子供に向かって「お前のことを誇りに思っているよ」などと言うことは滅多にありません。父親は自分ではそうだと思っていても，子供が年ごろになってしまうと，そんなことは口に出しません。親は恥ずかしいのかあるいは控え目なのか，内心そう考えていても，自慢げな気持ちを言葉で表現することには，ためらいを感ずるのです。

an arrogant person. To express pride in, or praise to
family members is also considered ridiculous or awkward. So the father would seldom say to his son or
daughter, "I'm proud of you," though he really is, especially after the child has grown up to puberty. This
is because the parents hesitate, whether from shyness
or modesty, to express their pride even though they
are proud of their children in their hearts. (KA)

Eating　Japanese diet, now evaluated as "healthy,"
is characterized by the close-to-ideal balance in calorie
ratio of protein, fat and carbohydrate : 59.6%, 27.4%
and 13.0%, respectively. It is also marked by a shift
from rather high-calorie fatty diet to low-calorie less
fatty diet as people age : young people prefer Chinese
and European meat dishes, while people of middle age
and older prefer Japanese dishes consisting of fish and
vegetables. These two characteristics of the Japanese
diet partially account for the average life span in Japan
being longer than that in the U.S.A. : 80.9 vs. 78.5
for women, and 75.2 vs. 71.1 for men (1986). In fact,
the average life span in Japan is now the highest in
the world.

The traditional daily diet in Japan consists of staple
food and side dishes : boiled rice, fish and vegetables,
miso soup, and pickles. On a typical Japanese breakfast
table, for example, will be found a bowl of rice, a
raw egg or a slice of cooked salted salmon, dried sea
vegetable, soup, and pickles. The primary staple food

食の文化　　現在，日本の食事は"健康食"として評価されています。蛋白質と脂肪と炭水化物の割合が，それぞれ 59.6％，27.4％，13.0％，と理想的な割合になっているからです。また，食事の質は，年を取るにつれて，カロリーが高めで，脂肪の多いものから，カロリーが低めで，脂肪の少ないものへと変わります。若者は，中国料理や西洋風の肉料理のほうを好みますが，中高年者には，魚や野菜を使った日本料理のほうが合うのです。日本人の食事に，このような 2 つの特徴があるために，日本のほうがアメリカより平均寿命が長くなっており，1986 年に女性で 80.9 歳対 78.5 歳，男性で 75.2 歳対 71.1 歳です。日本の平均寿命は，今や世界一なのです。

　日本の伝統的な日常の食事は，主食と副食からなっています。ご飯，魚と野菜，みそ汁と漬物等です。朝の食卓には，ご飯，生卵または焼いた塩鮭 1 切れ，干しのり，汁と漬物がよく並びます。主食によく使われる米は，粘りけが多く，粒の短いジャポニカ米の一種です。米は通常，水で炊き，味を付けずに，温かいものを食卓に出します。副食で人気があるのは，魚と野菜で，醬油で味付けして出す場合が多いようです。牛肉，豚肉，鶏肉も今はよく使われますが，中世から 19 世紀末までは，仏教の影響でほとんど食べませんでした。牛肉は人気が出ていますが，値段が高く，

is the rather glutenous short-grained japonica variety of rice, which is boiled and normally served unseasoned and warm. Popular side dishes are fish and vegetables that are often served seasoned with soy sauce. Beef, pork, and chicken are now also popular, but were not eaten from the Middle Ages until the last half of the 19th century because of Buddhist influence. Although beef is growing in popularity, its price can be prohibitive. In Tokyo supermarkets a pound of lean beef can be $18. Food is eaten normally with wooden chopsticks, although the use of western cutlery is growing.

Economic growth triggered an increase in the consumption of meat and milk products. Japanese diet has been further diversified with the introduction of Chinese and Western culinary traditions including "fast-foods" such as hamburger and pizza. Rice consumption, on the other hand, has been reduced by half during the last twenty years. This trend is apparent in the increasing popularity of a small rice bowl of about 4.1 inches (10.5 centimeters) in diameter.

People, however, are still fond of rice and 87% are said to eat rice more than once a day. Although they have acquired new eating habits, they keep the old one, a rather frugal and healthy diet with an average daily intake of 2,075 calories (1987). (MO)

Economic reconstruction, secrets of post-war
Several elements led to Japan's post-war economic mir-

東京のスーパーで，牛肉の赤身450グラム（1ポンド）が約2,400円（18ドル）する場合があります。食事には通常，木製の箸を使いますが，西洋風のスプーン類を使う場合も多くなっています。

　経済が成長するにつれて，肉や乳製品の消費が増えています。中国料理や，ハンバーガーやピッツァ等の西洋料理がとり入れられ，日本の食事は多様になっています。一方，米の消費量は，過去20年間に半減しています。この傾向は，直径10.5センチ（4.1インチ）ほどの小さなご飯茶碗の人気が高まっていることにも示されています。

　しかし，日本人は相変わらずご飯が好きで，調査回答者の87％が，1日2回以上食べています。新しい食習慣をとり入れても，従来の食習慣も残し，1987年には，1日平均2,075カロリーの，質素で健康的な食事をしているのです。

経済再建，戦後復興の秘密　　第2次世界大戦の荒廃から世界第2位の経済力に到達した戦後日本の経済奇跡にはいろいろな要

acle, which has seen Japan rise from the ruins of World War II to the position of the second most powerful economy in the world. The first is the set of reforms that General MacArthur initiated, such as redistribution of agricultural land, democratization of labor, and dissolution of the *zaibatsu* (financial cliques). These were essential to creating and increasing purchasing power among the Japanese.

The second is the priority production system of the early 1950s, in which Japan concentrated on increasing production of coal and steel. Almost all imported oil was put into furthering the production of coal, which in turn was used for the production of steel.

Third, technological innovation started in 1956, when a White Paper report declared the post-war age was over. Mass production was realized by much investment in plants and equipments, and during the following decade the much longed-for appliances called "Three Sacred Treasures" (i.e., black and white TV sets, refrigerators, and washing-machines) came into wide use. In the early 1960s, the doubling-income policy effectively shifted Japan's economy from an investment-oriented to a consumer-oriented one. In 1968 Japan's Gross National Product outstripped that of West Germany, having previously surpassed those of Great Britain and France, while in terms of individual income, Japan ranked 20th in the world. The GNP and the National Income Per Capita in 1970 were 73.0461 trillion yen and 570 thousand yen ($202.9 billion and $1,583 at the exchange

因があります。第1に，マッカーサー元帥の始めたいろいろな改革，つまり農地解放，労働組合の民主化，財閥解体等です。このような処置によって日本人の購買力が増しました。

　第2に，1950年代の初めの傾斜生産体制です。これで，日本は石炭と鉄鋼の増産に集中しました。ほとんどすべての輸入石油を石炭増産のために投入し，その石炭を使用して鉄鋼を生産しました。

　第3は，戦後は終わったと白書が宣言した1956年（昭和31年）に始まった技術開発です。工場に多大な設備投資をした結果，大量生産が可能になりました。昭和30年代には，三種の神器と言われた白黒テレビ，冷蔵庫，洗濯機が普及しました。また，昭和35年以後の所得倍増政策が功を奏し，日本経済が投資型から消費型に変わりました。イギリス，フランスのGNPを抜き，昭和43年についに西ドイツを抜きましたが，個人所得では世界で20位でした。昭和45年のGNPと年間平均個人所得は73兆461億円と57万円，昭和50年には149兆5010億円と113万9000円，昭和55年は245兆1627億円と170万3000円，昭和60年には320兆7748億円と210万4000円でした。昭和50年，ランブイエで開催された第1回西側先進国経済首脳会談に出席を要請されて，初めて日本は西側先進国の一員になったように感じました。

　4番目の要素は，日本人の生活様式に内在しています。天然資源に乏しいことからくる不安と将来万一の貧困に対する恐怖感のため，たとえ余裕があっても生活を楽しむための消費はおさえ，貯蓄する傾向があるのです。貯蓄のためのいろいろなサービスが整っています。例えば，郵便局が預金や保険の業務をしており，全国津々浦々まで行き渡っています。しかも，一般の銀行と違い，郵政省の管理下にある郵便局には納税の義務がないため，預貯金が集めやすく，それが再投資され生産を高めることになるのです。

　また，儒教の伝統が日本にはあり，教育や，家族，友人，支配

rate of 360 yen to the dollar) respectively, in 1975 149. 501 trillion yen and 1,139 thousand yen ($482.3 billion and $3,674 at the exchange rate of 310 yen to the dollar), in 1980 245.1627 trillion yen and 1,703 thousand yen, ($1,021.5 billion and $7,096 at the exchange rate of 240 yen to the dollar) and in 1985 320.7748 trillion yen and 2,104 thousand yen ($1,603.9 billion and $10,520 at the exchange rate of 200 yen to the dollar). In 1971 the exchange rate began to float. In 1975 when Japan was advised to attend the First Economic Summit Conference at Rambouillet, the Japanese felt for the first time that Japan had become a member of "Western industrialized nations."

A fourth factor has been innate in the Japanese way of life. A sense of insecurity due to the lack of natural resources and the fear of possible impoverishment in the future has made people hesitate to spend money freely on the enjoyment of life, even if they could afford to. They have tended to save more, encouraged by some special facilities. For example, there have been services provided by the public post office, such as savings and insurance, which were carried out all over Japan, even in the remotest area of the countryside. In addition, unlike regular private banks, the postal branches of the government need not pay tax. This has been very helpful in collecting money, which was reinvested to increase production.

Besides, Japan has a long tradition of Confucianism stressing education, loyalty to one's family, friends and

者に対しての忠誠が重視され，縦社会の人間関係によって調和が保たれてきました。第2次世界大戦末には大多数の日本人は少なくとも6年間の義務教育を受けており，文盲率がほとんどゼロであり，急速な産業の近代化に対応するだけの準備が十分できていました。

　以上が日本の復興の主要な理由です。しかし，それ以上に重要なのは日本の経済復興にアメリカが寛大な態度をとったことでしょう。

rulers, and harmonious, hierarchical interpersonal relationships. At the end of World War Ⅱ most of the Japanese population had received at least a compulsory six year education, which lowered the illiteracy rate to almost zero. They were well prepared for the rapid modernization of Japanese industry.

These are the major reasons for Japan's successful post-war reconstruction. But no less important is an international environment favorable to Japan's economic recovery and growth resulting mainly from the United States' generous attitude to Japan. (MK)

Education as a means of social promotion

The Japanese emphasize the quality of schools attended from kindergarten on through the university level. The prestige of the university a person attends often determines the status he/she will ultimately achieve in life. Graduates of the prestigious universities are benefited both in their careers and in their social lives through the good reputation and the strong alumni connections of their universities.

The push to enter the highest quality schools possible begins at the kindergarten level. Beginning with the entrance tests for kindergarten, the Japanese are in a long educational race that takes them over a series of entrance examinations to each higher level. "Education mamas" or *kyōiku mamas* have been in the media in recent years for their efforts to guarantee their sons and daughters every chance for the best possible education.

学歴社会　　日本では幼稚園から大学に至るまで，どんな学校に行ったかが重要視されます。名門大学を卒業したかどうかで，出世が左右されることもしばしばです。名門大学を出ると評判も良く，また学閥も強いので，仕事の面や社会生活の面で得をすることが多いと言えます。

　できる限り良い学校に子供を入学させたいという競争は，幼稚園から始まります。幼稚園の入園試験から始まって，志望の小学校，中学校，高校，大学への入試に追われる長い教育レースを闘わなければなりません。最近のマスコミでは，子供に何が何でも良い教育を受けさせようと奔走する「教育ママ」が取り沙汰されています。そのような「教育ママ」の中には，病気で休んでいる子供にかわって授業を聴講し，子供の勉強をみてやって授業におくれないようにする母親さえいるほどです。良い小学校に行けば，良い中学校に入りやすくなり，良い中学校に行けば，良い高校に入りやすくなる，というように良い大学への道は続きます。「教育ママ」に限らず，どんな親でも子供をできるだけ良い学校に入れたいと思っているのです。

For example, some attend their child's class when he/she is sick so that they can help the child keep up with the class. The chances of entering a top university are better if the student has attended a top high school. A top elementary school makes it easier to enter a top middle school and so on through the system. All parents, not just "education mamas," would like to see their children in the best school possible.

Ironically, enrollment at a top university is usually sufficient to get quality job offers in the business world; the courses and grades are not so important. Japanese college life, then, at times looks like a four-year vacation between the days of cramming in secondary school and those of serious competition in their work after college graduation.

The Japanese school system is being criticized these days for several reasons : too much rote memory work, too little creative or individualistic thinking, too many hours at school with little time for leisure or personal development, and so on. However, even though changes may be proposed, the system has served the country's economic growth in pragmatic terms. (MH)

Emotional expression Facial expressions are a major factor in communication. The face is usually the first part of the body that is observed in social interaction. But correct facial interpretation is an extremely difficult and complicated task even among those people who share a common system of facial meanings. The

86

皮肉なことに，一旦名門大学に入学してしまうと，それでもう一流会社へのパスポートが手に入ったことになります。どんな講座を履修して，どんな成績をあげたかということはそれほど重要ではありません。時としてこのような日本の大学生の生活は，高校までのつめこみ勉強と卒業後の熾烈な企業競争との狭間にある４年間の休暇のようにもみえます。

　今日では，日本の学校制度は次のような点で批判されています。知識をつめこみ暗記させるような教育が多すぎ，創造的で個性的な思考力が育ちにくいこと，学校の授業時間が長すぎ，余暇や個性を伸ばす時間がほとんどないこと，などです。しかしながら，たとえ何らかの変革が提案されたとしても，このような学校制度が今日の日本の経済的発展に実際に貢献してきたことは否めません。

　感情の表現　　顔の表情はコミュニケーションで重要な働きをします。人々は相手の顔を注意深く観察します。しかし，顔の表情が伝達する意味を正しく解釈することは，同国人のあいだでも，大変やっかいなことです。文化的背景が異なる人々と接触すると，問題はますます複雑になります。

　専門家の話では，人間は喜び，悲しみ，怒り，恐れ，侮辱，嫌

problem becomes more conspicuous in an encounter with people from a different culture.

Scholars agree that normal expressions of ten basic emotions (happiness, sorrow, anger, fear, contempt, disgust, bewilderment, interest, determinaton, and surprise) are fairly easily interpreted in similar ways across cultures. Difficulty multiplies when people try to "mask" their true feeling. Masking is the use of one facial expression in an effort to conceal another facial expression.

People employ an interesting set of masking techniques. They "modulate" their facial message by controlling its intensity and duration. They "falsify" their true emotion by not expressing it (poker face) or expressing it differently (feeling angry but looking happy). They also "modify" their facial expression by adding another one.

In social interaction, Japanese people generally are expected to restrain, if not suppress, the strong or direct expression of emotion. Those who cannot control their emotion are considered to be immature as human beings. Strong expression (verbal or nonverbal) of such negative emotions as anger, disgust, or contempt could embarrass other people. Direct expression of sorrow or fear could cause feelings of insecurity in other people. Expression of even happiness should be controlled so that it does not displease other people.

The best way to comply with this social code of behavior is to utilize masking techniques. Thus, Japanese

悪，当惑，興味，決意，そして驚きの10種の基本的情動をもち，それぞれの表情は文化を越えて，ほぼ同じように解釈されるそうです。しかし，人々は本当の感情を表に出さないようにするために，仮面をかぶることもあります。そうなると，表情の解釈は非常に困難になります。仮面をかぶるということは，本当の感情をかくすために，別の表情をつくろうことです。

仮面操作の技術には興味深いものがいろいろあります。人々は感情表示を加減して，表情の強弱や時間をコントロールします。本当の気持ちを偽造して，ポーカーフェースのように無表情をよそおったり，怒りを感じているのに笑顔をふりまき，まるで違った表情を見せることもあります。また，とっさの表情を修正して，新たな表情を付け加えることもあります。

社会的な交わりでは，日本人は感情を強く，直接的に表現してはならないとされています。感情を抑制できないと，人間として未熟であると思われます。怒り，嫌悪，侮辱といった不快な感情をことばや身振りで強く表に出すと，回りの人はいやな気持ちになるものです。悲しみや恐怖感も，他人に不安感を引き起こします。うれしいときでさえ，他人を傷つけないように抑えた表現が大切です。

こういった行動規範に順応するためには，仮面をかぶる必要があります。その結果，日本人は無意識のうちに，無表情になってしまいます。西洋人は日本人のこの表情を「不可解」といいますが，それは強い感情を露骨に出して，他人を当惑させたり，不安に落とし入れたりしないための慎みの結果なのです。

「ミステリアス」と呼ばれるジャパニーズスマイルも，このような社会的背景を考慮に入れて考えなければなりません。日本人はバスに乗りおくれると，笑みを浮かべることがあります。しかし，それは他人が回りにいる場合です。ほかにだれもいなければ，悪態すらつきます。同じように，テレビのインタビューアーが政

people, although unaware, frequently display apparent lack of a meaningful facial expression, often referred to as "inscrutable" by Western people. It is an attempt to neutralize strong emotions to avoid displeasure or embarrassment on the part of other people.

The "mysterious" Japanese smile should be understood in the context of the social situation. When a Japanese commuter misses a bus, he smiles if there are other people on the site, but he does curse if there is nobody around. He has to hide his embarrassment in public, but he can let out his emotion in private. Similarly, a TV interviewer may keep smiling while asking a politician harsh questions in an effort to show that however cruel he may sound, he does not mean to be. (NH)

English loan words   The Japanese language is replete with English loan words. While many loans retain their original English meaning and form (though written in the Japanese orthographical system), still more go through a variety of semantic and structural changes. For the latter, at least seven types of borrowing patterns are noticed.

The first type is characterized by a shift or narrowing of meaning. For example, *hyūman* from "human" often means "humanly," "humanistic," or "humane," as in *hyūman konpyūtā* (human computer).

The second type consists of what can be referred to as "Japanese English." Japanese uses borrowed words and phrases to create new English items which may or

治家に厳しい質問をしているさいに，笑顔を絶やさないことがあります。それは，質問は厳しいかもしれないが，相手に悪意があるわけではないことを示すためです。

英語借用語　日本語には英語からの借用語がたくさんあります。借用にあたっては日本語の書き方になりますが，英語のもとの意味と形を残しているものもあれば，意味や形がいろいろと変わるものもあります。後者のほうがずっと多く，それには少なくても7種のパターンが見られます。

第1のタイプはもとの意味が変わったり，狭くなったりする場合です。「ヒューマン」は「ヒューマン・コンピューター」のように使い，人間の（human）という意味よりも，人間らしい（humanly, humanistic, humane）といった意味合いを強調します。

第2のタイプはジャパニーズ・イングリッシュと呼ばれるものです。日本語は英語の語句を借りて，新しい英語らしいことばを造ります。それは英語のネイティブ・スピーカーにわかることもあれば，わからないこともあります。「ワンマン・バス」という

may not be understandable to the native English speaker. *Wan man basu* (one-man-bus) is a bus in which the driver must collect the fares rather than having a conductor. *Furumūn* (full moon) is, by analogy to "honeymoon," a journey by a long married couple.

The third type of example abbreviates all syllables after the first two or three. Thus, "apartment" becomes *apātomento*, then *apāto*, which is seen spelled back in English as "apart" in real estate ads. Other examples are *biru* (building), *infure* (inflation), *defure* (deflation), *kone* (connection), *nega* (negative), *sando* (sandwich), *gyara* (guarantee), and so on.

The fourth type uses initials. "O.L." is from "office lady" (working woman). "DK" occurs in current house ads for "dining kitchen," a Western-style organization of rooms. "OB" may sound to the English ear like the hospital room, "obstetrics," but in Japanese it refers to a fellow alumnus, an "Old Boy."

The fifth type of English loan utilizes the traditional Japanese abbreviation rule of compound words. Classic examples include a wide range of words from *sufu* (from *suteipuru fuaibā* for "staple fiber") to *ensuto* (from *enjin sutoppu* for "engine stop" meaning "engine failure"). The use of this simplification method is proliferating in the field of computers and other high technology products. Thus, "word processor" becomes *wāpuro*, while "personal computer" is *pasokon*.

The sixth type of borrowing involves English loans and Japanese vocabulary. Combining loans and native

のは運転手が車掌の仕事もして，料金を集めるバスのことです。「フルムーン」は「ハネムーン」をまねて造ったことばで，熟年カップルの旅行をさします。

　第3のタイプは最初のいくつかのシラブルを残して，あとを省略する方法です。その結果，apartment はまず「アパートメント」となり，次に「アパート」となります。これを英語で apart と書くのも，不動産屋の広告で見かけます。同じように，building は「ビル」，inflation は「インフレ」，deflation は「デフレ」，connection は「コネ」，negative は「ネガ」，sandwitch は「サンド」，guarantee は「ギャラ」になります。

　第4のタイプではイニシアルを使います。「OL」は "office lady" の省略で，働く女性の意味です。「DK」は "dining kitchen" の省略で，洋式の間取りをもつ家の広告によく見かけます。「OB」は英語では病院の産科（obstetrics）のように聞こえるかもしれませんが，日本語ではそうではなく，大学などの卒業生，すなわち "Old Boy" のことです。

　第5のタイプでは日本語の複合語の省略法を利用します。これにはいろいろな実例があります。「スフ」は「ステープル・ファイバー」（staple　fiber），「エンスト」は「エンジン・ストップ」（engine stop）からできたものです。このような省略法は現在，コンピューターや他のハイテク製品の分野で広まっています。たとえば，ワード・プロセッサーは「ワープロ」となり，パーソナル・コンピューターは「パソコン」になります。

　第6のタイプは英語と日本語を組み合わせる方法で，広く使われています。「ハブラシ」は日本語の歯と英語のブラシを組み合わせたことばで，完全な日本語になっています。「ノミニケーション」は日本語の飲むと英語のコミュニケーションをくっつけたものですが，まだ新語の段階です。

　第7のタイプは第6のタイプの発展したものです。借用語と日

words is also one of the most popular practices in the current use of the Japanese language. *Haburashi* (Japanese "tooth" connected with "brush" is now a perfect Japanese word, while *nominikēshon* (Japanese "drinking" related by "communication") is a neologism.

The seventh type of English loan is an evolution of the sixth. When loans and vernacular are homophonous, their combinations create more sophisticated phrases. For example, in *Getsuyōbi-wa-suwanai-dē*, *dē* is bilingually ambiguous. It is possible to interpret it as a loan from the English word "day" or as a Japanese particle conveying request. In the first interpretation, the whole sentence is read as "Monday is a non-smoking day," and in the latter as "Please do not smoke on Monday." (BH/NH)

Equality and discrimination   The group, not the individual, is of primary importance in Japanese society. When applied to Japanese society, equality is often taken to mean that one is treated just like other members in a group to which one belongs, and fair treatment is guaranteed as long as one observes the group's internal rules. However, once idiosyncratic aspects which may deviate from the mainstream norm of behavior surface, one is subject to discrimination by the group. Such aspects may be sexual, religious, political, or academic.

To the majority of Japanese, the worst way in which they can be discriminated against is by what is referred

本語が同音の場合，両方を重ねるとおもしろいことばが生まれます。「月曜日はすわないデー」では，「デー」は英語の day にも，日本語の願望を表す助詞にもとれます。そこで，この文は，前者の解釈では「月曜日は禁煙日」となり，後者の解釈では「月曜日にはたばこをすわないでください」といったふうになります。

平等と差別　　日本社会では，個人よりグループが極めて重要です。普通，平等とはグループの他のメンバーと同じように処遇されること，と日本では解釈されています。したがって，グループ内のルールを守っている限り公平な待遇が約束されます。しかし，男女差別であろうと，宗教上，政治上あるいは学問上のことであろうと，一旦グループと異なる独自性を出すようなことがあれば，その人はグループからの差別の対象になります。

　ほとんどの日本人にとって，最も耐え難い差別は村八分と言われるものです。昔は，自分の村の人々との交流を一切断たれることを意味しましたが，現代では，グループから仲間はずれにされることを意味します。村八分にあうと，グループの社交的な集まりからはずされたり，必要な時に助けてもらえなかったり，職場での昇進を遅らされたりといったことがよくおこります。

to as *mura-hachibu* or village ostracism. In olden times, this meant exclusion from social interaction with others in one's village. In modern Japan, it means to be excluded from one's group, so that ostracized members are likely to face difficulties. They may not be invited to social gatherings. They may not be offered help when needed. They may have delayed promotions at work, and so on.

In Japan, it can be disadvantageous if one is not a member of a dominant group. Anyone who is on the outside, such as a minority ethnic group, can be subject to discrimination in Japanese society, unless his/her efforts to conform to the ways of the community are acknowledged by the insiders. The Japanese concepts of equality and discrimination are defined by feelings based on case-by-case situations rather than by clear-cut laws and/or principles. (YN)

Examination as a social institution   One of the problems in the Japanese educational system is that students are primarily motivated to study by examinations. The most important one is the entrance examination to the university given in February or March of high school students' senior year.

It is not too much of an exaggeration to say that almost everything in Japanese secondary education is focused on the university entrance examination. Since admission to a good university often determines a large part of a students' future career and life, everyone is

96

日本では，主流派のメンバーでないと極めて不利になります。日本社会においては，民族的少数者など，多数派に属さない者はすべて差別の対象となり得るのです。日本人の平等・差別の概念は，明確に定義された法やプリンシプルに基づいたものではなく，その場その場の感情に左右されるものなのです。

　入学試験と就職試験　　日本の教育制度の問題の一つは，学生が試験によってまず勉強するように動機付けられているということです。最も重要な試験は，高校3年生の2月か3月に行われる大学の入学試験です。

　日本の高校教育のほとんど全てが大学の入学試験に焦点を当てていると言っても過言ではありません。名門大学への入学が学生の将来を左右することも多いので，誰でも入試については大変真剣です。

　一般に入学試験は記述式の問題ではなく択一式の問題によって，学生の勉学の成果を測ろうとします。画一的な基準に国民を合わせようとする教育制度とあいまって，このような試験のやり方は

very serious about it.

The examination usually attempts to measure student's scholastic achievements by multiple-choice questions rather than essay-type written tests. Coupled with an educational system which tends to shape a whole population to a national standard, this tendency in the examination promotes the rote memory work and discourages creativity or individuality in Japanese students. Also, the process cannot detect other abilities of the examinees either in their curricular or extracurricular activities. It seems that such matters do not count in an education which focuses on memory.

Several attempts have been made to improve examination processes at the government as well as each university level. Some universities give essay-type written tests to the examinees who have passed the first screening. There are other universities which select students according to interviews and recommendation letters.

In Japan, students may also take a company examination before being hired, but it is normally easier than a university entrance examination. The selection process of companies varies from one to another . Many companies conduct interviews in which they examine a student's motivation, enthusiasm, personality, and so on. Personal connections to the company through parents, relatives, friends, and alumni association sometimes favor the candidates. However, it is usually the prestige of the student's university that is most impor-

丸暗記を助長し，学生の創造性や個性を潰してしまう結果になりがちです。またこうしたペーパー・テストによる入学試験では，例えばクラブ活動における学生の活躍などについては評価の対象とされません。

政府レベルでも各大学レベルでも入試改革の試みがなされてきました。2次試験で，記述式の筆記試験を課す大学や，面接や推薦状によって学生を選抜する大学もあります。

大学生は卒業年度に就職のための入社試験も受けますが，これは大学入試よりもずっと楽のようです。入社試験のやり方は会社によって違います。たいがいの会社は面接を行って，志願者の動機，熱意，個性などをみます。親や親戚や友人や先輩のコネがきく場合もあります。しかし，通常，最も重要なのは志願者の通う大学の名声です。

tant. (MH)

Family　　The typical Japanese family today is an independent nuclear family, with father, mother, and one or two children. According to a survey conducted by the Ministry of Health and Welfare in 1986, more than a half of parents wanted to have a big cheerful three-generation family with three children. Actually, however, the average number of children is 1.7 and only 30% of the parents have a three-generation family, due to economic, housing, and occupational factors.

Post-war Japan has witnessed tremendous changes in the types of households, as is revealed in the 1987 White Paper on People's Livelihood released by the Economic Planning Agency. First, the size of households shrank, owing to an increase in nuclear families and a decrease in the number of children. In a 1964 survey, 54.9% of the respondents had nuclear families, while in 1985 61.1% did. The average size of households changed from 4.97 persons in 1955 to 3.23 persons in 1985.

Second, the divorce rate has gone up and created more fatherless and motherless families. Third, an increasing number of mothers are holding jobs.

All these changes in the types of households have affected family functions.

For example, traditionally in Japan the roles of husband and wife are rather clearly defined : to earn money for living for the former and to take care of household chores for the latter. However, the number of

家　族　　今日の日本で，典型的なのは，独立した核家族であり，父親と母親，子供1人または2人の構成になっています。厚生省調査（1986年）によると，子持ちの夫婦回答者の半数以上が，子供3人と大勢で賑やかな三世代同居を理想としています。しかし，実際には，経済上の理由や住宅事情，仕事上の都合などから，子供の数は平均1.7人で，三世代同居も30％だけとなっています。

　戦後，日本の家族形態は，大きく変化しました。1987年度版『国民生活白書』（経済企画庁編）によると，変化の1つは，世帯規模の縮小であって，核家族の増加と子供の数の減少によるものです。1964年の調査では，回答者の54.9％が核家族でしたが，1985年には，61.1％に増加しています。家族の平均人数は減少して，1955年に4.97人，1985年には3.23人となっています。

　2つ目の変化は，離婚率の上昇と母子，父子世帯数の増加です。3つ目の変化は，仕事を持つ母親の増加です。

　このような家族形態の変化から，家族の果たす機能も変化し始めています。例えば，日本では伝統的に，夫婦の役割分担がはっきりしていて，夫は生活費を稼ぎ，妻は家事を担当してきました。けれども，総理府の調査によると，このような役割分担を認める人の数が減少しているのです。1972年には，男女の80％が伝統的な役割を認めていましたが，1984年には，認める人の割合が，男性の60％，女性の50％となっています。同じような傾向が，最近行われた新聞社の世論調査にも見られ，役割分担を認める男女の割合は，1980年に72％，1985年に60％，そして1987年には54％となっています。

people accepting such role differentiation decreased. According to a Prime Minister's Office survey, 80% of both men and women favored the traditional roles in 1972, while 60% of men and 50% of women did so in 1984. A similar trend is observed in a recent newspaper survey: 72% of men and women in 1980, 60% in 1985, and 54% in 1987. (MO)

Foreign aid　　Japan is administering two types of economic aid to developing countries: official development assistance, which evolved from reparation that Japan started to make in 1954 and continued until 1977 to Asian nations for damage which she had caused during World War Ⅱ, and private-sector assistance, which developed from attempts to secure agricultural and raw material supplies from abroad in the 1960s.

According to the 1988 White Paper on official development assistance published by the Ministry of Foreign Affairs, Japan ranks the second after the United States in economic aid. In several developing countries where Japan is the biggest donor, the Japanese government thinks that Japan will start to advise such countries on development and macroeconomic policies instead of merely granting requests for aid by the governments of developing countries as has been done so far.

The government-funded Japan International Cooperation Agency and Overseas Economic Cooperation Fund together with the Export-Import Bank of Japan carry out the official development assistance. The Japanese Diet

対外援助　　日本の対外援助には2種類あります。1954年に始まり1977年まで続いたアジア諸国に対する賠償から発展したODA（政府開発援助）と1960年代に農産物と原材料の供給を確保するために始まった民間援助とです。

　外務省発行のODAに関する昭和63年度白書によると経済援助分野で日本はアメリカについで第2位になっています。日本政府は，日本の援助がトップになっている数ヵ国では，今までのように援助要求にただ応じるだけではなく，開発とマクロ経済政策の面で助言をするつもりでいます。

　ODAを実施するのは外郭団体の国際協力事業団や海外経済協力基金で，日本輸出入銀行と協力して当たることになっています。対外援助予算は毎年国会で次のように割り当てられます。

　(I)　2国間援助の約40%は無償供与です。それらは(1)農業，水資源，教育，研究，医療，福祉の分野における施設の建設と資材供給，(2)漁業産業の振興のための援助で，漁港の開発，漁夫の訓練のための漁船提供，(3)災害に遭った地域への援助，(4)教育の振興と，固有文化の保護のための援助，(5)穀物供与援助，(6)食料増産援助です。

　(II)　2国間援助の残り約60%は長期円借款です。これらは(1)道路や発電所建設のためのプログラム借款，(2)機具や肥料を購入するための商品借款，(3)債務が払えなくなった国に対する債

allocates foreign assistance funds every year in the following way.

I. About 40% of the bilateral aid is in the form of free grants. They cover : (1) general assistance in order to build facilities and supply materials for developing agricultural programs, water resources, education, research facilities, medicine and welfare ; (2) assistance in order to promote fishing industries by way of developing fishing ports and providing ships for training fishermen ; (3) assistance to areas hit by natural disasters ; (4) cultural assistance to promote education and to preserve traditional cultures ; (5) food assistance to supply grain ; and (6) programs for increasing food production.

II. The remainder of about 60% of the bilateral aid is yen credit, a long term loan. The program of the yen credit consists of three parts : (1) loans to projects such as the construction of roads and power plants, (2) loans to purchase merchandise such as machinery and fertilizer and (3) loans to debtor nations in order for them to be able to defer payments.

III. In addition to bilateral assistance, the government makes investments and donations through international organizations such as the World Bank, the Asian Development Bank, and the United Nations.

Besides the official development assistance, there are also private-sector assistance programs. The most important are credit and investment. Supplier credit is funded by the Export-Import Bank of Japan and private city

務救済です。

　㈽　2国間援助のほかに，世銀，アジア開発銀行，国連のような国際機関を通じて，投資や寄付を行っています。

　ODAのほかに民間での援助もあります。最も重要なのは融資と投資です。サプライヤー・クレディットは日本輸出入銀行と都市銀行でまかなわれています。発展途上国の購入者はサプライヤー・クレディットを使い，金融機関はバンク・ローンを利用するわけです。日本企業は，いろいろなプロジェクトに単独または合弁で参加しています。

　また，民間の援助団体も宗教，主婦，学生，市民団体といったボランティア・グループが200ぐらいあります。例えば，清潔な水を供給するのにアジア諸国で井戸を掘る運動をする団体や，世界の貧しい人々へ食物と衣類を送る品川区の主婦団体のマザーランド・アカデミーがあります。相手国の自助努力を助けるのが目的です。

　1983年の日本の対外援助はGNPの0.75％で，その60％は東南アジア向きです。最大の援助国は韓国，インドネシアと台湾でしたが，韓国への援助は経済力がつくにつれて，減ってきています。

banks. Buyers in developing countries use supplier credit and financial institutions make use of bank loans. The semi-official and city banks extend loans or buy bonds issued by international organizations. Also, Japanese companies invest in various projects in developing countries alone or in joint ventures.

There are also about 200 non-governmental organizations, involving religious groups, housewives, students and other citizens' organizations. They are very adaptable, giving aid largely on a voluntary basis. One group advocates movements in various Asian nations to dig wells to provide clean water. "Motherland Academy," a group composed of housewives in Shinagawa Ward in Tokyo sends food and clothing to poor people all over the world. These organizations have as their aim assisting the developing nations to help themselves.

Foreign aid occupies 0.75% of Japan's GNP as of 1983 and about 60% of the total flow of resources goes to East and Southeast Asia. Japan gave the most economic aid to the Republic of Korea, Indonesia and Taiwan, but aid to Korea was decreased as it became increasingly independent economically. (MK)

Foreign culture and country: attitudes toward

The Japanese are very curious people. They always want to know what other people are like. Their curiosity is intensified even more when it comes to things foreign.

In the past, Japan had a lot of catching-up to do for

異文化・外国観　　　日本人は非常に好奇心の強い国民で，いつ
も他人のことを知りたがります。外来のものということになると，
その好奇心はとりわけ旺盛になります。

　これまで，日本は近代化を進めるうえで，やらねばならぬこと
がたくさんありました。大多数の日本人にとって，近代化は西洋
化そのものでした。ですから，日本人は外来思想・文化，わけて

modernization, which meant Westernization to the vast majority of Japanese people. Therefore, the Japanese craved foreign ideas, culture, and more importantly the advanced technology of the West. As many have claimed, Japanese absorbed, adapted, and improved these things with breath-taking speed and success. Japan's fascination with anything foreign has never come to an end. Even today, the Japanese keep telling themselves to be more international-minded and tend to believe that the importation of foreign ideas and culture is an effective way to achieve this goal. The degree of openness that the Japanese show to outside ideas and culture is extraordinary. Whether it is religion, political systems, food, music, or fashion, they are open-minded toward non-Japanese things. However, it is important to bear in mind that this remarkable readiness for things foreign is not likewise applied to people from abroad.

On one hand, foreign visitors to Japan often remarks that the Japanese are polite and kind. Japanese people are quite pleased to hear such statements. In fact, they would be disappointed if no such compliment came from foreign visitors. On the other hand, many foreign nationals complain that the Japanese are xenophobic, probably because they are almost always treated as guests and not as regular members of the society. It may be that things foreign are much less threatening than foreign people to the unity of Japanese people. (YN)

Friendship   Friendship has been regarded as a re-

も西洋の進んだ技術を貪欲なまでに求めたのです。よく言われるように，日本人は外来文化・技術をあっという間に巧みに吸収・改良していったのです。日本人の外来の事物へのあこがれは止まることを知りませんでした。現在でも，日本人は，もっと国際的になるようにと自分たちに言い聞かせていますし，外国の考え方・文化を摂取することが効果的な国際化への道だと信じているようです。日本人の異国の考え方・文化に対する開放性には目を見張るものがあります。宗教であろうと，政治制度，食べもの，音楽あるいはファッションであろうと，外来のものなら何でも知りたがります。しかし，外来のものをこれほどまでに受け入れる用意があるにもかかわらず，外国人となると話は別です。

　「日本人は礼儀正しく親切だ」と日本を訪れる外国人はよく言います。それを聞いて日本人は大変喜びます。実際，外国人の口からそのようなことが聞かれないと，がっかりしてしまいます。その一方で，多くの外国人が，「日本人は外国人嫌いだ」と不平をもらします。これは，おそらく，彼らが日本社会の一員というよりゲストとしてあつかわれることが多いからだと思われます。いずれにしても，外来の事物は，外国人ほどには日本人のハーモニーを脅かすものではないということなのでしょう。

友　情　　日本の社会では，女性同士よりも男性同士のほうが

al existence more between men than women in Japanese society. For Japanese people a real friendship is established after they have shared experiences for long enough, attending the same class or belonging to the same club in their school days, working in the same office, or fighting as comrades in the war, and so on. The companions of one's youth are described as *onaji kama no meshi wo kutta nakama* (fellows who ate at the same mess), which implies that they shared each other's hardship or sweat and tears.

Here the sense of insiders and outsiders can be seen reflected in the association with others. Once a close friendship is established between two people and they are emotionally tied, they feel at home with each other. They are then ready to give or obtain as much help as they want to even in private matters. The materialization of the friendship is seen in the phrase, "your business is my business and my business is yours," which is the concept of mutual dependency. In times of trouble, they will meet and talk about the problem over a glass of *sake* (rice wine). Even though they could not find any solution, the friendship is reconfirmed by the fact that they talked from the bottom of their hearts and drowned the sorrow by drinking together. This process has a kind of psychotherapeutical effect.

Friendship is often a favorite theme of novels and songs. Japanese popular songs, often called *enka*, deal rather exaggeratingly with the friendship among

110

本当の友情が存在するといわれています。日本人は，たとえば昔学校で同じクラスにいたとか，同じクラブに所属していたとか，戦争で一緒に戦ったとか，会社の同僚であったとかいうように，長い間ある経験を共にしたもの同士が友情で結ばれるようです。食住を共にし，同じ喜び，悲しみを分かち合ったもの同士という意味の「同じ釜の飯を食った仲間」という表現は，若き日に結ばれた固い友情を端的に示しています。

　一旦固い友情で結ばれ，感情的にも相手を受け入れてしまうとお互い心を許すことができるのです。ここには「ウチ」と「ソト」という意識があります。そしてお互いの私的なことまで助け合うことができます。相互依存の考え方である「君のものは私のもの，私のものは君のもの」という文句は，この友情のあり方をよく示しています。困ったときは，時間を工面して会い，酒を飲みながらその悩みを語り合うのです。たとえよい解決法が見出せなかったとしても，心の底から語り合い，酒とともに悲しみを飲み干したということによって，さらにその友情は堅固なものとなります。この過程には，いわば精神療法のような価値も見出すことができます。

　友情は，小説や歌のテーマとしてもしばしばとり上げられます。演歌と呼ばれる流行歌の中には，この相手の内面にまで入っていく友情，特に漁師，芸人，そしてやくざなどに見られる友情を誇張しながらも，熱を込めて思い入れたっぷりに歌いあげているものもあります。そこでは血縁よりも義理や人情に重きが置かれ，男の友情を基にした忠義や自己犠牲の心が強調されるのです。

fishermen, artists, *yakuza* (social outcasts), and so on. Since such people tend to regard relationship formed by *giri* (mutual dependency and obligation) and *ninjō* (human feelings) as more important than that by *ketsuen* (a blood relation), self-renunciation or self-sacrifice arising from friendship is emphasized in these sentimental songs. (KA)

Generation gap   One of the major generation gaps in Japan occurs because of the fact that more than 60 % of Japan's population was born after the last war. There seem to be clear distinctions in thinking and behavioral patterns between those educated under the influence of the Emperor system and the Old Civil Law and those educated under democratic ideas, Americanism, and the New Family Rights Law.

The former, born before the war, are now over fifty and many have already retired, though some of them who are in their 50's or early 60's still hold important posts in their work as managers or executives. Early in their lives they devoted themselves to the Emperor or the country, and then after the war they transferred their attitudes of selfless devotion to their work. They were trained to be conscious of the seniority system and aware of the hierarchical social order, so they are respectful to the superiors and in return expect their inferiors to be the same. Having experienced a time when it was necessary to practice frugalities and austerities, they tend to forgo all luxuries. The latter,

世代の断絶　　日本の全人口の6割以上が第2次大戦以降に生まれたということは，世代の断絶に大きな意味を与えています。それゆえ天皇制や旧憲法のもとで教育を受けた戦前派の世代と，民主主義，アメリカの影響，新家族法などのもとで教育を受けた戦後派の世代の間には明確な違いが見られます。戦前派の人々の多くはもう退職・引退をしていますが，50代，60代前半の人の中には，社長や取締役などの要職に就いている人もいます。戦前若いうちは天皇や国に忠誠を誓い，戦後は仕事に対して無私の忠誠を誓ってきた人たちです。これらの人々は，目上のものを敬い，見返りに目下のものからの敬意を期待するという，年功序列，社会的な階級制度を重んずるように訓育されてきたのです。また節約・耐乏生活を余儀なくされたことから，彼らはあらゆるぜいたくを排しようとします。一方，新憲法，民主教育制度のもとで自らの権利や自己判断・自己主張をすることを約束された戦後派は，徐々に自分の個人的な生活に重きを置くようになってきています。

　さらにこれらに加え，戦争中，終戦直前・直後に生まれ育った世代があります。一般に戦中派と呼ばれますが，彼らはある種の感傷を込めて自らを「焼け跡派」と呼びます。この人々は今や40，50代の前半ですが，自らの信念，見解を時代の流れの中で確実に実行できなかったが故に，いざ決定を下す際にしばしばためらいや困惑を感じることさえあります。新しい社会の急激な価

post-war people who were ensured of their own rights of self-determination and self-expression under the New Constitution and the democratic education system, have gradually come to put emphasis on their private lives.

The people of the so-called mid-war generation, who were born during the war or just before or after it, often call themselves *yakeato-ha* (the generation of war ruins). They are now in their 40's or early 50's, and in a position to make decision in their work, but they are often said to have hesitation and perplexity in this job. This is because they cannot be firm in their beliefs and views. They have difficulty readjusting themselves to the drastically changed values of the new society.

People who are now in their twenties appear to be so different from preceding generations that they are referred to by a fashionable term as *shin-jinrui* (new human beings). They are often criticized by older generations for being hard to understand and deal with. They are at the same time sceptical yet easily pretend to be going with the tide. Born into a world of prosperity and affluence, they tend to attach much importance to their private lives, seeking and enjoying their happiness in their own small circles or groups. (KA)

Giri and on in a business setting   Japanese business management is known for its efficiency. Yet what underlie this efficiency are *giri* and *on*, deep-root-

値観の変化に対応できなかったのです。また現在の若者，特に20代の人々は，彼らより上の人々とあまりに思考・行動形態が異なっているといわれ，それゆえ理解しにくい，扱いにくいと批評されます。彼らは総称的に「新人類」という流行語で形容されますが，一般に世間の事物に対し冷笑的である一方，自己主張をせず，社会の流れ，体制に容易に歩調を合わせてしまうといわれています。繁栄の中，物の有り余る時代に生まれ育ち，自分たちの回りの小さな集団の中に幸せを求め，またこれを享受しながら，自分たちの私的な生活に重点を置き，これを中心に考える傾向があるともいわれています。

ビジネスにおける義理と恩　　日本の企業経営はその能率の良さで知られています。でも，その底には日本文化に深く根ざした倫理，つまり義理と恩の概念が流れています。義理は社会関係に

ed concepts of Japanese ethics. *Giri* implies the give-and-take principle in social interaction. It is a concept which drives a person to fulfill one of life's duties as a Japanese. A Japanese feels morally obligated to return a favor to those who have helped him in some way. *On*, on the other hand, refers to the social and psychological indebtedness incurred upon receiving a favor from those in superior positions. In Japanese society, which is still basically vertically structured, those in higher ranks are expected to do a paternal type of favor for their subordinates publicly and privately. In return, inferiors are expected to feel *on* and demonstrate respect and loyalty.

A business firm is often described as a "family," where the management plays the role of father and the employees that of children. The management provides the employees with the security of lifetime employment, in-service training, recreational facilities, and various welfare plans, just as a father takes care of his children. In return, the employees feel loyal to the company, have a strong sense of belonging to it, and work hard for it. This father-and-son type relationship is maintained between the immediate boss and his men as well, and the boss often takes his men out for a drink after work. The concepts of *giri* and *on* are deeply rooted in the minds of the Japanese.

The feelings of obligation also extend to relations between businesses, for example, between a firm and a supplier. If the two have done business together for

116

おける相互扶助の原理を意味しますが，日本人はこの概念のために日本人としての責務を果たさなければならないと感じるのです。また，助けてくれた人にはその好意に報いなければならないと思っています。一方，恩は目上の人から受けた恩恵に対して，社会的，心理的義理を負うことをいいます。日本の社会はまだ基本的には縦構造なのですが，そこでは目上の者は父親のように目下の者を公私にわたって面倒見なければなりません。代わりに，目下の者は目上の者に恩を感じ，敬意をはらい，忠誠をつくすのです。

　日本の企業はよく家族にたとえられますが，そこでは経営者側が父親の役を演じ，社員が子供の役を演じます。経営者側は，ちょうど父親が子供の面倒を見るように，社員に終身雇用制，社内研修，保養所などの福利施設，福祉事業などを提供します。お返しに，社員は会社に忠誠をつくし，強い帰属意識をもち，会社のためにけんめいに働きます。この親子のような関係は上司と部下のあいだにも見られ，上司は仕事のあとでよく部下を飲みに連れていきます。このように，義理と恩の概念は日本人の心に深く根ざしているのです。

　義理の意識は，メーカーと商社のような取引関係にも見られます。取引関係がある期間続くと，たとえ別のメーカーがもっと安い価格で取引を持ちかけても，その商社はおそらくいままでのメーカーとの取引を続けるでしょう。

　「新人類」と呼ばれる今日の若者は，会社のような人間関係の密な組織体においてさえ義理と恩に縛られていないように見受けられます。でも，そういう若者も，勤勉で忠実な「会社人間」に育っていく間に，義理と恩が日本の社会でいかに重要であるかを学んでいくことでしょう。

some time, the firm is most likely to retain the supplier even if another supplier proposes a somewhat better offer.

Present-day young people, called "a new breed," seem to be rather free from *giri* and *on* even in a tight-knit organization like a company. In the process of growing to be hard-working and loyal "company men," however, they too will learn how important these concepts are in Japanese society. (YY)

Government and bureaucracy　　Among the words that signify government and bureaucracy are *okami* and *yakunin*, respectively. *Okami* literally means the top or the upper part. *Yakunin* is a bureaucrat with all the same bad connotations as exist in English.

The government as *okami* is somewhat detached from the people and has some absolute authority over them. It tries to control their lives by talking down to them except at the time of electioneering. The ruling party members running in elections often coax the electorate to vote for them by committing themselves to appealing policies and pledges. But the voters are more often than not betrayed. In many cases, the Diet members, once elected, give evasive answers and avoid fulfilling their campaign pledges. This is why people often speak of what *okami* says or does as being unreliable.

Bureaucracy is associated with so-called red-tapism. Bureaucrats are rule-governed, inflexible, and insolent under the cover of politeness, and stick with sectional-

政府と官僚　　日本では，政府のことを「お上」，また官僚の
ことを「役人」と言うことがあります。「お上」は文字どおり
「上」を意味し，「役人」は官僚のことですが，英語の場合と同
様，悪いニュアンスを持っています。

　日本人が政府のことを「お上」と言うときには，何か自分たち
とは遊離した，絶対的な権威を持つ存在と位置付けているときで
す。「お上」は高飛車に国民の生活を規制しようとしますが，た
だ一つ例外となるケースがあります。それは選挙のときです。選
挙民である国民の利益にかかわる政策を発表することはできても，
実際に国会で法案を通し実行する能力のない野党候補とは異なり，
与党自民党の公認候補は，政権担当政党の候補であることをちら
つかせ，魅力ある政策や公約を並べたてて投票のお願いをします。
しかし選挙民の期待は裏切られてきました。いったん選出され国
会議員になってしまうと，釈然としない態度で自分の選挙公約を
はぐらかそうとするケースが多いようです。だから，「お上の言
うことだから」とか「お上のやることだから」などという言葉が
よく聞かれるのです。

　「官僚」と聞くと「官僚主義」（あるいは「お役所仕事」）という
言葉が連想されます。官僚は，杓子定規で融通が利かず，慇懃無

ism and a "safety first" principle. They are called public "officials," but not public "servants."

Despite the unfavorable impressions that people have of them, Japanese bureaucrats are rated as top-notch, since the bureaucracy is more or less monopolized by graduates of Tokyo University, which rests on the top of the pyramid structure of all the Japanese universities and colleges.

What is peculiar to Japanese bureaucrats is that they work together in a large room in their own ministry or agency instead of in a private office. This means among other things that duties and qualifications are not specified in detail for each post or person, but that all the clerks belonging to a section perform office duties according to their collective responsibility. Yet, ambitious government employees, while working in cooperation with each other, are actually competing for the highest-ranking position in their office. (MAT)

Group consciousness　　To a significant degree, group activities are encouraged and practiced in Japan. Nothing illustrates this more clearly than the way Japanese people travel. The Japanese prefer to travel in groups both domestically and internationally. At school and work, too, the supreme emphasis is placed on teamwork. Some Japanese feel that too much emphasis on group activities leaves little room for individual freedom and creativity. However, the great majority of Japanese people find it a virtue to conform to the group to

120

礼な派閥主義者，ことなかれ主義者だと思われています。彼らは，「公務員」でしかなく，「公僕」ではないのです。

　こうした国民感情とは裏腹に，日本の官僚は一流との評価を受けています。その理由は，日本の大学制度の頂点に立つ東京大学の卒業生がもっぱらその職を独占しているからです。

　日本の官僚の特徴は，「大部屋」主義ということです。欧米の官僚が個室を与えられ，そこで執務するのとは対照的です。「大部屋」主義は，各個人あるいは地位に関する職務及び職務権限が細かく規定されずに，ある課に配属されたもの全員が連帯責任の名のもとに一丸となって職務を遂行することにつながっています。しかし，こうした協調の精神の陰には激しい出世競争があり，彼らにとっての省内最高の職である事務次官を目指してしのぎを削っているのです。

みんなで渡れば怖くない　　日本では，集団行動はごく普通です。このことは，日本人の旅行を考えればすぐわかります。国内旅行でも海外旅行でも，日本人はグループで旅をするのを好みます。学校や職場でもチームワークが極めて重要です。過度のグループ優先主義は，個人の自由や創造性をなくしてしまうと心配する人たちもいますが，大多数の日本人は学校・会社・政党など自分の所属団体にならうことが美徳だと考えています。

　順応主義は帰属集団の仲間うちで非常に強固な連帯感を育てます。そうしたなかで，各成員はグループ内のルールに従うことを求められます。ルールに則して行動するかぎり，グループの支持

which they belong, whether it is a school, a company, or a political party.

Conformism fosters a great sense of oneness shared by all the members in the same group. Consequently, each member is subject to the group's internal rules and conversely protected by the group as long as he observes those rules and behaves accordingly. A member who deviates from the group norms or disturbs the group consensus may have to take the risk of being excluded from the group. In fact, there is a Japanese saying which goes, "The nail that stands up will be pounded down."

There is no doubt that harmony within the group is a key value in Japanese society, so that Japanese people tend to think and behave as a group. By conforming to the group, an individual gets group protection. On the other hand, however, the emphasis on the group often causes a Japanese to refrain from standing up for himself and follow the group instead. When this group psychology is carried to extremes, the Japanese as a group may even behave rudely. For instance, traffic offenses such as jaywalking and speeding are frequent occurrences and littering in public places is a common sight in Japan. Group psychology tells the Japanese, "You can do it, because everyone else is doing it." (YN)

Happiness People vary in how they seek happiness, but in general they are happiest when they find

を得ることができます。しかし，集団規範から逸脱したり，グループのコンセンサスを乱すようなことがあれば，グループからしめ出される危険があります。日本のことわざにもあるように，出る杭は打たれるというわけです。

日本社会ではグループの調和が重要ですし，日本人は集団で考え，行動する傾向が強いことははっきりしています。グループと同調することで成員はグループの保護を受けます。しかし，その一方で，日本人はグループに頼るあまり自立できないことがよくあります。こうした集団意識が度を過ぎると，日本人は集団で破廉恥な振舞におよぶことがあります。例えば，信号無視やスピード違反はよくあることですし，公共の場に物を投げすてるのもよく見かける光景です。「やったっていいよ，どうせみんなやっているんだから」と集団意識が働くようです。

幸福感　　幸福を何に求めるかは，人によってもちろん異なります。しかし，自分の人生が生き甲斐のあるものだと分かったり，

their lives worth living or when their purposes in life are attained. One's living conditions also affect one's sense of happiness, and to some people improvement of them seems to be the sole reason for living.

Japan is now regarded as one of the economic giants of the world, but few people feel that they are really enjoying the resulting affluence. For many, the living has become more difficult due to the rising costs of land and housing, lower saving interests rates, and concern about their lives after retirement, among other factors. In fact, recent surveys show that people are less satisfied with their present lives than they used to be. In 1985, 70.6% of the respondents to a questionnaire conducted by the Prime Minister's Office thought they were happy with their lives, while in 1987, 64.6% were satisfied with the present state of their lives.

In 1973 when role differentiation between husbands and wives was more clear-cut than now, men tended to find happiness in work and women in family. In 1987, however, the family became increasingly important both for men and for women. About half of the respondents believed family to have the primary importance in their lives. Physical and mental health is also considered indispensable to a happy life.

The surveys show further that about half of the respondents want to lead a cozy and peaceful life. Many of them would feel happy if they have a successful marriage, a child or two, and a promising job. These are undoubtedly moderate rather than inordinate desires,

人生の諸目標を達成した時に，一番幸せに思うのが普通です。生活の諸条件もまた，その人の幸福感を左右するものです。このような生活条件の改善が，唯一の生き甲斐になっているような人もあります。

　日本は今や，世界の経済大国の一つとみなされています。しかし，その結果手に入るはずの豊かさを，本当に享受していると感じている国民は少ないのです。生活がこれまでより，しにくくなっている人が多く，その要因として，土地建物の価格高騰，預貯金の利率低下，定年後の生活に対する不安などがあげられます。事実，最近行われた調査は，人々が現在の生活に，以前ほど満足していないことを示しています。総理府が実施したアンケート調査によりますと，回答者の自分たちの生活に対する満足度は，1985 年には 70.6% だったものが，1987 年には，64.6% となっています。

　1973 年には，夫婦の役割分担が，今よりもっとはっきり分かれていましたが，この年に，男性は「仕事」に，女性は「家庭」に幸せを見出す傾向が見られました。しかし，1987 年になると，男女両方に，「家族」重視の考え方が強まり，回答者の約半数が，自分たちの生活で「家族」が一番大切だと信じています。心身の健康もまた，幸せな生活に欠くことのできないものとされています。

　調査結果からさらに分かることは，回答者の約半数が，「心にゆとりを持って生きたい」と願っていることです。幸せな結婚，子供が 1 人か 2 人，そして将来性のある仕事があれば「幸せ」，と感じる人が多いのです。こういう願いは，高過ぎるものではなく，むしろ慎ましいくらいです。しかし，このような願いを満たすことは，必ずしも容易ではありません。それで，今はやりの新興宗教に救いを求める人があるのかもしれません。この世で神から与えられるとされる，御加護を求めているのです。

but it is not necessarily easy to gratify them. This may be why some people resort to newly-risen religions now in fashion, seeking after divine favors believed to be granted in this world. (MO/TS)

Health, management of　Since the establishment of a nationwide health insurance system in 1961, medical care has been made more accessible to the Japanese. They tend to go to see a doctor for minor symptoms, such as a slight cold or headache, and to depend excessively on medicine. According to the 1987 report by the Health and Welfare Ministry, nearly 30% of Japan's 120 million people suffer from various ailments such as high blood pressure, soreness in the hips, stiff shoulders, and eye problems, caused by aging, stress, overwork, and so on. However, many of them consider themselves basically healthy and do their usual work.

Recently there has been one incident after another in which well-known business executives, writers, or actors who were in the prime of life died of heart attacks or cancer. Suicides in 1986 reached a record high and particularly conspicuous among middle-aged men. These facts get wide media coverage and awaken the public to the importance of physical and mental health care. Moreover, to cope with the nation's yearly increase in medical expenditures, the government has revised the health insurance scheme, thereby making the patients bear a larger part of their medical expenses than before.

健康管理　　1961年に国民皆保険制度が成立して以来，日本人にとって医療を受けることが容易になりました。軽い風邪や頭痛のような症状でも医師に診てもらい，薬に頼りすぎる傾向があります。1987年の厚生省の発表によれば，1億2000万人の日本人のうち，約30％が高齢化，ストレス，過労などが原因で，高血圧，腰痛，肩こり，目の異常など何らかの症状を持っています。しかし，このうちの多くの人は自分が基本的には健康だと考え，平常の仕事をしています。

　最近，働き盛りの有名な実業家，作家，俳優が心臓まひやガンで相次いで亡くなりました。1986年には自殺者数が過去最高となり，特に中年男性の自殺が目立ちました。これらの事実が広くマスコミにより報道され，心身の健康管理の重要さが認識されるようになりました。その上，年々増大する国民医療費の抑制策として，政府は保険制度を改正して，患者の医療費自己負担分を以前より大きくしました。

　その結果として，人々は予防的な健康管理にいっそう注意を払わざるを得ないのです。十分な睡眠，バランスのとれた食事，適度の運動を心がけています。定期的な健康診断の必要性も感じています。各職場では雇主が従業員のために健康診断を実施することが法律上義務づけられています。健康やスポーツに関連したクラブや施設は空前のブームとなっていて，テニス，水泳，ゴルフ，ジョギング，その他さまざまな運動が，いろいろの年代の人々の人気を集めています。ゲートボールは特に高齢者に好まれています。成人男子の喫煙率は他の先進諸国に比べるとまだ高いのです

As a result, people are obliged to pay more attention to preventive health care. They try to get enough sleep, well-balanced meals, and moderate exercise. They feel they need to undergo regular health examination which every workplace is required by law to provide for the employees. Clubs and facilities related to health and exercise are enjoying an unprecedented boom. Tennis, swimming, golf, jogging, and many other activities are popular among different age-groups. *Gētobōru* (a ball game modeled after English croquet) is favored exclusively by senior citizens . Nonsmoking campaigns are gradually gaining strength, though the smoking rate among male adults is still higher than those in other developed countries. (MT)

High technology Amazingly rapid and wide-ranging are the recent developments in Japan's high technology. New discoveries and inventions in electronics, computer science, telecommunication, biotechnology, medical engineering and so on are so constantly appearing in the news headlines that it is often hard for non-experts to keep up with the latest developments. "High-tech" products, however, have already filtered into daily life, and people are unknowingly using them.

One of the most remarkable and familiar fields, electronics has produced, besides laser disks and compact disks, various kinds of home appliances, which are of smaller size and lighter weight than their predecessors and are available at lower prices. They suit the trend

が，禁煙運動は次第に強力になってきています。

　ハイテクノロジー（**高度先端技術**）　最近の日本のハイテクノ
ロジーの発達は驚くほど早く，広範囲にわたっています。電子工
学，コンピューター科学，通信技術，生物工学，医療工学などの
発見や発明が連日のようにニュースになっているので，専門家で
もなければ最新の事情についていくのが大変なくらいです。しか
し，「ハイテク」製品はすでに日常生活に浸透していて，みんな
がそれとは知らずに使っています。
　電子工学は最もよく知られており，最もめざましい分野ですが，
レーザーディスクやコンパクトディスクのほかに，以前のものよ
りも小さくて軽く，値段も安い電気製品をいろいろ生産していま
す。そうした製品は「軽薄短小」を求める今日の風潮にあってい
ます。ニューメディアの分野もそれに劣らず豊かな成果をあげて
います。例えばNTTはキャプテンシステムを開発し，職場や家
庭と情報センターのデータバンクとを結んで，「情報時代」の要

of the times when *kei-haku-tan-shō* (light weight, thin volume, short length, and small size) is much sought after. No less fruitful has been the field of new mass-communication media. For example, NTT (Nippon Telegraph and Telephone Corporation) has developed a videotex system called CAPTAIN (Character and Pattern Telephone Access Information Network System). Connecting individual homes and offices with computer data banks at the information center, it is now meeting the demands of the "Information Age".

Other developments have also become the topics of the day—FMS (Flexible Manufacturing System) with its industrial robots automating many of the processes used in manufacturing industrial goods, laser surgical knives now in use in many hospitals, and various kinds of new materials, such as shape-memory alloys, used in making bras. Furthermore, hopes are laid on an electrical storage system utilizing superconductivity, on a hyperthermic cure for cancer using microwaves, and on monoclonal antibodies produced by cellular engineering for cures of other diseases incurable at present.

Technology in some fields is so much advanced that the American government proposed a technical tie-up for SDI (Strategic Defence Initiative), but many people here are against Japan's involvement in "Star Wars." They insist that high technology products and techniques must be used with great caution and only for peaceful purposes. (TS)

求に応えています。

その他の分野の開発も話題になっています。例えば，工業製品の生産過程の多くを自動化する工業用ロボットを使うFMS（フレキシブル生産システム），多くの病院で使われているレーザーメス，ブラジャーに使われる形状記憶合金のような新素材などです。さらに，超電導を利用した電力貯蔵システムや，マイクロウェーブを利用した癌治療のための温熱療法や，現在不治とされているいろいろな病気を治療するために細胞工学が生みだしたモノクローナル抗体などに期待がかけられています。

ある分野の技術は高度に進んでいるので，SDI（戦略防衛構想）のためにアメリカが技術提携を申し入れてきたほどです。しかし，日本が「スターウォーズ」に関与すべきではないと反対する人もたくさんいます。ハイテクノロジーの製品や技術は慎重に，平和的な目的のためだけに使うべきだと彼らは主張しています。

Holding back   *Enryo*, or holding back, is a form
of politeness, a device for maintaining a certain distance
from those one does not know well or one considers as
one's superiors. When the Japanese meet someone for
the first time, they tend to avoid close contact, such
as expressed by Americans through a firm hand-shake
or an arm around the shoulders. A polite bow is the
usual greeting. The distance does not necessarily mean
unfriendliness. Rather, it expresses a sense of deference.

Since aggressiveness and frankness are considered
rather negatively in Japanese social etiquette, it is
graceful to behave in a "holding back" way. For example, when they are offered a drink or food, it is cour-
teous to refuse what is offered at least once in order
to show that they are "holding back," that is, they are
polite. It should be remembered, however, that a flat
"no" never works. To show that they are not really
declining the offer, they should add something like
"that would be troubling you too much." The offerer,
on the other hand, is not to take their words of refusal
at their face value. He will repeat the offer, saying,
"Please don't hold back." And then, they finally accept
the offer. Subtle exchanges of courtesy of this kind
can be sometimes too difficult even for Japanese to
perform perfectly.

Enryo in behavior and honorifics in the language correspond to each other. *Enryo* is practiced where honorifics are employed in speech, and vice versa. There

132

遠　慮　遠慮というのはていねいさの表現の一つで，よく知らない人や目上の人との間にある種の距離を作る行動を言います。初対面の人に対して日本人は，アメリカ人のように固い握手をしたり肩を抱いたりして親密さを表すことはしません。ふつうていねいにおじぎをするだけです。距離を置くというのは必ずしもよそよそしいということではありません。むしろ，かしこまった気持ちを表現しているのです。

　積極性や率直さは，日本人の社会ではむしろあまり好ましくないとされています。ですから，遠慮がちにふるまうことが上品なのです。例えば，飲み物や食事を勧められた時，遠慮しているのだということ，つまりていねいさを表すために少なくとも一度は相手の勧めをことわることが礼儀にかなっています。しかしながら，そっけなく「結構です」と言ってしまってはいけません。勧めを本当はことわっているわけではないということを表すために，「それではご迷惑でしょうから」というようなことを言いそえます。そして最後には勧めに応じるのです。日本人にとってさえ，このような微妙な対応は時にはむずかしく感じられます。

　行動における遠慮と言語における敬語とは互いに対応しています。敬語を使う相手には遠慮がちな行動をし，その逆もまた成り立ちます。親しい間柄では遠慮は必要ありません。そのような間柄で遠慮していると，かえってよそよそしいとされてしまいます。

is no need to "hold back" among intimates. Those who behave in a holding-back way toward their close friends are criticized as unfriendly. (MH)

Hometown   Twice a year, there is a grand exodus from the big cities back to the countryside. At New Year, millions of city dwellers who originally came from rural areas throughout Japan return to their hometowns to be reunited with their family. The second exodus takes place during August for the *Bon* Festival (a traditional Buddhist festival), during which people celebrate the return of the souls of their ancestors. On these occasions, major metropolitan railway and bus terminals, highways, and airports get overcrowded with passengers returning to their hometowns. Traffic tie-ups on major highways have become a common sight. In spite of the huge crowds, people still want to return home for these two special festive seasons of the year.

For those who cannot go home, there is an easy way to get a taste of home. Recently, many villages and towns have been promoting products for which they are famous, such as farm and handmade products. Coupled with this "village goods promotion campaign," quite a large number of companies offer a door-to-door service, delivering specialities from various villages and towns across the nation. Thus, one can enjoy a taste of his hometown without actually going home.

But why is one's hometown so important to the Japanese? In olden times, one's village was everything to

134

故　郷　　年に２度，都会から田舎への大移動が見られます。正月には，家族と一緒に過ごそうと何百万もの人が都会を離れて生まれ故郷へ帰ります。８月の伝統的仏教行事である盆の時期にも，先祖の霊を迎えるために大勢の人がそれぞれの郷里へ帰ります。こうした盆・正月のシーズンには，主な駅・バスターミナル・高速道路・空港は帰省客で大混雑します。交通渋滞もいたるところで見受けられます。そうした混雑にもめげず，年に２回，正月と盆には多くの人が里帰りするのです。

　帰省できない人にとっては，故郷を手軽に味わえる方法があります。最近，多くの村・町が農産物・手工芸品などの振興に力をそそいでいます。こうした村おこし運動とあいまって，数多くの企業が宅配便のサービスを行っています。全国各地の村や町の特産物を家庭まで届けてくれるもので，実際に帰省しなくても，ふるさとをちょっぴり味わうことができます。

　しかし，なぜ，ふるさとは日本人にとってこんなにも大切なものなのでしょうか。昔は，日本人にとって村がすべてでした。村こそが生まれてから死ぬまでの一生を過ごす唯一の場所だったのです。しかし，工業化・都市化が進むにつれて，都会で職を得るために，人々は故郷をあとにするようになったのです。でも，彼らにとって，都会は一時的な場所でしかありませんでした。多くの人々が，故郷に思いをはせながら，都会で一生懸命に働きました。今日見られる年に２度の帰省はその名残りと言えます。

the Japanese. It was the place where they were born, raised and buried. With the advancement of industry and urbanization, the Japanese began to leave their hometowns to work in the big cities. In their minds, however, their life in the big cities was not permanent. With a strong nostalgia for their birthplaces, many Japanese worked hard in the city, hoping to return to the place from where they originally came. Even today, this fits the Japanese scene, if only for two brief visits a year. (YN)

Hopelessness, feeling of Any culture is greatly influenced by its natural environment, and this seems true in the case of Japanese culture, particularly the environment's psychological effects. One of the most striking of them is a feeling of helplessness. This state of mind cannot be explained without referring to Japan's geographical and climatic features.

The history of Japan is marked by natural disasters— volcanic eruptions , earthquakes , typhoons , floods , landslides, snowslides and *tsunami* tidal waves (in fact, "tsunami" comes from the Japanese language). These disasters cause great destruction of life and property in various parts of the country every year. For example, a large amount of hard work for the year's rice crop is brought to nothing in a night by typhoons, which are frequent in Japan at flowering time and harvest time. The Japanese have had to bow before the force of nature and have developed a deep-rooted feeling of

諦めの気持ち　　どの文化も自然環境から大きな影響を受けます。日本文化の場合, とりわけ環境が及ぼす心理的影響という点で, このことが当てはまるように思われます。最も顕著な影響の1つに諦めの気持ちがあります。この心理状態は日本の風土に言及することなしには説明できません。

　日本の歴史は, 火山の噴火, 地震, 台風, 洪水, 地すべり, 雪崩, 津波（英語でも tsunami と言いますが, 日本語から来ています）などの自然災害によって特徴づけられています。これらの天災は毎年国内各地で多くの人命を奪い財産を破壊しています。例えば, 米作のために注がれた1年間の労苦が, 開花期や収穫期に襲う台風のせいで, 一夜のうちに無に帰してしまいます。日本人は自然の力の前に平伏し, 根深い諦めの気持ちを抱くようになりました。日本人は基本的には悲観的な国民だとよく指摘されます。

　「仕方がない」と言って, 抵抗し難いものを容易に受容してしまう日本人の傾向は, 権威への服従という形でも表れます。日本には「泣く子と地頭には勝てぬ」とか「長いものには巻かれろ」という諺があります。一見安易と見える従順は, あまりにも受動的で服従的に思われるでしょうが, 時にはそれが事態がいっそう

helplessness. It is often pointed out that the Japanese are basically a pessimistic and melancholy people.

Their tendency to easily accept what is hard to resist, saying "It can't be helped," is also seen in their obedience to authority. Japanese proverbs say, "It is impossible to reason with a crying child or government officials," and "Get ready to be rolled up when you see something long" (i.e. "Yield to the powerful"). This seemingly ready obedience may appear too passive and submissive, but it can sometimes serve as a kind of traditional wisdom which prevents a situation from getting more troublesome. Some people can even feel relieved, excusing themselves from making greater efforts or fighting against authorities. They often try to be satisfied with what they are and what they have, thus keeping their mental balance. Though in actual fact the Japanese have risen anew after every disaster and devastation in their long history, yet they have always had a sense of resignation deep in their heart. (MT)

Housing　The traditional Japanese house is wooden, airy and light and of one or two stories, a combination which is suited to the hot, humid summer of Japan. Structurally, it features a joined skeleton frame of post-and-beam construction, elevated floor and the posts placed on foundation stones for protection from moisture and earthquakes. Only the natural colors and textures of the building materials are used for the house. A

面倒になるのを防ぐ伝統的な知恵として役立つこともあります。新しい努力や権威に逆らう闘いを免れて，ほっと安心する人さえいます。自分の現状に満足しようとし，それによって精神のバランスを保っているのです。日本人は実際は長い歴史において災害や荒廃のたびに立ち直ってきましたが，心の奥底にはいつも一種の諦観があります。

住の文化　　伝統的な日本の家屋は木造で，通風と採光が良く，一，二階建で，暑くて湿気の多い気候に向いています。構造上の特徴として，柱と梁の骨組みと，高い床，それに湿気予防や地震に備えて土台に据えた柱が，あげられます。建築資材には，色合いも，手触りも，自然のものを使います。茅葺き屋根の伝統的な茶室がその典型です。

　伝統的な家の内部は，中心に座敷（客間）があり，人は部屋から部屋へ移動するようになっています。部屋はいろいろの目的に

typical example is the traditional *chashitsu* (tea house) with a thatched roof.

The interior of the traditional house is characterized by *zashiki* (a special reception room) at the center, room-to-room passage, multipurpose rooms with *tatami* (thick straw mats covered with woven rushes) and partitioned by *fusuma* or *shōji* (sliding doors). The size of living space is measured in terms of the number of *tatami* (approximately 18 square feet each).

Western influence and rapid urbanization, among other factors, have caused a drastic change in Japanese housing in this century: the replacement of *zashiki* with *ima* (the living room) as the center of the home; the introduction of the corridor and the specialization of room functions; the use of a Western style living-dining room; a shift from an airy housing model to a closed one with aluminum sashes and other materials; multiunit dwellings as the norm in large cities.

There were 34,705,000 housing units in Japan in 1983, with an average of 3.3 persons per unit. Of this total, 64% were single family dwellings and 36% multiple-unit dwellings. Of the single-family units 87.6% were owned and 12.4% rented; of the multiple-unit dwellings (especially of apartment house type) 22.6% were owned and 77.4% were rented. The total area of each dwelling averages 924.3 square feet (85.9 square meters). The cost of a house in Japan and especially that in Tokyo is among the highest in the world. For example, the cost for a housing lot within an hour and

使われ，畳敷きになっています（畳は芯台に，イグサで編んだカバーをかけたものです）。部屋の仕切りには，襖や障子の引戸が使われています。部屋の広さは，畳の枚数で表します（畳1枚は，約1.6平方メートル〔18平方フィート〕の広さです）。

今世紀に，特に西洋の影響と急速な都市化のために，日本家屋は大きく変わりました。家の中心は，座敷から居間に移り，廊下がとり入れられました。各部屋の機能が固定して，洋風の居間兼食堂が使われるようになりました。風通しの良い家から，アルミサッシその他の資材を使った気密性の高い家へと変わりました。また，大都市では，集合住宅が標準になりました。

日本には1983年に，住宅が34,705,000軒あり，1軒平均3.3人となっていました。この軒数の64％が一戸建で，36％が集合住宅です。一戸建の住宅の87.6％は持家で，12.4％は賃貸です。集合住宅（特にアパート形式のもの）の22.6％は分譲で，77.4％は賃貸となっています。1戸あたりの総床面積は，平均85.9平方メートル（924.3平方フィート）です。特に東京での住宅取得費は，世界最高です。例えば，都心から1時間半以内の湘南地方のようなところに土地を求めると，0.09平方メートル（1平方フット）につき約45,278円（337.9ドル）に達します。この地方の一戸建の建築費は，0.09平方メートル（1平方フィート）につき15,008円（112ドル）かかります。

a half from downtown Tokyo, such as that in Shōnan, could reach $337.90 per square foot. The average construction cost for a single-family unit in the same area is $112 per square foot. (MO)

Humility   In Japanese society people are expected to be humble and modest regardless of their age and social position . Least favored are those who are aggressive and self-assertive and who display their ability, knowledge, or wealth.

Japanese society developed from an agrarian society, where it was necessary to work in groups and have a system of cooperation. Accordingly, harmony and the consensus of the entire community were of prime importance, and confronting others openly in order to get one's own way was discouraged. Even a person in charge, in making a decision, was not supposed to insist on his own way but to seek the consensus of those who were evolved.

Above all, humility and modesty are required of leaders. As the saying goes, "The boughs that bear most hang lowest." Therefore, Japanese business firms use bottom-up management rather than top-down management, which is common in the Western business world. The decision-making process goes like this : the person in charge draws up the original plan and informally discusses it with his seniors in ascending order, from supervisor to manager to general manager. In the process which is traditionally called *nemawashi* or *ringi*

謙　虚　　日本の社会では，人は年齢や社会的地位に関係なく謙虚で控えめであることが良いとされています。攻撃的で自己主張が強く，能力や知識や富をひけらかす人物は嫌われます。

　日本の社会は農耕社会を原型としています。そこでは，共同で仕事をしなければならないので，そのための協力体制が必要でした。したがって，共同体全体の調和と合意がもっとも大切で，自分の思い通りにしようと他人とおおっぴらに対決することは抑えられました。長でさえ，何かを決めるときには，自分勝手に決めず，関係者の合意を取りつけなければなりませんでした。

　とくに，指導者には謙虚で控えめであることが望ましいとされています。諺にも「実るほど頭のさがる稲穂かな」と言います。それで，日本の企業は，欧米のビジネス界でいっぱんに用いられているトップダウン方式ではなく，ボトムアップ方式の経営を行っているわけです。したがって，ものごとを決めるのは次のような手順で行われます。担当者が計画書を作り，非公式に係長，課長，部長と順に上の上司に相談していきます。伝統的に「根回し」とか「稟議制度」とか呼ばれているこの過程で計画は修正され，正式に会議に提案された時点では関係者全員の賛同を得られるものになっているというわけです。

　このような手順の背後には，人がそれぞれもっている名誉は大切であり，尊重されなければならないという考えがあります。たとえば，ある年配者にその地位に要求される指導力が欠けていても，周りが彼を辞めさせることはしません。彼が自分の名誉を損なわずに自ら辞任できるよういろいろと気を配ってあげるのです。

143

seido, the plan is revised, and by the time it is brought to a formal meeting for discussion, it is acceptable to all the people concerned.

Behind this practice lies the assumption that everybody's honor is important and must be respected. For example, even when a senior leader lacks the leadership required in his position, people will not force him out. Instead, they will try to help him decide to resign on his own without losing face. (YY)

Humor　　Japanese are often said to have little sense of humor. It is true that statesmen, government officials, and financial magnates rarely make jokes on formal occassions, but this is simply because they consider it inappropriate to provoke laughter on such occasions. The apparent lack of humor in political or ceremonial speeches delivered by Japanese leaders may be a vestige of Confucian influence. Confucianism, popular among the ancient warrior class, advocated gravity and discouraged laughter in public, and consequently the making of jokes during work or in serious communication came to be considered insincere or imprudent.

The common people, however, knowing that humor can be a lubricant which helps smooth stiff conversations and personal relations, not only enjoy jokes on casual and relaxed occasions, but also appreciate the novelty and charm of humorous phraseology in business transactions. They know that humor can reduce frictions and foster the conciliatory atmosphere needed in

ユーモア　　日本人はユーモアのセンスがないとよく言われます。確かに政治家や官僚や財界人が公式の場で冗談を言うことはめったにありませんが，それは公式の場で人を笑わせるようなことは不適切だと考えられているからにすぎません。政治や儀式の場で日本のリーダーがする演説にユーモアが欠けているのは儒教の影響かもしれません。昔の武士階級に人気のあった儒教は謹厳を唱道し，公の場での笑いをよくないこととしました。その結果，仕事中や真面目な話の最中に冗談を言ったりするのは不真面目で不謹慎と考えられるようになりました。

　しかし，一般庶民はユーモアが堅苦しい会話や人間関係を和らげるのに役立つということを知っていて，くだけた，くつろいだ場で冗談を楽しむだけではなく，商談の場でも気の利いた面白い言葉づかいを楽しみます。ユーモアによって摩擦を少なくし，仕事のやりとりで同意を得るのに必要な和気あいあいの雰囲気を作り出せることを知っているのです。

　日本のユーモア（諧虐または滑稽）は何世紀にもわたってさまざまな種類の文学的，演芸的娯楽を生み出してきました。例えば，狂言，狂歌，川柳，落語，漫才などです。このようなユーモアの伝統的なジャンルは主として庶民の文化でしたが，時に皮肉やペ

reaching business agreements.

Japanese humor (*kaigyaku* or *kokkei*) has produced over the centuries many forms of literary and theatrical entertainments, such as *kyōgen* (comic interludes performed between *nō* plays), *kyōka* (satirical short poems in *tanka* style), *senryū* (short humorous poems in *haiku* style), *rakugo* (comic story telling), and *manzai* (comic stage dialogues). These traditional genres of humor, which reveal the truth in life sometimes with a touch of irony and pathos, have been largely part of the common people's culture.

Every known type of humor is enjoyed by people today — punning jokes, parodies, satires, tall tales, impersonation, and so on. Comics and humorous novels are among the bestselling books, and slapstick comedies and rollicking gags performed by funny TV personalities and cutups, though not always irresistible, are getting the highest audience ratings. Probably the best way to see what kinds of humor are attracting people is to watch TV commercials. (TS)

Imitation and creation Japanese people have been often criticized as clever at imitating foreign inventions and styles but lacking in originality. It is common to all countries, however, to adopt foreign culture with appropriate modifications introduced to make it suit to their own. For example, Japanese fine arts of the 19th century, *ukiyoe* in particular, influenced Western artists including impressionistic painters such as Monet

146

ーソスで味付けをして人生の真実を垣間見せてくれます。

　現在では，人々はあらゆる種類のユーモアを楽しんでいます。それには駄洒落，パロディー，風刺，ほら話，もの真似などがあります。漫画やユーモア小説がベストセラーに入っていますし，いつも爆笑というわけではありませんが，面白いタレントやひょうきん者が演じるドタバタ喜劇やギャグが，テレビの高視聴率を稼いでいます。どんな種類のユーモアが受けているか，それを知るのに一番いい方法はたぶんテレビのコマーシャルを見ることでしょう。

　模倣と創造　　日本人は，外国の発明ややり方を真似るのは巧いけれど，創造性に欠ける，とよく批判されてきました。けれども，自国の文化に合うように，外国文化に適宜修正を加え，これを採用することは，どの国にも共通して見られることです。例えば，19世紀の日本美術，特に浮世絵は，モネやゴッホなどの印象派画家も含めて，西洋の芸術家に影響を与えました。この芸術家たちは，浮世絵をそっくり真似はしませんでしたが，創造的に真似たと言えるでしょう。

and van Gogh. Though they did not copy *ukiyoe* slavishly, they can be said to have imitated it creatively.

Japan has been active in transferring and adopting superior culture and technology from foreign countries since ancient times. Above all, the adoption of highly developed Chinese Tang culture beginning in the 7th century enabled Japan to become a more civilized, law-governed country. Japan's technological modernization and advancement also owe much to its ability to revise and refine the original model as well as its imitative attitude. At the core of the Japanese culture lies the idea that imitation is an important process of basic education. The words *manabu* (to learn) and *maneru* (to imitate) are said to have derived from the same origin, *manebu*, and students and apprentices are often told to follow their masters' models before they acquire their own ideas and skills.

Nor do Japanese always distinguish clearly between imitation and creation. Rather, they regard practical application of science and refinement of prototypes of technology as no less creative than discoveries and inventions. As Professor H. Hironaka, a Field's Medal winner, once remarked in a TV interview, coming up with a new idea is not creative enough unless it is put into practice, which also requires a creative mind.

On the other hand, Japan is slower than the U.S. and European countries in fundamental scientific research. This may be shown by the ratio of technologists to scientists, which is 4 : 1 in Japan and 3 : 2 in

昔から日本では，外国の優れた文化や技術を積極的にとり入れてきました。中でも，7世紀初頭に高度に発達した中国の唐文化を採用することにより，日本はそれまでよりも文化的な法治国家になることができました。日本の科学技術が近代化し，発展したのも，良いものに習おうとする姿勢に加えて，元となるモデルを修正・洗練する能力があることによるのです。日本文化の根底には，模倣は基本的な教育の大切な一過程であるとする考え方があります。「まなぶ」と「まねる」は，共通の語源である「まねぶ」から派生したと言われます。そして，弟子は，自らの考え方や技を身につけるのに先立ち，師の手本に習うよう，教えられることが多いのです。

　日本人は，また，模倣と創造も，常にはっきり区別しているわけではありません。むしろ，科学の実際的応用や，科学技術の原型改良は，発明・発見と同じくらい創造的な業であるとみなしているのです。フィールズ・メダル受賞者の広中平祐教授も，テレビ・インタビューに答え，こう述べています。思いついただけなら，それっきり，それを受けて実行するほうも独創である，と。

　他方，基礎科学研究の面で，日本は欧米に遅れをとっています。この遅れは，技術者と科学者の割合に示されており，日本では4対1，アメリカでは3対2となっています。しかし，日本の研究開発費増加の割合は，アメリカの場合の2倍となっているのです。また，日本の文部省は，福井謙一教授や利根川進教授級のノーベル賞受賞者がもっと出ることを期待してか，基礎研究促進のために，いろいろの措置を講じています。

the U. S. However, the rate of increase in research and development costs in Japan doubles that of the U.S., and the Ministry of Education is taking measures to promote fundamental research in the hope of producing more of Nobel Prize winners like Professors K. Fukui and S. Tonegawa. (MO/TS)

Inheritance　　The post-war Constitution of Japan prohibits discrimination based on "race, creed, sex, social status or family origin." According to this constitutional mandate, the Civil Code was revised in 1947 to abolish the age-old "family-head inheritance system" under which the eldest son, as the head of a clan, usually took all of the descedent's estate. The Code now provides, in an ordinary intestate case (where a person dies without leaving a will), that a spouse inherits half of a decedent's estate and children equally share the rest.

However, old customs are hard to change, particularly in rural areas where farmland has customarily been inherited by one person, preferably the eldest son. To achieve this, the usual practice, even in urban areas when a person dies leaving real property of some value, is that the other heirs waive their inheritance claim when they pay inheritance tax and register the change of land ownership to depict the new owner. But, this practice, based on an amicable agreement among family members, has been under attack recently. The growth of the Japanese economy has brought about a tremen-

150

相　続　戦後の日本国憲法は「人種，信条，性別，社会的身分又は門地」にもとづく差別を禁止しました。この憲法の要求に従い，1947年に民法典が改正され，古くからあったいわゆる「家督相続制」は廃止になりました。家督相続制のもとでは，通例，長男子が一族の長として，被相続人の財産をすべて承継することになっていました。現行の民法典は，通常の無遺言の事例（すなわち，人が遺言書を残さずに死亡した場合）において，配偶者が被相続人の財産の二分の一を相続し，残りを子供達が平等に分けることと定めています。

　しかしながら，古くからの慣行を変えることは，とりわけ農地が一人の者，できれば長男によって相続されることが望ましいと従来から考えられてきた農村部においては，大変難しいことです。そこで，1人の相続を達成するために，たとえ都市部であっても人がいくばくかの価値ある不動産を残して死亡した場合には，相続税の支払いと土地所有権の変更の登記にあたって，他の相続人が相続の権利を放棄するということがよく行われています。しかし，この家族のメンバー間の平和的な合意にもとづくやり方は，近年攻撃をうけるようになりました。日本経済の発展がどこでも土地価格のすさまじい高騰をもたらし，土地が富の主要な源泉となったからです。日本における土地の異常なまでの高い価値のために，長男が家族の他のメンバーに，自分または被相続人の現金あるいは動産を提供して，自分の相続の埋め合わせをするという

dous rise in land prices everywhere and land has become an important source of wealth. Because of the unusually high worth of land in Japan, an eldest son can no longer offset his inheritance by offering other members of his family cash or other non-real properties of his own or of the decedent, and as a result, issues of land inheritance are increasingly the cause of family conflict.

To avoid family conflict as well as piecemeal devision of an estate, more and more people are preparing wills which devise ways of distributing land to a particular person, a method which until recently was not common among ordinary Japanese people. However, the Civil Code provides for a so-called "forced inheritance" or "legal reserve" system, under which persons desinherited by an otherwise valid will are still authorized to claim as their right half of their legal entitlement to the descedent's estate. In addition, the rising inheritance taxes which come with the hightened value of real property have become another cause of distress among Japanese heirs. Thus, land price and inheritance taxes have inevitably raised the Japanese awareness toward inheritance issues. It is expected, therefore, that in the future an elaborate estate planning of the Western type will become part of Japanese life. (IT)

Internationalization　　Japanese have long been interested in foreign culture. Books, magazines, newspaper articles, TV programs, or any kind of information

ことはもはや不可能になりました。その結果，土地の相続問題が家族の争いのもととなることが増えています。

　家族の争いを避け，合わせて財産の細切れ的な分割を避けるために，ますます多くの人が，特定の者に土地を相続させる方法として遺言書を作成するようになってきましたが，これは最近までは日本の普通の人々にとってあまり一般的ではありませんでした。しかし，民法典はいわゆる「遺留分」の制度を定めており，この下では，有効な遺言書によって相続を否定された者であっても，依然として被相続人の財産に対する法定相続分の半分について権利を主張することを認められています。これに加えて，不動産価格の高騰にともなう相続税の高騰が，日本の相続人にとってもう一つの悩みの種となっています。このように，土地価格と相続税は，必然的に相続問題に対する日本人の意識を高めることになりました。それゆえ，近い将来において西欧型の巧妙なエステイト・プランニング（相続財産計画）が日本人の生活の一部となることが予想されるのです。

　　国際化　　日本人は外国の文化には強い関心を抱いてきました。外国の生活を伝える書物はよく売れていますし，テレビ番組はいつも高い視聴率を誇っています。海外情報はとりわけ重要視され

153

that deals with foreign ways of life have been attracting a large audience from all sections of Japanese society. Foreign products are bought and used, exotic foods tasted and favored, different ways of life experimented with and incorporated into traditional Japanese customs.

For many years in Japan, internationalization was actually associated with Westernization in general and Americanization in particular. Japanese took to this renovative process for the benefit of themselves. They adopted those parts of Western and American civilization and culture that suited their own needs in modernizing and enriching their ways of life. They selected what they considered would contribute to progress in economic and social functions, but they kept their traditional core intact as much as possible. They sought and found what they wanted to advance their society.

The recent tendency for Japan's greater internationalization is a gavernment response to strong pressures from all over the world for her increased fair trade practice. The current international economic situation demands that Japanese change their ways of life for the benefit of other people. They are asked to change their industrial system, distribution structure, labor condition and even communication style in order to facilitate increased foreign participation in Japanese markets of all sorts.

While established interest groups express fear, consumers welcome a free flow of goods, information, and

154

ているのです。外国製品の愛好者も多く，異国情緒のある食べ物にも人気があります。外国の生活様式もいろいろな形で日本の習慣に取り入れられています。

　日本では，長い間，国際化というと，西洋式の生活，特にアメリカ式の生活を取り入れることを意味していました。日本人は自分自身の利益のために，そのような改革に着手したのです。日本人は西洋とアメリカの文明・文化の中から，自分の生活を近代化させ向上させるのに必要な部分だけを採用してきました。主眼は自国の経済と社会の進歩にあり，その他の部分では日本の伝統を強く守ってきました。他国の利益のために国際化したわけではないのです。

　日本政府が最近力を入れている国際化は，諸外国が日本に対して公平な貿易慣行をさらに確実に実行するようにと求めてきたからであります。現在の国際経済の状況から判断すると，日本人は他の国の人々のために，今までの生活習慣を変えるように求められているのです。外国人が日本市場に自由に参加できるようにするには，日本人は伝統的な産業構造，流通機構，労働条件，さらにはコミュニケーションの様式さえも変えなければならないところまできています。

　既存のさまざまな利益集団は危機感をつのらせていますが，消費者は製品，情報，人間の自由な交流を歓迎しています。新しい国際主義によって諸外国の人々との接触が強まることを予想して，各企業では社員教育の一環として，異文化理解のプログラムを導入しはじめました。多くの市民もさまざまな文化的背景をもつ人々と交際することが，有意義であると感じているようです。

people. Anticipating greater contact both here and overseas with people from different national backgrounds to be brought forth by the new age of internationalism, companies are introducing cross-cultural communication programs for their employees. Citizens are finding it enlightening and enriching to get to know people with different cultural backgrounds. (NH)

Japan as an information society　On July 4, 1987, Japan started the world's first twenty-four-hour direct satellite broadcasting. Today Japan's home viewers, who have purchased special small parabolic antennas and tuners for nearly $800, can enjoy watching, for example, a tennis match at Wimbledon and a performance from the Paris Opera House in digital sound, all live and in real time. One of the major programs of this new direct satellite service is the "World News" which begins as early as at 3 a.m. and is broadcast four times a day for a total of eleven and a half hours. This program features the latest news in English from the United States' ABC and CNN and Britain's BBC networks with simultaneous Japanese captions, as well as the firsthand news in Japanese direct from Japan Broadcasting Corporation's New York and London studios.

Along with these most recent achievements in telecommunications technology, Japan is also a land of newspapers. A total of 72.2 million copies of about 160 national and local newspapers is printed everyday,

情報社会　　1987年7月4日，日本は放送衛星を使った世界最初の24時間テレビ放送を開始した。視聴者は，衛星放送用の小さなパラボラアンテナとチューナーを約10万円で購入して備え付けさえすれば，今や家庭に居ながらにしてウインブルドンのテニスの試合やパリのオペラ座の出し物を，生放送でしかもリアルタイムのまま楽しむことができるのです。この衛星放送の目玉番組の一つは，深夜3時から始まり，1日4回，11時間半にわたって流される「ワールド・ニュース」です。NHKのニューヨークやロンドン支局のスタジオから，最新のニュースが日本語によって直接茶の間に送られてくるだけでなく，アメリカのABCやCNN，イギリスのBBCなどのネットワークを通して，世界のホットなニュースが日本語の字幕入りで生放送されています。

　こうした最先端の遠距離通信技術の成果と並んで，日本はまた新聞王国でもあります。およそ160紙もある全国紙・地方紙の総発行部数は朝刊，夕刊を含めると実に1日7,220万部にも達します。そのうち1874年創立の読売新聞は，1日1,387万部という世界最多販売部数を誇っています。これはアメリカのウォールストリート・ジャーナルやニューヨーク・デイリーニューズ，イギリスのザ・サンやソ連のプラウダの各紙を凌ぐものです。

　さらに，990万部，14種の主要スポーツ紙と，約3,500種の業界紙，年間9億冊もの新刊書，さらに多種多様な内容を盛った膨

including morning and evening editions. The best-selling newspaper, *Yomiuri Shimbun*, for example, which was established in 1874, boasts of the world's largest daily circulation of 13,869,000, surpassing the United States' *Wall Street Journal* and *New York Daily News*, Britain's *The Sun*, and even Soviet Union's *Pravda*.

To these must be added 14 major sports newspapers with a combined circulation of 9.9 million copies, and some 3,500 trade newspapers. Besides, nearly 900 million books and an enormous number of magazines with a large variety of contents are sold every year. This immense flood of information makes average Japanese really well-informed and sometimes too-informed people, confusing them in their ability to collate and choose between reality and fiction. (ON)

Journey　　　Many people like to travel. Two possibilities about where to go suggest themselves—in Japan or outside Japan. Elderly folks prefer to make a domestic trip, while young people prefer to travel overseas.

Mental relaxation as well as physical rest is what most travellers seek for. Hot spring resorts meet both these needs and are now very popular, much more so than ever before among Japanese people. Lots of spa advertizements appear in newspapers and in magazines, and travel brochures abound at travel agencies.

There are some hot spring resorts that have been well known throughout Japan, but there are countless

大な数の雑誌がこれに加わります。こうした氾濫する情報の海の中で，平均的日本人は実に情報通なのですが，他方情報過多に陥って，現実と虚構の見分けがつきにくくなる危険も存在しています。

　　旅　　旅行好きな人はたくさんいます。行き先は大きく言って二つに分かれます。国内と海外です。ある程度年齢のいった人たちは国内旅行が主でしょう。しかし，若者は海外旅行ということになります。

　旅行者の多くは，体を休めるだけでなく，心も休めたいのです。温泉はこの条件にぴったりで，現在，かつてないほど日本人の間で人気を集めています。新聞，雑誌には必ずといっていいほど，温泉の広告が載っています。また，旅行代理店には旅行用のパンフレットがあふれています。

　全国に知れわたるほど有名な温泉地もあります。それほど有名でないものなら無数にあります。数年前なら，骨休めには，皆有名で大きな温泉地に行ったものです。ところが最近はちょっと事情が変わって，今まで無名だった温泉地が多くの人でにぎわうよ

others that are not so well known. Some years ago, people used to choose the former when they wanted to relax. But things have changed and the latter have come to attract a large number of people these days. This is because hot spring resorts are places where they go for mental relaxation as well as for physical rest, so that they do not feel like going to crowded places. Elderly people are most likely to enjoy these places. However, young people, who have itchy feet, have been making trips to them in increasing numbers lately.

Overseas travel is booming, particularly among the youth. Young office workers are said to spend a large part of their money on traveling. University students, most of whom have some kind of part-time jobs these days, make a journey abroad, taking advantage of the long summer and spring vacation. A shift in people's preference in their choice of the places to visit can be recognized. As in the case of hot spring resorts, they tend to want to visit places which have been less known so far. Thus, while many Japanese tourists can still be seen in the United States, Europe and Southeast Asia, you will also find them in Africa, South America and in islands in the South Sea. Journeys abroad are mainly for enjoyment rather than for relaxation. (MAT)

Labor union　　Labor unions began to be formed in Japan among the skilled workers in the 1890s after the

うになりました。これは，温泉は体だけでなく，心を休めるにも
いい，ということと関係しています。心の安らぎを求めるのに，
だれが好き好んで混雑した場所へ行くでしょう。人里はなれた温
泉地は，お年寄りならまず間違いなく楽しめます。でも，最近は，
旅行好きで鳴らした若者たちがこのような温泉に旅するケースが
ますます増えています。

　海外旅行は，特に若者の間でブームを巻き起こしています。若
いサラリーマンは給料の多くを旅行につぎ込んでいるそうです。
大学生も，学生の特権である長い夏休みや春休みを利用して，ア
ルバイトで稼いだお金で海外旅行します。ここでもまた，温泉地
の場合と同様，行き先の好みが変わってきました。つまり，これ
までさほど知られていない場所に行くようになったのです。日本
人旅行者の姿は，相変わらずアメリカ，ヨーロッパ，そして東南
アジアでも見かけますが，今までと違ってアフリカや南米や南洋
諸島でもずいぶん見かけるようになったのです。こうした海外旅
行は，休むことよりも楽しむことが目的だといっていいでしょう。

労働組合　　1889（明治22年）年に明治憲法が交付された後，
明治20年代に熟練工の間で労働組合が組織されました。大正元

LABOR UNION

Meiji Constitution was promulgated in 1889. In 1912, the first nation-wide labor federation was established, modeled on the American Federation of Labor. This developmemt supported the concept of company unions, in which white- and blue-collar workers were unionized by company rather than by industry or craft. This has remained a characteristic of unions to the present in Japan, where life-time employment and the seniority system in companies have been the norm.

In 1950, the General Council of Trade Unions of Japan, affiliated with the Japan Socialist Party, was formed, soon taking a leftist position against the United Nations' military interference in the Korean War. In 1954 some important unions in the private sector left the Council and formed the Japanese Confederation of Labor, lending support to the Democratic Socialist Party. In 1956 some unions, tired of the Council and the Confederation, formed the Federation of Independent Unions. As of 1987, the General Council consists of about 4. 27 million members, the Confederation, of about 1. 9 million, the Federation, of about 1. 4 million, and others, of about one million.

Since 1955 a "spring offensive" designed for the collective bargaining of wages has been effective in increasing wages every year. However, in general the people have not supported a general walkout of public transportation workers and have become somewhat critical of labor movements. Union membership has declined gradually during the past decade.

年に AFL（アメリカ労働総同盟）によって初めて全国規模の労働組合が形成されました。ホワイト・カラーとブルー・カラー労働者が産業や技術別ではなく，会社別の組合を作ったのです。これは今日まで日本の労働組合の特徴です。なぜなら，日本では，終身雇用や年功序列が普通だからです。

1950年（昭和25年），日本社会党系の総評が組織され，朝鮮動乱に介入する国連軍に反対する左翼の立場をとりました。1954年に民間の主要組合が総評を脱退して同盟を形成し，民社党を支持しました。1956年に総評と同盟に飽いた組合が中立労連を作りました。1987年には総評の組合員数は約427万人，同盟は190万人，中立労連は140万人，残りが100万人です。

1955年以来，春闘は毎年賃金上昇に役立ってきました。しかし，一般大衆は公共輸送の組合員の総ストライキには支持を与えなくなり，労働運動に批判的になってきました。組合員数は過去10年ぐらい徐々に減少しています。

1987年に同盟と中立労連が解散して新しく民間組合の連合を結成しました。組合員数は555万に達するでしょう。総評は3年以内に解散予定です。連合の目標はイデオロギーや政治闘争よりも，労働者の「家庭の幸せ」の実現を目指しています。労働組合再編は日本の政界の再編成につながるかもしれません。

In 1987 the Confederation of Labor and the Federation of Independent Unions were disbanded and united in the newly born Japanese Private Sector Trade Union Confederation with a membership expected to reach about 5.55 million. The General Council is expected to disband itself in three years. The Confederation aims at achieving laborers' "Happiness at Home" rather than engaging in ideological and political struggles. This new move may have an effect on the political parties out of power in Japan. (MK)

Language, social functions of　Language plays a limited role in Japanese society. People generally believe that it is needless to speak precisely and explicitly with one another because they take it for granted that they share a lot of common assumptions. The function of language as a means of social communication in this country, then, is to emphasize and reinforce the feeling of homogeneity.

In daily conversations, messages become telegraphic. Time, space, and logical relations are often unexpressed. Even major points are sometimes left unsaid. People are expected to understand meanings in view of the context of situation in which they are embedded.

Tacit understanding is more important than elaborate speech. People who cannot understand speech in its social context are frowned upon. People who resort to elaborate speech are felt as noise makers. Many Japanese would like to believe that if they are Japanese,

164

ことばの社会的機能　　日本では，ことばは伝達の手段として，必ずしも重要視されているわけではありません。人々はコミュニケーションにおいて，ものごとを正確に明示的に表現する必要はないと考えています。なぜならば，人々はおたがいに了解事項をたくさん共有しているという前提に立っているからです。この意味で，ことばは日本人の同族意識を強調し，それを強化する働きをしているといえます。

　日常の会話では，ことばはずいぶん省略されます。時間，空間，論理関係は表現されないこともあります。要点さえ，省略されることもあります。意味は発話の状況のなかで解釈されます。

　暗黙の了解が可能と思われているので，こまかに説明する必要は感じられないのです。察しを働かせることができない人は，よく思われません。こまかな説明をする人は，うとんじられます。多くの日本人は，おたがいに日本人であれば，ことばを使わなくても理解できるはずだくらいに思っているのです。親しい仲では，意志の疎通に欠けると，「こんなこと，言わなければ，わからないのか」といって，おたがいに相手を責めます。

　察しを強調すると，ことばはそのとおりの意味を表現するとは

they should be able to understand each other without words. When a communications failure occurs between two close friends, the one often accuses the other by saying "Don't you understand my intention if I don't express it?"

Emphasis on tacit understanding has led to belief that words may not say what they mean say. To understand what words mean, people are supposed to look for a variety of nonverbal cues. In an effort to discover the meaning of words, the hearer will carefully but instantly examine the speaker's psychological state which may be realized in his facial expression and tone of speech. Appropriate background interpretation is extremely important as well.

Dependence on tacit understanding endorsed by contextual interpretation discourages the development of a disposition to convey messages in an expository manner. The speakers or writers are so preoccupied with their knowledge that they find it extremely difficult and annoying to provide orderly and precise explanation for an unknowing audience.

Recently, however, this custom of language use has been causing a lot of serious problems abroad. English-language manuals of Japanese hi-tech products are found unintelligible and unserviceable . These manuals is translated into English from the Japanese which are originally characterized by the lack of preciseness and explicitness, a product of the traditional communication style in this country. Recognizing the significance of

かぎらないという気持ちを生みます。人々は真意を理解するために，ことば以外の手掛かりを探します。聞き手は話し手の心をさぐるために，顔の表情やことばの音調に注意します。ことばの背後にある状況を適切に判断することも，きわめて重要です。

状況理解に支えられた察しの働きに依存するようになると，くわしく説明しようという気がおきなくなります。話し手や書き手は自分が知っていることは他人も知っていると思いがちで，なにも知らない人を対象にものごとを順序正しく正確に説明することが，うっとうしく，めんどうになるものです。

しかし，最近，このような日本人の言語習慣は，外国で深刻な問題を引き起こしています。日本のハイテク製品の英文マニュアルがまったく不明瞭で，用をなさず，不評をかっているのです。これらは日本語のマニュアルから英訳されたものです。そのかんじんの日本語のマニュアルが，日本式コミュニケーションの方法にもとづき，明確性と明示性を欠いているのです。日本人はこの問題の重要性を強く認識しはじめています。そして，ことばをもっと広く，効果的に運用する技術の習得に目を向けはじめています。

the matter, Japanese are now beginning to learn how to use language for wider and better communication. (NH)

Leadership model   A key to the understanding of the Japanese concept of leadership is the *oyabun-kobun* or parent-child relationship. An extension of this relationship can be readily observed in the relationships between teacher and student, boss and subordinate, employer and employee, and so on. Whether in business, academic, or political sectors, it is commonly understood that the *oyabun* (one with the status of parent) gives protection and security to the *kobun* (one with the status of child) who, in return, works faithfully for the *oyabun*. According to many successful leaders in Japan, it is in the *oyabun* role within this relationship that their leadership can be exerted to the full extent.

To be recognized as a leader, one must, while operating on the *oyabun-kobun* principle, act fair to every member, and be sensitive to each member's interest and ability. It is quite vital for a leader to be able to assess what each one of his subordinates can and cannot do, and assign tasks in accordance with the individual capability for work. It is a must for a leader to understand his subordinates' personalities and even to be aware of their personal problems. When his subordinates happen to make errors, a leader must be ready to take full responsibility for them without too much complaint. On the other hand, successes are to be

指導者像　　日本人のリーダーシップの概念を理解するうえで，親分－子分の関係は極めて重要なカギになります。この親分－子分関係は，恩師と教え子，上司と部下，雇主と従業員といった関係などどこにでも見受けられます。経済界であれ，学界あるいは政界であれ，親分は子分に生活保障と安全を与えるものであり，そのお返しに子分は忠実に働くというのが一般常識になっています。日本で指導的立場にある多くの人は，この親分－子分関係の中でこそ，リーダーシップを存分に発揮できるのだと言います。

リーダーとして認められるためには，あくまで親分－子分の原則に基づき，えこひいきのないようにし，部下の関心事・能力をしっかり察知することが求められます。部下1人ひとりの力量を見極め，能力に応じて責任ある仕事を割り当てることがリーダーの大切な役目です。部下の性格からプライベートな問題にいたるまで把握することはリーダーとしての必須条件です。部下が失敗をするようなことがあれば，文句を言わずに代わりに全責任をとるくらいの用意が必要ですし，その一方で，うまくいった時にはリーダーとしての役割を持ち上げることなく，成功をグループ全員で分け合うことが肝要です。よく言われるように，日本ではグループの協力が基本です。したがって，この社会的価値観にそわないようなリーダーは部下の信用を失ってしまいます。日本人のもつ指導者像は，ものわかりが良く，寛大で親切，思いやりがあって信頼できる親分ということになるようです。

shared by the entire group, and the credit not solely given to the leader even if he deserves it. As often pointed out, group cooperation is basic for the Japanese. Therefore, a leader who goes against this social value is certain to lose trust among his subordinates. It can be said that the Japanese image of the leader is the *oyabun* who is understanding, tolerant, kind, altruistic, and trustworthy. (YN)

Learning   Japan has traditionally upheld the Confucian attitude toward learning as an ideal. In some branches of learning, for example math and science, Japanese students rank among the best in the world. The number of international awards, including Nobel Prizes, won by Japanese has been growing. There are many scholars and researchers who devote all their time to their studies and researches. For the motivated college students and graduate students, there is an opportunity to study with some of the best professors in the world. There is also a dedication to learning in the best businesses and other institutions as well as in the schools.

In addition to the schools and universities which are true centers of learning, there are some which have been labeled "recreation centers" providing college diplomas. That is, in some universities, students may idle away four years and still graduate. One cause of this situation is that businesses tend to hire college graduates not according to what they have learned, but ac-

学　問　　日本では学問に対して儒教的な態度で接するのを理想とする伝統があります。数学や科学など，分野によっては日本の学生は世界最高のレベルに達しています。ノーベル賞などの国際的な賞を受賞する日本人の数は年々増えています。多くの学者や研究者が時間を忘れて学問や研究に没頭しています。やる気のある大学生や大学院生には世界最高の教授陣について学ぶ機会が与えられています。大学だけでなく，優秀な企業や研究所が学問に大きな貢献をしています。

　真の学問の府である大学に加えて，学生に「大卒」の資格を乱発する「レジャーランド」と呼ばれるところもあります。つまり，学生は4年間遊びほうけて，それでも卒業できる，そういう大学もあるのです。原因の一つは，企業が大学で何を学んだかではなく，大学卒という学歴だけで学生を採用しがちだということにあります。大学入試を突破した学生なら受け入れてよかろうと思っているのです。どうせ社内研修で「会社人間」に鍛えあげていくのですから。もう一つの原因は，日本の企業や社会で同窓会ネットワークが重要な役割を果たしていることでしょう。大学の数が増え，学生が増え過ぎたのです。結果として，学生の能力よりも「大卒」の肩書のほうが大事になってきたようです。その肩書があれば，卒業生はいろいろな同窓関係の利益を得ることができる

cording to their mere educational background. A student who has met the entrance requirements of a higher institution is assumed to be acceptable since the company will train him or her to become a "company person" anyway. Another cause may be the important role the alumni network plays in the Japanese business and social world. Universities have grown numerous and have perhaps admitted too many students. As a result, the ability of the student may be less important than the college diploma, which permits him or her to benefit from various alumni relations.

The emphasis on learning in Japanese society does have one saving grace in that it produces every year excellent and serious students who go on to graduate schools to pursue their studies further. They dedicate themselves to careers in research and teaching at institutes and universities, even though their working conditions are often not satisfactory in terms of facilities and finance. So long as there is such a group of scholars and researchers, Japan is able to maintain its high academic standards in their fields. (YY)

Legal profession　To become a lawyer in Japan, one usually begins by studying law in university. Annually about 30,000 law majors graduate from some 70 universities in Japan. However, the majority of these law graduates go into business and have no contact with the law for the rest of their lives. To become a licensed lawyer, one must pass the state bar

のです。

　しかしながら，毎年大学院へ進んでさらに勉強しようという優秀で真面目な学生もいます。そしてそのことが日本社会において学問を重視することについて救いになっています。彼らは卒業して，大学や研究所で研究や教育に専念します。残念ながら，たいていの場合，設備の面でも，資金面でも研究条件はあまり満足のいくものではありません。でも，このような学者・研究者がいるかぎり，少なくとも彼らの分野では日本は高い学問的水準を保っていけるでしょう。

　法　曹　　日本で法律家になるには，通例，大学で法律を学ぶことに始まります。毎年，約3万人の法学部の学生が，日本国内の70余りの大学を卒業します。しかし，その大多数の卒業生は企業に就職し，人生の残りのあいだ法律とは関係のない生活を送ります。認可をうけた法律家になるためには，司法試験に合格し，第2次大戦後最高裁判所によって設立された司法研修所で，専門的な研修過程を経なければなりません。ところが，毎年司法試験

exam and complete the professional training program at the Institute of Legal Research and Training, which was established after the War by the Supreme Court of Japan. However, each year only about 500 of 25,000 applicants pass the requisite bar exam. Some law graduates repeatedly attempt the exam: the average age of those who have passed in recent years is 28, thus making the Japanese bar exam one of the most difficult professional examination in the world.

Those who enroll in the Institute receive emoluments from the public fund during the two-year training course. They receive classroom instructions at the Institute for the first and the last semesters, and on-the-job training in a court, a prosecutor's office and in an attorney's office for the middle semesters. After two years, about 80 of 500 are appointed as judges, 30 as prosecutors, and the rest choose to become attorneys.

Today, the Japanese legal profession consists of about 2,000 judges and a little more than 1,100 prosecutors (excluding judges and prosecutors without lawyer's qualification), and about 14,000 attorneys. In addition to this relatively small number of licensed lawyers, the demand for legal services in Japanese society is met by so-called "quasilawyers." Some graduates with law majors who went to work corporations do legal work in their company's legal department, drafting contracts and giving in-house legal advice. Some of those who became government employees perform legal duties for the government, including legislative drafting and legal

に合格するのは，2万5,000名の受験者のうち約500名にすぎないのです。何度も繰り返して試験を受ける法学部卒業生もおり，その結果，最近の合格者の平均年令は28歳となっています。これが，日本の司法試験を世界で最も難しい専門家試験の一つにしている理由です。

　司法研修所に入所した者は，2年間の研修期間のあいだ公費から給与の支給を受けます。彼らは，最初と最後の半年間は研修所で教室授業をうけ，中間の1年間は裁判官，検察官，弁護士について実務修習をうけます。2年後，500人のうち約80名は裁判官として任官し，約30名は検察官に任官し，残りは弁護士となる道を選びます。

　今日，日本の法曹は約2,000名の裁判官，1,100名より少し多い検察官（これらの数には，法律家としての資格をもたない裁判官，検察官は含まれていません），約1万4,000名の弁護士からなっています。この認可をうけた法律家の数が比較的少ないことを補うために，日本社会の法律サービスに対する需要は，いわゆる「準法律家」の助けを必要としています。法学部の卒業生で企業で働く者のある部分は，それぞれの会社の法務部で契約書を作成したり社内の法的助言を与えたりして，法律業務に従事しています。政府役人になった者のある部分は，立法作業や法律相談を含めて，政府のための法律家として職務を遂行しています。さらに，司法書士や税理士は，特に資格ある法律家の数の少ない地方においては，しばしば一般の人々から法についての情報源とみなされ，交通事故の損害賠償，不動産取引，相続など様々な問題について法律的な助言を求められることがあります。

counseling. Also, judicial scriveners and tax attorneys, particularly in local areas where qualified lawyers are scarce, are quite often considered the source of legal information and are sought for their legal advice by ordinary people on various matters, such as traffic accident damages, real property transactions, inheritance and so on. (IT)

Logic   The Japanese language, in contrast to other languages, is often perceived as illogical. A primary reason for this false perception seems to lie not in the structure of the Japanese language but in the way the Japanese use the language to express themselves.

In comparison with Western people, who generally prefer to state their opinions as explicitly, logically, and objectively as possible by following a "step-by-step" approach, the Japanese favor a "roundabout" way of approach. Japanese people choose to speak and behave in a vague, ambiguous, and indirect manner when making requests, settling business deals, and so on. They are more likely to consider other people's feelings and hesitate to make "either-or" decisions or give definite "yes-no" answers. They feel more comfortable if there is a little room for compromise so that adjustments can be made when circumstances change. Therefore, those who are too persistent in logical reasoning and clear-cut argumentation are often reproached as *rikutsuppoi* (going beyond the point of being reasonably logical).

Too often, Japanese reluctance to be explicit and di-

論　理　　他の言語に比べて，日本語は非論理的だと思われがちですが，このような誤った考え方は日本語の構造上の問題というより日本人の言葉のつかい方に起因するようです。

順を踏まえながら意見をできるだけ明確に論理的に，そして客観的に述べようとする西洋人に比べて，日本人は遠回しなアプローチを好みます。頼み事や商談などの際，はっきりしない間接的な発言・行動を選び，相手の気持ちを察してどちらか一方に割り切ったり諾否をはっきり表現することを避ける傾向があります。妥協の余地を残しているほうが，日本人には気分的に楽なのです。そうすれば，必要な時，状況に応じて調整できるからです。したがって，日本では，あまり物事を理詰めで考えたり，理路整然とした論議に固執すると，理屈っぽい人間ということで敬遠されることがよくあります。

日本人はストレートに表現することを避けるために，国際的なコミュニケーションの場においてよく誤解を受けます。事実，「日本人は本音を言わない」とか，「日本人というのは何を考えているのかわからない」といった不評を買っています。

日本式論理と西洋でいう論理とは違います。日本人は白黒をはっきりさせるやり方よりも，妥協によって物事の解決をはかろうとする柔軟性のある方法を好みます。「論理には，正しい論理，誤った論理，そして日本式の論理がある」というようなことを冗

rect results in misunderstandings when the Japanese interact with foreign people in international communicative settings. In fact, it is frequently voiced that the Japanese hide their true feelings or that they are hard to understand.

Japanese logic is, as noted, different from logic as understood in the Western sense. Instead of a "black and white" approach, the Japanese like to have the flexibility of settling disputes through compromise. This may be why some say jestingly that there is a right way, a wrong way, and a Japanese way. (YN)

Majority decision　Decisions in a democratic society are made according to "majority rule," which is based on the idea that the judgment of the many is likely to be better than that of the few. In a Western society, when people draw up a project, they try to achieve agreement among fellow workers through discussion at a meeting. In the end, decisions are made according to the majority rule even if some people are persistent in their opposition.

In Japanese society, on the contrary, decisions are made on the basis of "unanimity rule." Japanese society operates by group consensus and discourages open confrontation. Therefore, a person proposing a plan meets people concerned individually and informally, revises the plan, and enlists support, before the formal proposal. In this way, by the time the plan is brought to the formal meeting for discussion, it is usually made ac-

談まじりに言う人がいるのもこうした相違があるからでしょう。

多数決　　民主社会ではものごとは「多数決の原則」に基づいて決定されます。この原則は，多数の人の判断は少数の人の判断より良いだろうという考えに基づいています。西欧社会では，ある企画ができると会議を開き，いろいろ議論をして同僚のなかで合意にいたるようにつとめます。しかし，最後にはたとえ強く反対する人がいても多数決で決めます。

　一方，日本の社会では，ものごとは「満場一致の原則」に基づいて決定されます。日本の社会では，ことは集団の合意ではこばれ，面と向かっての対決は避けられます。それで，ある企画を提案する場合には，正式に提案する前に関係者一人ひとりに会って相談し，案を修正し，支持を取りつけます。こうして，案件が正式に会議にかけられた時には反対派にさえ受け入れられるものになっているわけです。この手順は日本の社会で「根回し」とか「稟議制度」といわれてきたものです。

　満場一致の原則は日本社会の原型である農耕社会から発達してきたと思われています。日本で行われてきた水田稲作では，田植えと収穫の時には集落全員の集中的共同作業と協力が必要でした

179

ceptable to all, including those who were originally opposed to it. This process is traditionally referred to as *nemawashi* or *ringi seido* in Japanese society.

The principle of unanimity is believed to have developed from an agrarian society, the prototype of Japanese society. The wet-paddy rice cultivation method used in Japan required intensive group work and cooperation of all the members of the community in the planting and harvesting of the rice. It also required group consensus for allocating the water for the paddies. All these factors instilled in the farmers the importance of cooperation and group consensus as well as a sense of belonging to their community.

The principle of unanimity is carried over to the present-day business world. Business firms use bottom-up, rather than top-down management so that their employees may have a feeling that they are involved in every important project. With such a system, the company can expect their full-fledged cooperation in its implementation. (YY)

Male-female relation　In the aristocratic society of Japan as in the Heian period (794-1192), the noble society was a polygamous one and women were visited by their boyfriends or husbands at their homes and they had little chance of controlling any aspect of life. Men of higher ranks often wrote beautiful love poems in praise of their loves or wives as described in *Genji Monogatari* (The Tale of Genji). However, women in

180

し，田に引く水の割当にも集団の合意が必要でした。これらの要因が農民に協力と集団の合意の重要性を吹きこみ，また集団への帰属意識を植えつけていったものと思われます。

満場一致の原則は今日のビジネス界に引きつがれています。企業は通常トップダウン方式よりボトムアップ方式経営によって，社員に重要な企画のひとつひとつに参加しているという意識をもたせています。そのようなシステムを通して，企業はそれら企画の実行の際に社員の全面的な協力を期待することができるのです。

男女関係　平安時代に見られるような貴族社会では一夫多妻の形態がとられ，女性の宅に恋人や夫が通う「通い婚」が一般的でした。そしてこのような社会では，女性が自分たちの生活のあらゆる面で，自らの意思によってことを成す機会はめったにありませんでした。地位のある男性は，『源氏物語』に描かれているように自分の恋人や妻をめでるために，自分の気持ちを美しい歌に託しました。同じく高い地位にいる女性は，しばしば家系を維持するための手段，あるいは自分の父親や男兄弟の出世のための

higher ranks were often considered as a means of family continuity or of advancement of their fathers or brothers in high society. Grassroots people enjoyed their male-female relations rather freely in spite of the fact that women were, in general, very passive, often having their marriage partners named by their parents. During warlike ages and feudal times (from the 13th century through 19th century), polygamy remained intact, especially in the warrior class. Women of reputable families were often forced into expedient marriage in their teens. Those of commoners were relatively free in forming a love relationship with their neighboring men, though still passive in the process and very sensitive to the talk of the town.

Though the modernization of Japan beginning in the 19th century replaced polygamy with monogamy, the keeping of a mistress or having extramarital affairs was overlooked to some extent. The old family system and primogeniture brought about the general tolerance of sexual promiscuity occasionally practiced by married males. In such an androcentric and family-centered society and under the influence of Confucianism, women, especially wives, were almost always obedient to their husbands or their parents-in-law. Women were, in general, very discreet in their speech and acts, and concerning their marriage they almost always obeyed their parents' decisions.

Since the New Constitution and the New Civil Law were enforced after the last war in 1947 and women ac-

手段として政略的に結婚させられたのです。一方，こういう時代においても庶民は，結婚に関して親の指示に従うこと，あるいは通婚の範囲が地域的に限られていたことなどはあったものの，ある程度まで自由に恋愛を楽しんでいました。

中世の戦国時代，幕府の時代を通じて，一夫多妻制は特に武士階級では続いていました。名家の女性たちは，しばしば幼いうちに政略結婚をさせられました。しかし一般庶民の女性たちは，近隣の男たちと比較的自由に恋愛関係を結んでいたようですが，やはりあくまで受け身的であり，回りの噂をも気にしていたようです。

19世紀に始まる日本の近代化は，一夫多妻制を一夫一婦制に変えましたが，古い家族制度や長子相続制度のため，妾を囲うこと，あるいは婚外交渉などはある程度まで大目に見られていました。そのような男性中心の社会，家中心の社会，そして儒教道徳の社会においては，女性，特に妻は常に夫や夫の両親に柔順でなければならなかったのです。一般に，女性は言葉づかいや行動とも控え目であることが要求され，特に結婚においては，ほとんどの場合両親の指示に従う必要がありました。

第2次大戦後の1947年に施行された新憲法によって，女性は結婚，離婚，財産などに関する多くの権利を獲得しましたが，自分の意思で伴侶を選ぶという意識も同時に持つようになりました。現在の日本で恋愛結婚は見合結婚と比べた場合，結婚全体の7割を越えています。10代や20代で異性の友達を持つことも社会的に認められてきました。この傾向にあわせて，同棲，婚前交渉，婚前妊娠・出産ももはやあまり非難されなくなってきています。最近，職場での既婚者との恋愛関係は，特に「不倫」という流行語で表されたりもしています。この言葉は，現在では女性からの積極的な働きかけをも含んでいるようです。

今や男女関係はかなり開放的な観念でとらえられ，性関係に対

quired many rights in regard to marriage, divorce, fortune, and so on, they have an awareness of choosing their partners according to their own will. The number of love marriages now exceeds that of arranged marriages by about 40%. Having friends of opposite sex in one's teens and twenties has been gradually accepted socially. In accordance with these trends, cohabitation, premarital relation, premarital pregnancy and childbirth, and divorce are no longer very reproachable. Secret love affairs, especially those arising in offices, are fashionably called *furin* (literally, "immorality"). People today use this word, often implying an active role on the part of the woman. Male-female relations have come to be viewed rather openly and people no longer seem to have a guilty conscience about sex. Yet there are still many who rely on go-betweens or private matching systems for arranged marriages. It is also said that there are many young people who enjoy their love affairs before they settle into arranged marriages. (KA)

Manners The basis of good manners may be the same everywhere, but their verbal and nonverbal manifestations vary from culture to culture. For example, when Japanese talk to somebody, particularly their social superior, they do not look at the other person's eyes. Eye contact is usually interpreted as an indication of the speaker's defiance, not of interest or respect. Casting one's eyes downward is an expression of one's humility.

しても，もはや以前のような罪悪感は感じられなくなっているようです。しかし他方で，見合結婚のための仲人や結婚相手を探すための組織の力を借りようとする人がかなりいるのも事実です。恋愛を十分楽しんだあと，最終的には確実な見合結婚をという若者もかなり多いといわれています。

　　礼儀作法　　礼儀作法の根本はどこにおいても同じでしょうが，言語的にも非言語的にもその表れ方は文化によって違います。例えば，日本人は誰かと話す時，特に目上の人と話す時には相手の目を見ません。視線を合わせることは，通常聞き手に対する関心や敬意を示すのではなく，話し手の反抗的態度を示すものと受け取られます。視線を下に向けることは謙譲を表します。
　　日本では謙虚さは高い評価を得る美徳です。自分のことや自分の持ち物を実際以上に軽く見るのが慣例です。贈物を差し出す時，たとえそれが高価なものであっても，日本人は「つまらないもの

MANNERS

Modesty is a highly valued virtue in Japan. It is customary to depreciate oneself and one's belongings beyond reality. In offering a gift, Japanese say, "Please accept this trifling little thing," even when it is very expensive. Enumerating one's abilities even at a job interview may give an unfavorable impression.

Foreign visitors who have noticed the good manners of Japanese are surprised to see such behavior as the pushings and shovings on and off jam-packed trains. However, individual Japanese have a distaste for physical contact. Bowing is their traditional way of greeting. Hand-shaking, though more common than ever, is still rather awkward or embarrassing to many Japanese. Kissing or hugging in public is improper and in fact rarely seen.

In Japanese society, people are primarily group-oriented. They give priority to group harmony and try to behave as expected by others, sometimes hiding their *honne* (true inner feelings). They conform to elaborate rules of proper behavior on such occasion as gift-giving, weddings, and funerals. The more formal the occasion, the more difficult people find it to disregard social conventions. Thus books on manners are always in great demand.

It is often pointed out that the Japanese make a clear distinction between the familiar *uchi* (insiders) and the unknown *soto* (outsiders) and are no good at associating with the latter. Because they do not know how to deal with foreign people, especially Westerners, they tend to

ですが，どうぞお納め下さい」と言います。求職の面接の時でさえ，自分の能力を数えたてると不利な印象を与えるでしょう。

日本人の礼儀正しさを指摘する外国人も，満員電車の乗り降りの際の押し合いへし合いを見て驚きます。しかし個々の日本人は体の接触を好みません。お辞儀が伝統的な挨拶の仕方です。握手は以前と比べれば普通に見られるようになりましたが，今なお多くの日本人はぎこちなく，とまどいを覚えます。人前でのキスや抱擁は無作法とされ，実際ほとんど見かけることはありません。

日本の社会では人々は元来集団志向です。集団の和を優先し，時には本音をかくして，他人から期待されるように行動します。贈物，結婚式，葬式などの際には詳細に規定された作法に従います。儀式が形式ばったものであれば，社会の慣行を無視することは困難です。礼儀作法に関する本はいつも大変需要があります。

よく指摘されることですが，日本人はなじみの「うち」と見慣れない「そと」とをはっきり区別し，「そと」の人々とのつき合いが下手です。外国人，特に西欧人に対しどのように振舞うかを知らないために，無関心になってしまうか，さもなければ改まったお客様のように丁重に応対する傾向があります。お客様に対して親切で礼儀正しいのは，日本の伝統だからです。

be indifferent to them, or treat them courteously like formal guests, toward whom Japanese are traditionally kind and polite. (MT)

Marriage and divorce   Beginning in the Meiji era (1868-1912), Japanese marriages were often arranged by a go-between who introduced the prospective bride and groom from appropriate families to each other. The modern system of marriage has been adjusted: after the introduction by the go-between, a couple date for a certain period of time before making their decision about marriage. The go-between is expected to continue to act as an intermediary, if the couple divorces or other future crises arise, for example.

The traditional idea of the household (*ie*) disappeared after World War II, but the child rather than the parents remains most important in family life, according to 54.5% of the respondents (Prime Minister's Office, February, 1987). Parents are said to pay half of the child's marriage expenses, which averaged from $48,000 - 56,000 (6 to 7 million yen) in 1986 (Ministry of Health and Welfare, 1987). The child, furthermore, is considered to bind the parents together, and 53.8% of the respondents are against divorce because of the effect on children (Prime Minister's Office, February, 1987).

As for recent attitudes toward marriage and divorce, 32.5% of men and 28% of women respondents think a woman's happiness lies in marriage, and 61% of the respondents think divorce is all right when unavoidable

結婚と離婚　日本では明治以来，見合結婚がよく行われ，仲人が釣り合う家族の子弟を，花嫁，花婿候補として，引き合わせました。現代風の見合結婚は，従来のものとは少し違い，若い2人は，仲人に紹介されてからしばらくつき合って，それから結婚の意思を固めるのです。将来，若い2人の結婚生活に離婚などの危機が生じると，仲人は仲裁役を務めることになっています。

　第2次世界大戦後，伝統的な家という概念はなくなりましたが，調査回答者の54.5％は，今の家族生活においても，親より子供のほうが大切であると考えています（総理府1987年2月）。1986年に子供の結婚費用は，平均600万円から700万円（48,000ドルから56,000ドル）かかり，親はその半分を負担していると言われます（厚生省1987年など）。さらに，子は親のかすがいとみなされ，調査回答者の53.8％が，子供への影響を理由に，離婚に反対しています（総理府1987年2月）。

　最近の結婚観と離婚観については，男性回答者の32.5％と女性回答者の28％が，女性の幸せは結婚にあると考えています。また，回答者の61％が，やむをえない場合には離婚を認めています（総理府1987年8月）。しかし，70％以上が未婚の母に反対，60％以上が未婚の男女の同棲に反対，となっています（総理府1987年2月）。

　結婚総件数は，1986年に710,962件，1987年に692,000件となっています。減った理由として，結婚可能な女性の数の減少と，初婚平均年齢の上昇（25.6歳）があげられます。離婚総件数は，1986年に166,000件，1987年に159,000件となっており，この減少は，中高年層の離婚減少によるものです（厚生省1987年）。

(Prime Minister's Office, August, 1987). More than 70% of the respondents, however, are against "unwed mothers," and more than 60% are against "men and women living together, unlisted in the family register" (Prime Minister's Office, February, 1987).

The total number of marriages in 1987 was 692,000 (compared with 710,962 for 1986), a decrease which is accounted for by the decreasing number of marriageable age women and a rise in the average age of first marriages (25.6 years old). The number of divorces in 1987 totaled 159,000 (166,000 in 1986), a drop due to a decrease in the number of divorces among the middle aged and older people (Ministry of Health and Welfare, 1987). (MO)

Mature age, becoming of   The word *jukunen* (the mature-aged) instead of *rōjin* (the aged) has come into use on TV commercials since about 1979. The word *jitsunen* (fruitful years) was coined for indicating people in their fifties and sixties by the Ministry of Health and Welfare in November 1985. Both are euphemisms to beautify the declining years and mask the melancholy aspect of the aged faced with the impending, inevitable end of life. The positive implications of these words— ripeness and fruitfulness—may encourage people of mature age to enjoy their "golden" years, but they do not solve the various social problems that the "graying society" has brought about.

The aging of Japan has progressed no less rapidly

熟　年　　1979 年頃からテレビのコマーシャルで「老人」に代わって「熟年」ということばが使われるようになりました。1985 年 11 月には 50 代，60 代の人を指す「実年」ということばが厚生省によって作られました。どちらのことばも老衰と避けられない人生の終わりにさしかかっている老人の暗い側面を覆い隠す婉曲語です。これらのことばには「熟していること」「実りのあること」という積極的な意味合がありますから，それによって自分の「黄金期」の人生をエンジョイする気力が熟年の人たちに湧き起こってくるかもしれません。しかし，それで「老齢社会」のもたらすさまざまな問題が解決するというわけではありません。

　日本の老齢化はヨーロッパやアメリカに劣らず早い速度で進んでいます。1986 年の平均寿命は男性で 75.23 歳，女性で 80.93歳です。2020 年には人口の 23.6％ が 65 歳以上になると推定されています。現在では，退職者の再就職が最も深刻で緊急の問題

than in Europe or America, and the average life span in 1986 was 75.23 years old for men, and 80.93 for women. It is estimated that 23.6% of the population will be over 65 in 2020. At present, reemployment of retired workers is one of the most serious and urgent problems, since the retirement age is under 60 in many companies whereas national pension begins at the age of 65. To fill the gap the government legally obliged companies to extend the retirement age to 60 in a few years' time. Other measures to promote the welfare of the aged are being taken—promotion of vocational education, advancement of continued employment, improvement of the pension insurance system and day care and life care systems, and encouragement of cultural and sports activities.

In accordance with the foundation of national pension, the elderly's income has improved, so their leisure hours have increased. This has served as an impetus to their desire to learn what they wished but failed to learn in their youth. To meet this unprecedented eager and varied demand for study, many local communities have established "Universities for the Third Age," and some universities have begun to offer a "Jukunen Postgraduate Program" for retired people over fifty, granting them Master's degrees. Neighborhood clubs for the elderly have been also organized in local towns and villages, whose members can often be seen enjoying *gēto-bōru* (gate-ball) or gardening in parks or green vacant lots. (OT/TS)

192

となっています。定年は多くの会社で60歳より前なのに国民年金の支給は65歳になってからでないと受けられないからです。このギャップを埋めるために政府は企業が数年のうちに定年を60歳以上に引き上げるように法的な措置を取りました。老人の福祉を促進するためにその他の手段もとられています。例えば，職業教育や，継続雇用の促進，年金保健制度の改善，デイケア・ライフケア制度の改善，文化・スポーツ活動の奨励などです。

　国民年金制度の創設にともなって，お年寄りの収入は改善され，その結果彼らの余暇も増えました。そのために，彼らの間に若い頃に学びたくても学べなかったことを改めて学びたいという望みが出てきました。以前にはみられなかったこのような熱心で多様な要求に応えるために，多くの地域で「高齢者大学」を設けています。またいくつかの大学も，50歳以上の定年退職者を対象に「熟年大学院プログラム」を設けて修士号を与えています。地方の都市や村には近所のお年寄りが集まるクラブがあり，メンバーが公演や空き地でゲートボールや園芸を楽しんでいるのがみられます。

Meiji Restoration   Overwhelmed by the increasing strength of the anti-shogunate forces, the 15th *shōgun* Tokugawa Yoshinobu voluntarily surrendered his sovereign power to the Emperor Meiji in 1867. The Restoration proclaimed in 1868 replaced feudalism by capitalistic systems and brought about drastic changes in Japanese politics, economy, and culture in the second half of the 19th century. The Meiji government, consisting chiefly of low-ranking *samurai*-class people of the Satsuma and Chōshu clans, made a series of reforms to secure national unity, build up the military strength, and modernize the country. This was imperative because Japan was exposed to the danger of colonization by the imperialistic World Powers.

First of all, in 1869 the government ordered feudal lords to return their domains and people to the Emperor and replaced the feudal clan system by a prefectural system administered by governors. Most *samurai* were to be paid off by government bonds worth less than their hereditary stipends. Thus disbanding feudal armed forces and adopting a draft system in 1873, the government advanced toward the creation of the national armies and navies trained and organized in the Western way.

Secondly, in 1872 the Meiji government adopted a compulsory education system on the benefit principle, which meant a great burden on farmers. And thirdly, it reformed the tax system on large scale and consoli-

明治維新　　1867年に第15代将軍徳川慶喜は倒幕の勢力が強大になったことに圧倒されて明治天皇に自ら大政を奉還しました。1868年に発布された王政復古は封建制度を資本主義体制に変え，19世紀後半に日本の政治，経済，文化に激しい変動をもたらしました。明治政府は主として薩摩，長州藩の下層武士階級の人たちで構成されていましたが，国家を統一し，軍事力を強め，現代化するための一連の改革を行いました。その頃日本は帝国主義的な世界の列強によって植民地化される危険にさらされていたので，これは否応なくしなければならないことでした。

まず第1に，1869年に政府は封建領主に対して領土と領民の返還を命じ，廃藩置県を行いました。たいていの武士は，代々の封録よりも少ない政府の金録公債を支給されて，解散させられました。このように，封建的軍隊を解体し，1873年には徴兵制度を採用し，政府は西洋式に訓練され編成された国家的な陸・海軍の創設を進めました。

第2に，1872年に明治政府は受益者負担制で義務教育制度を採用しました。これは農民には過酷な負担を強いることになりました。第3に，大規模な税制改革（地租改正）を行い，物納を廃止し，すべて金納とし，資本主義経済の地盤を固めました。第4に，西洋の技術を取り入れて産業の振興に努力し，資本主義の発展に不可欠な財産の私有と職業の自由を認めました。

これらの改革のあるものに対しては，武士も農民も非常な不満と激しい怒りを感じ，やがて全国各地で暴動や人権運動が起こりましたが，政府は鎮圧に成功しました。1889年には明治憲法が公布されました。これによって軍隊を天皇の指揮下に置く天皇制が確立され，人権や国会の権利は制限を受けました。このように，明治維新は日本の資本主義と天皇制の始まりを画すことになったのです。

dated the foundation of capitalistic economy, abolishing land tax in kind and introducing cash payment. Fourthly, it tried hard to develop industries by transplanting Western technology, while permitting private property and freedom of choice of occupation, which were both essential to capitalism.

Both *samurai* and farmers were so much dissatisfied with and infuriated at some of these reforms that there soon arose revolts and human-rights movements all over the country, but the government succeeded in putting them down. The Meiji Constitution was issued in 1889, and it established the Emperor system, bringing the armed forces under the control of the Emperor and placing limits on human rights and the rights of the Diet. In this way the Meiji Restoration marked the beginning of capitalism and the Emperor system in Japan. (OT/TS)

Middle-class consciousness　　A recent public opinion poll reports that nearly 90 percent of the Japanese believe that they belong to the "middle-class." This conviction arose from the idea that they have an average standard of living. In other words, they are "keeping up with the Joneses." But they never question what level of living the Japanese "Joneses" actually maintain. That one's standard of living is more or less that of the average Japanese is not necessarily the same as that he has a "middle-class" standard of living.

According to a sociologist, true "middle-class" people

中流意識　　最近の世論調査によると，日本人の90％近くが自分は「中流階級」に属していると信じているそうです。これは，自分たちは日本の平均的生活水準の暮らし，すなわち，隣近所の人たちに負けない暮らしをしているという考えからきているようです。しかし，彼らは平均的な暮らしの内容がどんなものであるかはいっさい問題にしていないのです。自分がほぼ日本の平均的な暮らしをしているからといってそれが必ずしも「中流階級」の生活程度とは言えません。

　ある社会学者によると，ほんとうの「中流階級」とは，平均水準より上の生活を楽しみ，相当の収入があり，社会的，知的活動をする時間もたっぷりあるような人のことを言うのだそうです。

enjoy an above-average standard of living with a comfortable income and with enough time for intellectual and social activities. They have not inherited great wealth but have enough means to maintain their present standard of living, even if their income stops due to injury, illness, or old age.

The average Japanese working in a big city lives in a small house, often called a "rabbit hutch," in the suburbs surrounded by polluted air, street noises, and few trees. He has to travel to his office, usually standing in a crowded commuter train for 90 minutes daily. He works hard to pay for his children's education and a house loan. He has to save for old age, too. In many cases, housewives also work to supplement their husbands' income, not for their own *raison de vivre* (fulfillment). Such a lifestyle does not seem to match the sociologist's definition of "middle-class."

The total amount of savings in Japan has reached the world's top. However, people save their money not for future pleasure but for injury, illness, and old age. Government expenditure on public welfare is so limited that people have to make provision for their future on a personal level. When affluence is measured in terms of the living environment and condition, the Japanese "middle-class" consciousness can hardly be justified by the reality. (YY)

Militarism　　After the Meiji Restoration, the Japanese government pushed forward *fukoku-kyōhei* (a rich

その人たちは大きな遺産は相続していないけれども，怪我や病気や高齢のために収入が途絶えてもその生活程度を維持していくだけの資産がある，そういう人のことを言うのだそうです。

　大都市で働いている平均的日本人は，排気ガスが充満し，通りの騒音がひどく，ほとんど樹木もない郊外の「兎小屋」に住み，毎日90分も満員電車に立ったままで通勤しています。子供の教育費と住宅ローンの返済に追われて必死に働いています。老後のための貯金もしなければなりません。多くの場合，主婦も生き甲斐のためではなく，夫の収入を補うために働いています。そのような暮らしはどうもさきほどの社会学者の「中流階級」の定義にマッチしないように思われます。

　日本の総貯蓄高は世界一になりました。しかし，悲しいかな，日本人がせっせと貯金するのは将来余暇を楽しむためではなく，怪我，病気，老齢に備えてなのです。政府の福祉予算は非常に限られているので，人々は個人個人で将来に備えなければならないのです。豊かさを住環境および生活状態を基準として計ってみると，日本人の「中流」意識はその現実からはとうてい認めがたいもののようです。

軍国主義　　明治維新後，日本の政府は世界の列強と対等の関係になって競争するために，文明開化と富国強兵政策を押し進め

country with a strong army) policy as well as *bunmei-kaika* (civilization and enlightenment) in order to rank and compete with the world powers. It invaded Korea in economic terms, forcing upon it an unequal commercial treaty, which eventually provoked the Sino-Japanese War of 1894-5. Japan's victory in this war established its militarism and imperialism, and incurred, on the other hand, imperialistic Russia's intrusion into China. The Russo-Japanese War of 1904-5 was fought, and again Japan gained a victory, which further strengthened military influence on the government. In 1910 Japan set up the Government-General of Korea and established Japanese rule in Korea.

Japanese militarism found its way to control over politics, economy, and education, especially after World War I. It related itself closely with Tennoism by invoking the name of the Emperor (*Tennō*) so that the Japanese people's reverence for the Emperor would cause them to go along with plans mapped out by military authorities. The steady expansion of armaments and the growth of insatiate territorial ambition made the military authorities boast of the Greater East Asia Co-Prosperity Sphere. Lacking in civilian control and pacifist movements strong enough to resist the general trend, the Japanese people allowed militarism to flourish, until it reached the zenith of its power just before World War II.

As the military took over the government, Japan became more and more totalitarian, and strict control over

ました。日本は朝鮮に不平等な通商条約を押しつけて経済侵略を
し，その結果1894年から85年にかけて日清戦争を引き起こしま
した。この戦争で日本が勝ったことにより軍国主義と帝国主義体
制が確立しました。また，これによって帝国主義ロシアの中国進
出を招く結果にもなりました。1904～05年に日露戦争が戦われ，
これにも日本が勝利をおさめ，日本の政府にはさらに軍国主義的
な影響が強まりました。1910年には日本は朝鮮総督府を設置し，
朝鮮支配を確立しました。

　日本の軍国主義は，特に第1次世界大戦後に政治，経済，教育
を支配するようになりました。国民が天皇に対する畏敬の念から
軍部の方針に従うように，軍国主義は天皇の名前を利用し，天皇
制と緊密に結び付きました。軍部は着実に拡大し，飽くことを知
らない領土的野心も増大し，軍隊の上層部は大東亜共栄圏を鼓吹
するまでになりました。文民統制と一般的な風潮に対抗するよう
な強力な反戦運動もなかったために，日本の国民は軍国主義が盛
んになるのをそのままにしていました。そして，第2次世界大戦
の直前には軍国主義はその絶頂に達したのです。

　軍部が政府を支配するにつれて，日本はますます全体主義的国
家になり，言論や出版に対して厳格な検閲が行われました。1931
年に満州で日本軍と住民との衝突があり，「満州事変」が勃発し
ました。これをはじめとして日本は東アジア全域に戦火を拡大し，
第2次世界大戦に突入したのです。

　敗戦によって日本は完全に非武装化され，1947年に制定され
た日本国憲法は戦争の放棄を唱っています。自衛隊はありますが，
それ以来ずっと日本は平和を愛する国民となっています。しかし，
最近では防衛費が急速に増加したり，何人かの政治家が戦前の軍
国主義的な信念を正当化または美化するような不謹慎な発言をし
たりするので，国内外で軍国主義復活に対する警告が発せられて
います。

speech and press was exercised. In 1931 a skirmish in Manchuria became known as "The Manchurian Incident," in which Japanese soldiers and Chinese locals came in conflict. With this as a starting point, Japan escalated war-fires all over East Asia and plunged into World War Ⅱ.

Japan's defeat in the last war brought about its complete demilitarization, and the Constitution of Japan enacted in 1947 stipulated renouncement of war. Though it preserved self-defense forces, it has been a peace-loving nation ever since. However, the arms budget is increasing so rapidly in recent years and some political leaders so often make inconsiderate statements that would justify or beautify the pre-war beliefs that warnings, both here and abroad, are raised against the possible revival of militarism. (OT/TS)

Moderation　*Setsudo*, the Japanese word for moderation or temperance, is connotative of 'a virtuous middle path,' 'a proper degree or amount,' 'a proper behavior' and the like. It is undoubtedly one of the most highly praised virtues in Japan, just as temperance is counted among the cardinal virtues in Western culture. The Japanese have a proverb that goes "Too much of a thing is as bad as too little," just as the Westerners have one that goes "The golden mean is best," or "Virtue is found in the middle." These proverbs also show that moderation holds a high place both in the Occident and the Orient.

節　度　　「節度」という日本語には「中庸」,「適度または適量」,「ふさわしい行動」などの含みがあります。西洋で中庸が七徳に数えられているように, 節度は日本でも高く評価されている美徳です。西洋には「中庸が最善」とか「美徳は中道にあり」という諺があるように, 日本には「過ぎたるは及ばざるが如し」という諺があります。これらの諺からも, 洋の東西を問わず節度は大切なものとされていることが分かります。

　節度に関する諺は世界中にあるかもしれませんが, この美徳についての日本人の考え方は, 過度な状態や極端な状態はいうまでもなく, 完全な状態をも嫌う日本人の性癖からきているようです。そうした状態は日本人の心を落ち着かせません。人々は物事の過不足は潮の満ち引きと同じように交互に繰り返されるものであり,

Although proverbs relating to moderation may be ubiquitous, the Japanese idea of the virtue seems to have derived from their dislike for fullness, not to speak of excessiveness, extravagance, or extremity, which will disturb the equilibrium of the Japanese mind. They vaguely sense that abundance and shortage of a thing will alternate like a full tide and an ebb tide and that lights are usually followed by shadows. Those who are at the zenith of their fortune are not necessarily the happiest, for they must inevitably be on the decline some day. *Hachibunme* (eight-tenths) of a thing is an ideal for many Japanese. Thus people of sensitive or refined taste would love cherry blossoms just short of full bloom more than those full-blown, and a thirteen-day-old moon more than a full moon.

Another aspect of moderation concerns one's self-restraint. Uncontrolled indulgence in drinking, eating, and other worldly pleasures is considered a moral weakness, if not a deadly sin, that is most likely to bring ruin upon oneself.

Moderation is also the key to good relations with others, especially with one's superordinates and colleagues in one's place of work. Modesty is all important in Japanese society, so that one who shows too much of self-confidence or self-assertion can easily become an object of general censure. (OT/TS)

Money game　Money game on a large scale which involves large companies, such as banks, real estate

光があれば必ず影があるということをなんとなく感じ取っているのです。好運の絶頂にいる人が最も幸福とは限りません。その人はいつかは必ず落ち目になるからです。多くの日本人は「八分目」を理想と考えています。ですから，趣味の洗練された人は満開の桜よりも八分咲の桜を好みますし，満月よりも十三夜を好みます。

　節度は節制にも関連しています。飲食をはじめ世俗の快楽に溺れることは，大罪とはされなくても破滅につながる道徳的な弱さとみなされます。

　節度はよい人間関係を保つ上でも重要です。特に職場での上司や同僚との関係においてはそうです。節度を忘れて自信たっぷりのところを見せたり，自己主張をし過ぎたりすると，みんなから批判されます。

マネーゲーム　　銀行，不動産業，投資信託といった大会社がらみの大規模なマネーゲームは，日本ばかりでなく国外でも社会

agents, and investment trusts, poses a serious social problem not only in Japan but also in other parts of the world.

A "surplus money" (*kane-amari*) phenomenon, which is caused by low money rates and low level of economic growth, is said to be currently plaguing Japan. Many financial institutions are seeking ways to put their money to lucrative use, while having to make constant efforts to accumulate money from customers.

One of the breakthroughs they have come up with is investment in real estate both domestic and foreign. For example, Japanese banks are cooperating with local agents to purchase famous hotels, department stores and corporations in New York, Hawaii and some other places. They play a central role in providing funds. There are cases where different Japanese banks tie up in taking over a company. In short, they make more money by selling properties at a higher price. The result of all this is the rise in the value of real estate properties. The people in Hawaii are said to be complaining that it is becoming very hard for them to buy land because Japanese companies have raised the price of land among themselves.

More or less the same situation is occurring in Japan, perhaps in a more atrocious and wicked way. A realtor finds a stretch of land which he believes is likely to fetch a high price. Upon finding one, he approaches a group of people called "*jiageya*" who are said to get five to ten percent of the market price of

問題を引き起こしています。

　日本経済には，低金利と経済の低成長路線の結果，金余り現象という歪が生じています。金融機関は，だぶつきぎみのお金の有効利用の方法を躍起になって探す一方，預貯金の目減りを避けるため，絶えず顧客からお金を集める算段をしなくてはなりません。

　そこで思いついた突破口は，国の内外を問わず不動産に投資することでした。たとえば，ニューヨークやハワイなどにある一流ホテルやデパートや企業を，地元の不動産業者などと協力して買収したりするのですが，その際資金提供者という形で中心的役割を演じるのです。企業を買収するのに数社の銀行が手を組むこともあれば，敵味方に分かれて争うこともあります。要するに，多額の金額をつぎ込んで値上がりさせ，その値上がり分を利益とするという手口です。ハワイやオーストラリアでは，日本の企業がこのように土地をどんどん値上がりさせてしまうので，地元の人の強い非難を浴びています。

　日本でも大体同じ様な状況ですが，手口はもっと悪らつです。たとえば，不動産業者は，めぼしい土地を見つけると，「地上げ屋」に話を持っていきます。すると「地上げ屋」はあらゆる手段を尽くして土地を明け渡すように仕向けるのです。こうして手に入れた土地は，オフィス建設用地を求めている企業や，マンション建設用地を求めている建設会社に，高い金額を上乗せして転売されるのです。

　しかし，この方法にはおのずと限界があります。適正な土地価格をはるかに超えてしまったために，買い手がつかなくなってしまったのです。欲に目が眩んで人の良識が見えなくなった報いでしょう。悪徳不動産業者の中には買収した土地をもてあますものが出てきました。土地買収費用の借金の利息や高い土地の税金に頭を抱えてしまっているのです。また，地上げ屋はもとより融資に一役かった銀行も，社会の非難を浴び，新聞紙上をにぎわして

the land in reward if they manage to drive the reluctant land owners away. In most cases, the land changes hands in the end, and the realtor gets the land. He then tries to sell it for more than it has cost him to a corporation or a construction company which wants to build there an office, a condominium, and the like. This results in the increase in the price of land in the neighborhood.

However, this method of making a profit is doomed. Land has come to be priced beyond the reach of almost everybody. People know better than to bite off more than they can chew. Some wicked realtors are at a loss what to do with the land they have taken over, while, at the same time, they are suffering from the interest on loans from the banks and the heavy land tax. Their accomplices, namely, banks and *jiageya*, are also socially accused of their conduct and are very much in the news. (MAT)

Mutability of the world   Originating in one of the fundamental Buddhist ideas, mutability of the world is usually termed as *shogyō-mujō* (all things flow and nothing is permanent). Japanese people in ancient times, seeing the rise and fall of clans or having ups and downs in their own lives, took mutability as a natural law governing this *ukiyo* (literally the "floating world" or the world of sufferings). The idea that things don't stay put permeates medieval literature. Typically, it furnished the dominant theme for *The*

います。

諸行無常　　「諸行無常」はもとは仏教の根本理念で，世の中の移り変わりを指します。古代の日本人は氏族の興亡を見たり，自分の人生で浮沈を体験したりして，転変はこの浮世を支配している自然法則であると考えました。諸行無常という考えは中世文学に広くみられます。13世紀に完成された『平家物語』は琵琶法師が語る叙事物語ですが，諸行無常は特にこの物語の主要なテーマとなりました。この物語は栄華を極めた平家の没落を同情的に描いたものですが，始終聞き手に人間の欲望の空しさを思い起こさせ，運命を受け入れるように説いています。

　一般的には，諸行無常と言えば，栄える者も必ず滅びなければ

Tale of the Taira Clan (compiled in the 13th century), the epic narrative recited by lute-playing minstrels. It sympathetically described the fall of the prosperous clan of Taira, constantly reminding the audience of the futility of human desire and advocating resignation to destiny.

The popular idea of mutability has it that the prosperous must decay, that things change from good to bad, that the vicissitudes of fortune are unstable, and that life in this transient world is fleeting and unreliable. Thus it is often regarded somewhat mistakenly as a pessimistic or hermistic view of life which emphasizes nothing but the vanity of the world.

According to Buddhist teachings, however, it does not necessarily imply a total negation of human endeavors in worldly affairs. Since life and the world are not stable, one can hope for a favorable turn of events and improvements in living conditions. The acceptance of the universal truth that all things are in flux and all beings mortal may lead one to attempt to explore one's fate or cultivate one's mind. One can also be liberated from pride, greed, or pursuit of worldly riches, consequently becoming very virtuous or even religious. Furthermore, by realizing that the future is very unreliable, one may try one's best to enrich every moment of the present life. (TS)

Mutual help Groups in Japanese society operate generally on what is referred to as 'reference group'

ならないこと，物事が良い状態から悪い状態へ変化すること，運命の転変は不安定であること，人生は束の間の頼りないものであることといった考えを指します。したがって，それはよく誤解されて，この世のはかなさを強調するだけの悲観的な，隠遁的な考えであるとされます。

　しかし，仏教の教えによれば，それは必ずしもこの世における人間の努力を全面的に否定するものではありません。人生もこの世も不安定なのですから，事態が好転したり，生活条件が改善されたりすることも望めるわけです。物事はすべて流動的であり，命あるものはすべて死ななければならないという普遍的な真理を受け入れれば，自分の運命を開拓し，精神の修養に努めるということにもなります。また，高慢や貪欲や富の追求から解放され，その結果非常に徳のある人になったり，信仰深い人になるかもしれません。さらに，未来は非常に頼りないということを認識して，現在の生活の一瞬一瞬を充実させようと最善を尽くすことになるかもしれません。

　助け合い　　日本社会における集団は，レファレンス・グループ，あるいは場と呼ばれるものに基づいて営まれています。レフ

or 'frame.' A reference group may be a family, a school, a company, or a community which integrates individuals into one collective body. These reference groups are very important when we consider mutual help or give-and-take in Japan.

Apart from human relations based purely on a one-to-one relationship as can be observed among intimate friends, a great majority of Japanese people belong to different reference groups at the same time and within these groups they develop a variety of human relationships. Once a relationship is established, a helping hand may be extended in various forms, from lending a lawn mower, finding a job, arranging an *omiai* (a meeting of a marriageable couple) to conducting a funeral. Conversely, acceptance of such help often creates on the part of its receiver a feeling of obligation to do something in return. This is partly because Japanese society expects that one should repay a favor done. In other words, the establishment of a relationship implies acceptance of a mutual relationship usually accompanied by various obligations to be fulfilled. Therefore, it may not be surprising that some Japanese perceive an offer of help as a nuisance.

To an outsider, the Japanese may appear "groupish" and exclusive in their relationships. It should be noted, however, that this exclusiveness is applied to everyone who does not belong to the same reference group. It is also a form of protection. Because repayment for help received is an integral part of maintaining Japanese re-

ァレンス・グループとは，学校・家族・会社・コミュニティーなど個々人を集約的に結びつけるグループのことです。これらのレファレンス・グループは日本における相互扶助を考えるうえで極めて重要です。

　対人関係は，親友同士の間で見られるように，一対一の関係で成立することもありますが，大多数の日本人はいくつかの異なったレファレンス・グループに同時に属し，その中でさまざまな人間関係を作り上げています。一旦関係が樹立されると，芝刈機から仕事・見合・葬式の世話にいたるまでいろいろな形で援助がさしのべられます。逆に，援助を受けた側には，お返ししなければという義務感が生じます。その理由の一つは，受けた好意は返すものと日本社会では考えられているからです。つまり，関係成立は互恵的間柄の受容を意味し，それにはいろいろ果たすべき義務がつきものです。したがって，他人からの援助をわずらわしいと感じる者がいたとしても別に不思議ではありません。

　外国人には，日本人は群をなし排他的と映るかもしれません。しかし，この排他性は同じレファレンス・グループに属さない者すべてに向けられるもので，同時にそれが一種の防衛機能を果たしていることを理解する必要があります。受けた好意を返すのは日本的人間関係を円滑に保つために不可欠です。そのなかで，排他性は互助関係を集団内の仲間に限定し，手に余るような範囲にまでつき合いを拡げないようにしてくれます。そうすることで，無理なく人の好意を受け，受けた好意のお返しをまちがいなく果たすことができるのです。

lationships, exclusivity protects a person from over-extending himself and limits reciprocity to in-group members. Thus, one can depend on help which is given to be mutually returned. (YN)

Nature The sense of harmony and identification with nature marks one of the most conspicuous differences between Japanese and Westerners. The Japanese, unlike Westerners, have viewed nature not as opposed to man but as a blessing under which he is allowed to live in harmony with his surroundings. This Japanese concept of nature seems to be correlated more or less to the following factors.

First, Japan's long rice-growing civilization developed blessed with clear-cut four seasons, temperate climate, and abundant rainfall. It also underwent occasional typhoons and earthquakes. In such an agricultural society, people have had to follow the natural seasonal rhythm of climatic change and at the same time live under the menace of nature.

Second, there has been the Japanese indigenous belief, since early *Shinto* times, in a superior and mysterious force of nature, the sacred, called *kami*, which resides in natural elements. For instance, in some farm communities of northern Aomori Prefecture, farmers offer beans, rice, seaweed, dried fish, and *sake* (rice wine) to the *ta no kami*, the traditional guardian deity of the rice fields, at the paddy's irrigation duct in the rice transplanting season in early summer.

自然観　　日本人が西欧人と最も著しく異なる点は，自然との調和・一体感とされています。日本人は自然を人間と対峙したものと見ないで恵みとしてとらえ，自らの置かれた環境と融け合うものとしてきました。この日本人の自然観は，以下のような点が関係しているものと思われます。

　1)　日本は台風や地震に見舞われることはあっても，一般に温暖な気候と豊かな雨量とに恵まれ，四季もはっきりしていて，長く農耕文明を育んできました。こうした農耕社会では，人々は自然のリズムに従って生き，自然の脅威にも耐えねばならなかったのです。

　2)　神道の昔から，自然の大きく不思議な力に対する素朴な民族信仰があり，日本人はこれを神として崇めてきました。この神は岩や木にも宿るものと考えられました。青森の北部の農村では，五月末の田植えの頃になると，今でも水口祭を行う集落がありますが，これは田に水を引き入れる水口で，米や豆，干魚や昆布などの自然の幸と酒を田の神に供える祭なのです。

　3)　一般に日本の伝統的家屋は，気象条件に合わせて開放的です。どこの家にも，掛け軸や花を活ける床の間をもったメインルームの座敷があり，手入れの行き届いた小さな庭に面しています。座敷は普通廊下をはさんで内側に障子，庭に面してガラス戸があり，換気や採光，また庭がよく見えるように工夫されています。こうして日本人は，自然に親しく触れながら何世紀にもわたって生活してきました。

　4)　日本人の間には，頭脳に対して心を重んじる傾向がありま

Third, adapted to the climatic condition, the Japanese traditional house is characterized by its "open" style. It typically has *zashiki*, a main Japanese-style room used on special occasions and for special guests, with *tatami*-covered floor and *tokonoma*, an alcove used for hanging a scroll and displaying arranged flowers. This main room faces the garden, usually partitioned by the corridors with two layers of wide-open sliding panels—*shōji*, paper sliding doors, on the inside and glass doors on the outside—which provide ventilation, light, and view of the elaborate garden. Japanese people lived for centuries in these environments which encouraged appreciation of—and living close to—nature.

Fourthly, the Japanese inclination to highly value *kokoro*, heart or soul, in contrast to brains is significant. *Kokoro* has been believed to dwell not only in human beings but also in physical objects as an essence which constitutes each entity. Based on this belief a great stress is placed upon a deep communion between people and nature. For instance, in any Japanese art such as painting or pottery, it is maintained that the ideal state is, paradoxically, *mushin*, a "no-mindedness" in which an artist and his object are one.

Fifthly, the amalgamation of *Shinto* and Buddhist beliefs should be pointed out. As Buddhism gained a foothold in Japan in the 7th century, people gradually accepted such a Buddhist belief as that not only human beings but all existing things, animate or inanimate, possess "Buddha-nature" in themselves. One can thus

す。心は人間だけでなく万物に宿っているという信仰が，人々の心に自然との深い交流や一体感を育んできました。例えば，絵画や陶芸などの日本芸術の分野では，「無心」ということが理想として強調されています。「無心」とは，一見逆説的ですが，芸術家が自分の向かい合っている対象と一つになった状態を指し，傑作とよばれるものは，この対象との深い交わり・一体化の結果にほかならないとされています。

5) 7世紀，仏教が日本に根を下ろすにつれて，神道との融合が行われました。人々は仏教の説く「一切衆生悉有仏性」といった考えを徐々に受け入れ，自然との一体化はさらに進んでいきました。

6) 英語では，動作主が何かを「する」ということをよくいいますが，日本語では動作主に言及せず，「なる」という言い方を好みます。例えば，英文の "I'll move out next month." （私は来月引っ越しをします）を，日本文では「来月引っ越すことになりました」という類です。日本人は，自ら進んで行う行為であっても，自然の成りゆきのようにとらえて表現しがちなのです。

extend oneself into nature with no barriers.

Last but not least, the Japanese language is a "become"-language that encourages its users to conform to the above-mentioned Japanese view of life in contrast to an agent-oriented "do"-language like English. An English sentence "I'll move out next month," for example, would be put in Japanese "The moving out will (be) come true next month" with no agent of moving out indicated. Japanese people thus tend to regard even an act of moving out as a "natural" outcome, not as an act made by their own choice. (ON)

Negotiation technique　　In negotiating with the Japanese, foreign businessmen are often perplexed by their silence and, when they speak, by their ambiguity. The Japanese say "I'll study it," when they turn down a proposal; "We'll do our best to solve the problem," when they know nothing can be done about it; and "We'll reply as soon as possible," when they don't know when they can.

The Japanese have traditionally placed an importance on honor. Consideration for the other party's honor and reputation is very important in Japanese human relations. Accordingly, they are extremely cautious not to disgrace the other person's honor and naturally they avoid open confrontation. This explains why Japanese are rather quiet and, when they speak, tend to be ambiguous.

In order to communicate in this way, the Japanese

交渉術　　日本人と交渉していて外国のビジネスマンがしばしば戸惑うのは，日本人がものを言わないことと，言った場合それが曖昧なことです。日本人は，答えがノーの時には「検討してみましょう」と言います。具体的な手立てがない時には「できるだけやってみましょう」と言い，いつ返答できるか分からない時には「できるだけ早くお返事いたします」などと言います。

　日本人は伝統的に名誉を重んじてきました。相手の名誉や信望にたいして心遣いをすることは日本での対人関係においてとても大切です。ですから，人の名誉を傷つけないよう細心の注意が払われ，面と向かった対決は避けられます。日本人が交渉の時に無口で，ものを言っても曖昧なのはそのせいでしょう。

　このようにして意思を通じあうために，日本人は「本音」と「建前」をたくみに操るのです。「己の説くところを実行せよ」というのが大切だと思っている西洋人にはがっかりすることですが，日本人はその場その場で本音と建前を使い分けます。したがって，交渉に長けた人は，声の調子とか言葉以外の手がかりなどから相手の真意を汲み取るよう期待されています。また，相手の

219

manipulate *honne* (what is intended) and *tatemae* (what is said). Much to the dismay of Westerners, who consider it important "to practice what you preach," the Japanese use these two forms of communication and occasionally switch from *tatemae* to *honne*, or vice versa, depending on the context of situation. Therefore, skilled negotiators are expected to determine, by the tone of voice and other nonverbal clues, the depth and subtlety of the other party's intentions. They are expected as well to learn quickly the other party's interests, desires, experiences and other background information which are useful in the negotiation. They are also expected to earn the trust and respect of the opponents by presenting themselves appropriately in the situation.

Another thing about the *honne-tatemae* dichotomy is that while *tatemae* is openly professed in the formal negotiation, *honne* is expressed privately in the informal setting, over a glass of beer, for example. Therefore, skilled negotiators often make the most of an informal private get-together with the negotiating opponents before the negotiation. (YY)

Nōkyō : **agricultural cooperatives**　In 1900 the first *nōkyō* in Japan were formed as farming and credit unions, and as sales and purchase cooperatives. The authorities discontinued these agricultural cooperatives during World War II, but they were re-established in 1947.

In postwar Japan, agriculture, especially rice farming,

関心事，やりたいこと，経験などの背景知識をすばやく学んで交渉に役立てることも期待されています。またその場にふさわしいパフォーマンスで相手の信用と尊敬を得ることも当然期待されています。

「本音」と「建前」についてもう一つ言っておくと，おおやけの交渉の場では対決を避けて建前が語られ，ビールを飲みながら，というような私的なやりとりの場で本音が出されます。それで，交渉に長けた人は本番前に交渉相手と私的に会い，それを最大限に利用するのです。

農 協　明治 33 年に最初の農協が農業信用組合，販売購買協同組合として成立しました。第 2 次世界大戦中に解体しましたが，昭和 22 年に再出発しました。

戦後，日本では農業，特に米作農業は聖域と考えられ，農業票は衆議院で過剰に代表され，その結果，農民の支持を得た自民党が 30 年以上にわたって与党となってきました。政府は農業を保護し，また食管法を導入することによって，生産者米価と消費者

was regarded as sacrosanct, that is to say, the agricultural votes were over-represented in the election of the members of the Lower House. This inequity has resulted in favoring the ruling Liberal Democratic Party for more than three decades. Agriculture has, therefore, been under the protection of the government, which, having enforced the Law of Governmental Food Management, makes up the balance between the producer price and the usually lower consumer price of rice. With stable cash income on the one hand and financial facilities and mutual benefit systems provided by the *nōkyō* on the other, the farmers began to enjoy growing prosperity. In the late 1960s and early 1970s, when cooperatives were at the peak of the boom, groups of tourists sponsored by the *nōkyō* were seen looking and shopping around in European and North American cities.

In 1971, however, the government started a program to arrange for production quotas of rice in order to reduce the heavy deficit caused by this system and make an adjustment of supply and demand. It encouraged farmers to reduce the rice paddy fields and grow other agricultural products by subsidizing them, because the farmers tended to overproduce the government-protected rice. One important function of the *nōkyō* was to increase the subsidy. Since the middle of the 1970s, therefore, the mass media have been very critical of the government subsidies, because they believed that the government's overprotection has made Japan's agriculture chronically inefficient and incompetitive in the

米価との差額を埋め合わせてきたのです。安定した収入，農協の金融便宜と相互利益体制のおかげで，農民は繁栄を享受し始めました。農協が全盛の1960年代の後半から1970年代前半にかけて，農協スポンサーの観光客がヨーロッパと北米諸都市を見物したり，買物したりする風景がよくみられました。

　しかし，昭和46年に，政府は食管赤字を削減するため米の生産割当をし，需給調整を始めました。米が過剰生産されたので政府は減反政策をとり，他の農産物に転作させようとしたのです。農協は援助金を増加しました。1970年代半ばから，マスメディアは政府の補助金をきびしく批判し，政府の過保護が日本の農業を慢性的に効率が悪く国際市場で太刀打ちできなくしていると指摘しました。昭和61年にカリフォルニアや発展途上国からもっと安い米を輸入せよとの外圧で，政府は初めて援助金を減らしました。

　農業と農協は，今日，多くの重大な問題に面しています。減少する農業人口，増大する老人・女性人口の問題です。これらの原因は，都市化，食生活の変化，大規模店舗の出現による卸売業界中心の流通機構の再編成などにあります。

international market. The government reduced the subsidy for the first time in 1986 due to the "foreign pressure" asking Japan to import rice at more reasonable prices from California and developing countries.

Japan's agriculture and *nōkyō* today face many problems, such as a decreasing number of farming population and an increasing number of aged and female farming workers. These problems arose in part because of urbanization in Japan, overproduction of rice partly due to changing Japanese food habits, and the reorganization of the distribution system, which was strongly controlled by the wholesale system but now is being replaced by the emerging big co-op stores and supermarkets. (MK)

Nonverbal communication Despite the striking industrialization during the last hundred years, Japan had long been an agricultural country with most of the population engaged in farming in small village communities. Strong emphasis was put on group work and cooperation, not only in rice cultivation but in other social activities. Though such rural community life has undergone drastic changes after World War Ⅱ and especially during the period of rapid economic growth, the underlying idea of group-orientedness still prevails in diverse aspects of Japanese society.

One of the typical examples is seen in the Japanese communication pattern in which speech is often unnecessary and sometimes even seems to obstruct harmonious

以心伝心　　日本はこの100年の間に著しく工業化しましたが，それ以前はずっと農業国であり，人口の大部分は小さな集落で農業に従事していました。稲作だけでなく，その他の社会活動においても，共同作業と協力が何よりも重要でした。このような地方共同体の生活は第2次大戦後，特に高度経済成長時に大きく変化しましたが，根底にある集団意識は，今なお日本社会のさまざまな面に見られます。

　その典型的な例の一つは，日本人のコミュニケーションの型です。この型では，言葉はしばしば不要で，時にはなごやかな人間関係の妨げになることさえあります。日本人は他人の感情を傷つけないように非常に気をつかいます。むき出しの対決が生じないように，自分の意見を言う前に，その意見に対する相手の反応を推測しがちです。断定的な話し方をする人は，「出る杭は打たれる」という諺のように，まわりから叩かれます。日本人は単刀直

225

interpersonal relations. The Japanese are very cautious not to hurt the feelings of others. Before giving their opinions, they tend to surmise the other party's reaction to them in an effort to avoid possible open confrontations. An assertive person, like a nail that sticks out, gets hammered down. Japanese would rather achieve mutual understanding by nonverbal cues rather than by outright questions or heated discussions.

To the Japanese, silence in conversation can often convey a far more profound meaning than eloquence. They have a lot of proverbial expressions concerning the effectiveness and wisdom of nonverbal communication, such as "The eyes tell as much as the mouth," *ishin-denshin* (communion of heart with heart), and *haragei* (literally, the belly art). By the unique technique of *haragei* a person makes the other party understand his real intentions without verbal interaction. This ability is regarded as indispensable to influential figures, particularly in political circles.

Unlike most other nations, Japan is a highly homogeneous society, where nonverbal forms of communication can be easily developed and conveniently used in various situations. However, in this internationalized world, more and more Japanese think it urgently necessary to change their tendency to implicitness and silence which can cause misunderstanding in intercultural communication. (MT)

Nuclear energy　　Japanese extreme sensitivity to

入な質問や激しい議論よりも，言葉によらない手がかりによって相互理解を得るほうを好みます。

　日本人にとって，会話中の沈黙はしばしば雄弁よりもはるかに深い意味を伝えるものです。言葉によらないコミュニケーションの効果と知恵に関する諺や言い回しがたくさんあります。例えば「目は口ほどにものを言い」「以心伝心」「腹芸」などです。「腹芸」という独特のテクニックによって，言葉をかわすことなしに自分の真意を相手に理解させます。これは有力者，特に政界においては不可欠の能力だと考えられています。

　他の国々と違って，日本は同質性の高い社会であり，言葉によらないコミュニケーションが成り立ちやすく，いろいろな状況で便利に行われています。しかし，国際化の進む世界では，はっきりと表現せず，沈黙を守る日本人の傾向は，異文化間コミュニケーションにおいて誤解を招きかねません。早急に改める必要があると考える日本人が増えています。

核エネルギー　　　昭和 20 年の広島，長崎の被爆体験のために，

nuclear energy used for both military and industrial purposes was formed by their experiences of atomic bombs at Hiroshima and Nagasaki in 1945. It was also enforced by the Lucky Dragon Incident, in which a Japanese small fishing boat outside of the warning zone was covered by "deadly ashes" as a result of an American testing of an atomic bomb at Bikini Island in 1954.

However, due to her total shortage of natural resources except for water, Japan has pursued research on nuclear power. In 1955 the Diet enacted the Basic Law on Atomic Energy, and in the following year it allocated funds in the budget to start research on atomic energy and founded the Atomic Energy Research Institute. In consideration of the general public's rising fear of the military use of atomic energy, the government repeatedly emphasized the three principles—renunciation of production, possession, and introduction of nuclear bombs. The government signed the Nuclear Nonproliferation Treaty in 1976 despite the concerns among many sectors that feared that it would hinder Japan from developing nuclear technology.

The first atomic power plant was built at Tōkaimura in 1957 and started to provide nuclear-powered electricity in 1963. In 1966 the first commercial reactor started. Since 1970 many reactors have been built all over Japan. As of 1987 thirty-three nuclear-generating reactors function in Japan. The number lags behind the United States, Russia, and France. This is partly due to rather strong opposition among environmentalists, pacifists,

日本人は軍事，産業目的の核利用に極端に敏感になりました。昭和29年，ビキニ島での核実験の危険水域外で漁船が死の灰を被った第五福竜丸事件でいっそう過敏になりました。

しかし，水資源以外の天然資源に乏しい日本は，原子力発電の研究を重ねてきました。昭和30年に原子力基本法を制定し，翌年原子力研究を始めるための予算を割り当て，日本原子力研究所を設立しました。原子力の軍事利用を恐れる一般国民を顧慮して，政府は非核3原則（核兵器の生産，所有，導入の破棄）を繰り返し強調しました。核技術開発を妨げるかもしれないとの懸念にもかかわらず，政府は昭和51年に核拡散防止条約に調印したのです。

昭和32年に最初の原子力発電所が東海村に設立され，以後昭和38年に電力供給を開始，昭和41年に商業発電炉が始動しました。昭和45年以来，全国で原子力発電所が建設されました。昭和62年には32の原子炉が稼働しています。アメリカ，ソ連，フランスに次ぐ数です。環境保護運動家，原子力発電所の放射能の危険に極端に過敏な平和主義者や住民の反対があるからです。昭和49年に原子力船陸奥が中性子を流失してから，反対が特に強くなりました。昭和63年，原子力発電にあまり反対しないと批判されてきた社会党が，ウラニウム運搬を監視する運動を組織しました。

日本は，昭和48年の第1次石油危機からエネルギー供給の多元化を図ってきましたが，昭和58年時点で原子力発電が，水力，石油，ガス，石炭発電より経費が安く済んでいます。同量の電気の生産のためには原子力発電はスペースが最も少なくてよいのです。ダム建設の必要もないし排気による空気汚染もありません。このため昭和54年のスリー・マイル島事件や昭和61年のチェルノブイリ事件のショックや恐怖にもかかわらず，日本は原子力発電所を建設していくでしょう。

and local people who have been extremely sensitive to possible dangers of radioactivity at nuclear plants. This opposition intensified, especially when it was found in 1974 that the nuclear-powered ship *Mutsu* (an experimental model) had a neutron leak. In 1988 the Japan Socialist Party, which was criticized for being less active in opposition against atomic power plants, organized a movement to keep an eye on the transportation of uranium.

Since the first Oil Crisis of 1973, Japan has tried to diversify her energy sources by developing solar systems. But as of 1983, nuclear power stations still remain cheaper than any of hydroelectric, oil thermal, gas thermal and coal thermal power plants. A nuclear power plant requires the smallest space in producing the same amount of electricity. Unlike the other types of plants, it neither entails the construction of dams nor causes air pollution by exhaust fumes, so that clean environment can be preserved. These factors may lead Japan to continue to construct more nuclear power plants, despite the great shock and subsequent fear among people caused by the Three Mile Island accident (1979) and the Chernobyl disaster (1986). (MK)

Parent-child relationship　　Physical and psychological closeness is the typical feature of the mother-child relationship and relationships among family members in Japan. The family members often sleep in the same room, especially while children are young, and

親子関係　　日本の母子関係や家族関係の特徴として，物理的，心理的な緊密さがあげられます。特に子供がまだ幼いうちは，家族が1つ部屋に寝ることが多く，出かけるのも一緒なのが普通です。それで，日本の子供は甘えがちになり，このような甘えは，かなり大きくなっても好ましいものとされています。子供は夫婦

231

they normally go out together. Thus Japanese children tend to be quite dependent and such dependency (*amae*) is encouraged well into adulthood. The children are said to bind the parents together, and for this reason 53.8% of the respondents are against divorce (Prime Minister's Office, February, 1987).

Contemporary Japan is experiencing an increase in nuclear families, a decrease in the number of children, overprotection, and "absence of fathers from home" owing to long commutes and a decline of paternal authority. Yet, 85% of the respondents think they communicate well with their children. They especially want their children to acquire manners for living and a sense of responsibility, independence and self-reliance for boys, and cooperativeness for girls. About 90% think parents should pay for the educational and living expenses of their children in college or university; about 70% are for paying children's wedding and reception expenses; about 40% are for making the initial payment on children's houses; and about 50% even think parents should pay the grown-up child's debts (Prime Minister's Office, February, 1987).

As for children's idea of their parents, about 90% of the respondents think their parents work hard; about 80% respect them; the father is gentler than the mother (67.5% and 63.9%, respectively); the mother is consulted more often than the father (60.3% and 30.3%, respectively) (Prime Minister's Office, September, 1987).

の絆とされ，このために離婚に反対する者の割合は，調査回答者の53.8％となっています（総理府1987年2月）。

　今日の日本には，核家族の増加，子供数の減少，過保護，そして長距離通勤や父権の衰退による「家庭における父親不在」の現象が見られます。けれども，調査回答者の85％は，子供との意思の疎通が良好であると考えています。この人たちは，子供に特に生活に必要な作法や責任感を身に付けることを望み，男の子には独立独歩を，女の子には，協調性を期待しています。また約90％の人たちは，大学在学中の子供の教育費と生活費を親が負担すべきだと考えます。「子供の結婚と披露宴の費用を負担すべし」が約70％，「子供の持家の頭金を支払うべし」が約40％，「成人した子供の借金も支払うべし」は約50％となっています。（総理府1987年2月）

　子供のほうは親をどう見ているのかというと，「良く働く」が約90％，「尊敬する」が約80％となっています。また，父親のほうが母親よりも優しいと考え，父親67.5％，母親63.9％となっています。ただし，相談する相手は，母親の場合のほうが多く，母親60.3％，父親30.3％となっています。（総務庁1987年9月）

　父親は普段家を留守にしているので，子供との緊密な関係が量質ともに欠けていますが，子供の回答者の62.4％が，家庭の中心は父親と考えています。（総務庁1987年6月）

The father does not have a close relationship with the child either in quantity or quality, since he is normally away. 62.4% of the child respondents, however, think the father is central figure of the home (Prime Minister's Office, June, 1987). (MO)

Play   Traditional Japanese culture is full of the spirits of play: Japanese poetry, particularly *waka* and *haiku*, tea ceremony, flower arrangement, theatrical arts like *nō* and *kabuki*, and even Japanese cooking. It used to be a good thing to lead a leisurely life of refined and chic tastes.

Despite the rich playful tradition, however, the Japanese have evolved some negative connotations around the concept of play. The word *asobi*, or play, originally meant any of "leisure," "pleasure," and "relaxation." Yet now, it often implies "no serious work," and suggests further negative meanings like "drinking, gambling, and buying a woman." Although many workaholic Japanese males occasionally indulge in one of these as a counteraction to their hectic work schedules, their conscience does not allow them to take a longer vacation. More than 52% of salaried workers feel uneasy about taking holidays, while only 36% do not. Of such workers 11% feel guilty even when they take a paid sick day (1987 Public Opinion Poll by the Prime Minister's Office).

Holiday plans the Japanese prefer are travelling, sports, watching TV at home, reading, listening to the

遊　び　　伝統的な日本文化は遊び心にあふれていると言えます。例えば，和歌や俳句などの詩歌，生け花，能や歌舞伎のような舞台芸術，そして日本料理にさえ，遊び心が感じられます。粋で洗練された趣味を持ち，風流な生き方をすることはむしろ好ましいことだとされていました。

　しかしながら，こうした豊かな遊び心の伝統にもかかわらず，「遊び」というと何かマイナスのイメージを持つもののように人人は考えるようになりました。「遊び」という言葉は「暇」「楽しみ」「余裕」などをもともとは意味していたのですが，今では「まじめな仕事ではないこと」を示すことも多く，さらに「飲む，打つ，買う」といったマイナスの意味をあらわすこともあります。仕事中毒の日本人男性の中には時にはこのような「遊び」をして過密な仕事のスケジュールの息ぬきにする人もいますが，長い休暇をとることには抵抗を感じる人も少なくありません。サラリーマンのうち52％以上の人が休暇をとるのを気がねしており，そうは思わない人は36％に過ぎません。11％のサラリーマンは病気で休暇をとる時でさえ，うしろめたい気持ちをいだいています。(1987年総理府の世論調査による)

　日本人が好む休暇の過ごし方は，旅行，スポーツ，テレビ，読書，音楽鑑賞などです。また，日本人は皆が一斉に休みをとる傾向にあります。例えば，お正月，ゴールデン・ウィーク，お盆には，行楽地はどこへ行っても込んでいます。ですから，外へ出かけるとかえって疲れてしまい，休養にはならないのです。最近の

music, and so on. They tend to take a holiday at the same time. Namely, a whole nation goes on a holiday around New Year's Day, in the first week of May, and in the middle of August. Pleasure resorts and places of interest are consequently so crowded everywhere that it can be exhausting rather than refreshing just to travel to and from one of these places. Nowadays younger generations are more apt to take holidays freely and know how to enjoy their holidays fully. (MH)

Political system   Japan's political system is a parliamentary democracy similar to the British system with two houses and a cabinet.

The Upper House (the House of Councillors) is composed of 252 members and serves for six years, half of whom are elected every three years. The Lower House (the House of Representatives), made up of 512 members serving for the maximum four years, has been elected every two years and a half on the average. The Lower House has more power in formulating bills into law.

There are several minor political parties in addition to one major one. In 1955 two conservative parties, the Democratic Party and the Liberal Party merged into the Liberal Democratic Party to counter the newly founded Japan Socialist Party. This Liberal Democratic Party has been in power ever since, although in the 1950s and 1960's the Japan Socialist Party gained popularity among intellectuals and became a threat to the ruling

236

若い世代は，休暇を自由にとり，心ゆくまで休暇を楽しむ方法を知っているようです。

　　政治制度　　日本の政治制度は二院制内閣のイギリスに似ています。

　参議院は 252 議席から成り，任期は 6 年で，半数ずつが 3 年ごとに選挙されます。衆議院は最長 4 年の任期で 512 議席から成っています。平均任期は 2 年半です。法案作成の影響力は衆議院のほうが大きいのです。

　政府は，与党自民党と，野党が数党あります。昭和 30 年に民主党と自由党が合同して自由民主党を作って，新生の日本社会党に対抗しました。1950 年代，1960 年代に社会党はインテリのあいだで人気を得て，与党に脅威となりましたが，自民党はずっと与党であり続けました。昭和 34 年に社会党の右派が分かれて民社党を設立しました。創価学会を母体とする公明党も少し勢力があります。日本共産党はごく少数です。

　1970 年代に高い生活水準を享受し始めた国民は，日本が西側の一員であることの重要さを悟り，日米友好関係を最重要視する自民党に強い支持を与えました。

　議会制民主主義制度では衆議院が内閣総理大臣を選出します。自民党が 30 年にわたり過半数を占めてきたので，この間，自民党総裁が内閣総理大臣になってきました。自民党には数派閥あり，

party. But the rightist element of the Japan Socialist Party split into the Social Democratic Party in 1959. The Clean Government Party (Kōmeito), more recently formed with its Buddhistic organization, has also gained some strength. The Japan Communist Party has remained marginal.

In the 1970's many people, who started to appreciate a high standard of living, realized the importance of Japan's membership in the Western block and gave staunch support to the Liberal Democratic Party, which emphasized Japan's friendly relations with the United States.

In a parliamentary democracy, the Lower House elects the prime Minister. Since the Liberal Democratic Party has had a majority for three decades, its President has been Prime Minister. This party has several factions and their heads, who are adept at raising funds to support as many other members of the party as possible, compete with each other to lead the party. (MK)

Praising　　The idea that modesty is a virtue has been so widespread in Japanese society that people are hesitant to accept praise, especially toward themselves, their family members, relatives and so on. People also take great care not to lavish undue praises on others, even though they are eager to praise others and are good at doing so. A tactful and due praise is always appreciated if it is given in a reasonable way. If not, it is considered as mere flattering or apple polishing.

238

各派閥のボスはできるだけ多くの子分を養う資金を収集する能力があり，お互いに自民党総裁を目指して競います。

　ほめる　　社会的に「謙譲の美徳」という考え方が広く行き渡っているため，日本人は特に自分や自分の家族，親戚などに対するほめ言葉を，そのまま受け入れるのには抵抗があります。これは自分の「身内」と考えられるもの一般についてもいえます。また，他人をほめたいと思っても，またそうすることが上手であっても，過度のほめ言葉を使うのには十分注意をはらいます。納得のいくようなほめ方をするのなら，それは常に感謝に価するものとなります。もしそうでないのなら，せっかくほめても単にお世辞やごますりになってしまいます。

PRAISING

In some cases excessive praising will be acceptable. For instance, in a letter of recommendation or at a wedding reception, the person concerned is often written or spoken very highly of. At wedding receptions several guests of honor offer their congratulations in such excessive praise that it may set one's teeth on edge. However, attendants are usually pleased with the praising even though the newly-weds hardly deserve it. They know that the speech of congratulations is ceremonial.

In daily life when being praised by others, the person praised often denies the merit by saying something like, "I don't deserve the praise." Otherwise, after expressing his/her thanks for the praise, the person adds some words in which he/she emphasizes good luck, a favor from others, or the help of his/her surroundings. By so doing, he/she tries to ascribe his/her virtue or achievements to the power of something other than his/her own ability or efforts. Thus the Japanese traditional attitude toward praise originates in the concept of self, which is regarded as "only a part of the whole organism."

Public commendation is very popular in Japanese society. From praising those who get high scores at school for tests of writing *kanji* (Chinese characters) to awarding distinguished persons the Cultural Medals for their achievements on the national level, the commendation is performed by reading a certificate of honor aloud in public. The winners accept them with gratitude, often

しかし，過度のほめ言葉も，場合においては受け入れられることもあります。例えば推薦状や結婚披露宴のスピーチなどの場合です。このような時，言及される本人は大いに持ち上げられます。特に結婚披露宴では，主賓格の招待者の何人かが歯の浮くような称賛の言葉でお祝いを述べますが，そもそもおめでたい席であるということもあり，ほかの招待者は，新郎新婦がその言葉には決して価しなくても，そのお祝いのスピーチに喜んで耳を傾けます。出席者はそれが儀礼的なものであることを知っているからです。

　一般に，他人からほめられると，当人は「いやあ，とんでもない」とか答えて，しばしばそれを否定しようとします。あるいはほめられたことに対して感謝したあと，幸運であったとか，みんなのおかげであるとかいうことを強調しようと言葉を付け加えます。そうすることによって，自分の人徳や業績を，自分の能力や努力以外の外部の力に帰そうとします。ほめられることに対して日本人が伝統的にとるこのような態度は，自分が全体のほんの部分でしかないという自己認識から生じているのです。

　みんなの前である個人をほめることは，日本の社会でもよくあることです。例えば，学校で漢字の書き取りがよくできた生徒を教師がほめることから，国のレベルでその個人の偉大な業績に対して文化勲章を与えることに至るまで，みんなの前で大きな声で賞状が読まれ，称賛されるのです。そしてこの場合も，ほめられる当人は，嬉しさを表す一方で，自分がそれにまだまだ価しないものであること，たまたま運が良かったことをしばしば強調しながら，その賛辞を受け入れるのです。

emphasizing their imperfection and good luck. (KA)

Private self and public self The disparity of
appearances between the private self and public self
seen in most Japanese people seems so confusing to
foreigners that the Japanese are sometimes mistakenly
considered two-faced. The same person can be both
rigidly formal in public and very frank and pleasant at
a privately held drinking party. He/she may give an
evasive or noncommittal reply to someone's business request, yet show his/her deep sympathy with that person's personal troubles.

Japanese habitually follow pluralistic behavioral patterns according to the occasion, but their private self
seems to be dominated by their public self which may
also be called "group self." Having a strong sense of
place and duty, they try to play the roles assigned to
them and live up to the expectations of the other members of their groups or organizations. In a business situation, they tend to behave "by the book" or according
to a certain model set to be followed by everyone in
their position. They usually place priority on their
company's interest over their own, and work hard,
suppressing their own egos and sometimes sacrificing
their private lives for their public roles. They become
not so much individuals as spokesmen for their
companies, and often act in a self-effacing way, masking their own feelings by means of traditional polite expressions. After-hours drinking parties given to entertain

私と公　　たいていの日本人には私的な場での自己と公的な場での自己の間に大きな差異がみられますが，外国人にはそのわけが分からず，日本人は二面性があると誤解しがちです。同じ人が公の場では非常に堅苦しいのに，私的な宴会の場では率直で愉快な人物になることがあります。また，仕事の上での要求には曖昧でどっちつかずの答えしかしないのに，相手の個人的な問題には深い同情を寄せることがあります。

　日本人は習慣的に場面に応じて複数の行動型に従って行動しますが，私的な自己はいつも公的な自己または「集団の自己」に支配されているようです。分限と義務を強く意識していて，自分に課せられた役割を果たし，集団や組織の期待にそって生きようとします。仕事の場合には，その地位にあるだれもが守るべき一定の「お手本」どおりに行動しがちです。たいていは，自分の利害よりも会社の利害を優先させて，利己心を抑え，時には公の役割のために私生活も犠牲にして勤勉に働きます。個人というよりは会社を代表する者になり，昔からある慇懃な言葉づかいによって自己を覆い隠して，自分が目だたないように振舞うことがあります。勤務時間中の商談では相手との間に溝ができがちですが，退社後に取引き先や仕事の関係者をもてなす酒宴が設けられ，その溝が埋められます。これは半ば公的で，半ば私的な場といえるでしょう。

　私的な自己と公的な自己との関係は，「内と外」とか「建前と本音」といった側面からも説明されています。だいたいのところ，内と本音が私的な自己にあたり，外と建前が公的な自己にあたります。

business customers and affiliations can be called half-business and half-private occasions for filling up the gaps likely to arise in the business communications held during office hours.

The relation between private and public selves may also be described in terms of *uchi-soto* (inside and outside) and *tatemae-honne* (official stand versus actual intention). *Uchi* and *honne* roughly correspond to the private self, and *soto* and *tatemae* to the public self. (TS)

Process of decision-making　The process of decision-making is of course varied according to the size and kind of the organization, the problem to be dealt with, or the project to be drawn up, but it may safely be said that the most conspicuous of Japanese ways are group approach and consensus seeking. In a business situation, though top-down management is excercised in small or newly-risen companies, bottom-up management is adopted to a certain degree by the board of directors in major companies.

Nemawashi and *ringi-seido* operate in group decision and in gaining the consensus of the concerned . *Nemawashi* is a process of securing informal consent from people concerned prior to a formal decision. Thus when a person in charge wants a project or a proposal to be pushed forward, he/she explains its general idea and outline to other members of the staff, particularly to the superordinates, asks for their opinion, and obtains their informal consent before it is submitted to a

244

意志決定　　意志決定の過程は組織の大きさと種類，対処する問題，企画の内容などによって，もちろん変わってきますが，日本で目だつ特徴は集団決定方式と全体の合意を求めるやり方です。中小企業ではトップダウン方式が行われていますが，大企業の重役会では，ある程度ボトムアップ方式が取り入れられています。

集団決定や関係者のコンセンサスを得るには根回しや稟議制度が効果を発揮します。根回しとは正式の決定前に関係者に非公式の同意を得ることです。例えば，ある責任者が企画や提言を実現させたいと思えば，その人は企画の趣旨や概要を職場の仲間，特に上司に説明して意見を求め，最終決定がされる重役会議にそれが提出される前に内諾を得ます。この過程で，もとの企画は十分に検討され，適当に修正されたり，改善されたりされます。

稟議制度は会議を必要としない比較的重要でない事柄に関するものです。これは責任者が作成した文書を回覧することによって企画に対する役職者の認可を得るやり方です。文書に役職者の印鑑が押されるとすぐに企画を実行に移すことができますから，この制度によって仕事の能率を上げ，すばやい対応ができるようになります。

生産管理のような構造的な問題については，コンピューターを

meeting of directors, where the final decision is made. In this process the project can be properly discussed, modified, or elaborated.

Ringi-seido concerns comparatively unimportant matters that require no meeting. It refers to a process of obtaining the sanction of executives to a plan by circulating the draft prepared by a person in charge. This system promotes promptitude in business, for the plan can be carried into execution as soon as the seals of the executives are stamped on the draft.

As for structured problems such as product control, the use of computers has made it much easier to find solutions for them. A proper output goal, for example, can be decided somewhat automatically by referring to the previously programed model stored in the computer data files. Notably, the computer system called MDSS (Management Decision-making Support System) aims at helping the human decision maker come to the best solutions for various problems arising in the company. The computer provides him/her with all the necessary and useful information and the human in turn inputs his /her own idea or judgment to the computer. Repeated debates follow between the human and the computer, until the former reaches the final conclusion. (OT/TS)

Proverbs Japanese like proverbs and seem to believe what they say. Thus, when they have to make a choice between a well-paying but little-known small company and a less-paying but well-established big com-

利用することによって解決が容易になりました。例えば適切な生産目標などは前もってコンピューターのデータファイルに保存されたモデルを参照して，ある程度自動的に決定することができます。特筆に値するのはMDSS（経営意志決定支援システム）と呼ばれるコンピューターシステムです。これは企業内のさまざまな問題について人間の意志決定者が最善の解決策に到達できるよう助けることを目的としています。コンピューターが人間にすべての有益で必要な情報を提供し，人間が自分の考えや判断をコンピューターに入力します。そして，人間が最終結論に達するまで両者の討論が繰り返されます。

ことわざ　　日本人はことわざが好きです。そして，ことわざを生活の指針にしているようです。たとえば，給料は高いが無名の小さな会社と，給料は低いが有名な大きな会社のどちらに就職したらよいかを考えるとき，たいがいの人は大会社のほうを選択

pany, they may take a big one, whispering to themselves "When you lean on a tree, find a big one" (A good tree is a good shelter). When they are in conflict with their superiors, they are apt to yield, saying to themselves "When you have something long, you'd better get yourself rolled up" (Don't kick against the nails). As these two proverbs suggest how Japanese look at social relations, there are many old sayings that indicate how people deal with language, pride, confrontation, cooperation, and many other aspects of life in this country.

The Japanese assumption on the use of language is represented in such sayings as "Silence is wisdom when speaking is folly," "Out of the mouth comes evil," or "No words but deeds." Similarly, they expect "that which comes from the heart" to "go to the heart," and see little need for effective elaboration for better communication.

Japanese hesitate to boast of themselves because they are often reminded that "Pride will have a fall." They also hesitate to be confrontive because they suppose "The best remedy against an ill man is much ground between," and they prefer to "let sleeping dogs lie," although some people elect to "go for broke," convinced of the wisdom of "Nothing ventured, nothing obtained."

Japanese value harmonious human relations. They assume that "Even a chance acquaintance is decreed by destiny." Cooperation among members is the goal of any group because "Two eyes can see more than one."

するようです。「寄らば大樹の陰」なのです。上役と意見が合わなければ、「長い物には巻かれろ」で，譲歩しがちです。これらのことわざが日本人の社会関係に対する考え方を示しているように，ことば，自慢，対決，助け合いなどといった生活の基本となることがらについて，日本人の態度を表すことわざがたくさんあります。

日本人のことばについての姿勢は，「言わぬが花」「口は禍の門」「不言実行」といった教訓によく出ています。また，日本人はことばを正確に使って，効果的なコミュニケーションをはかろうとすることがどうも苦手のようですが，それは「以心伝心」を期待しているからです。

日本人は自分の成功を他人に自慢するのを躊躇します。「驕る平家は久しからず」を思い出すからです。対決的な姿勢もあまり取ろうとしません。「君子危うきに近よらず」ですし，「触らぬ神に祟りなし」です。もっとも，「当たって砕けよ」を信条として，道を切り開く人もいます。たしかに，「虎穴に入らずんば虎子を得ず」です。

日本人は和をモットーとして，人間関係を築きます。そもそも，「袖振り合うのも他生の縁」なのです。どの集団でも，仲間はたがいに助け合うものとされています。「三人寄れば文珠の知恵」というのがあります。知ったかぶりをして，個人プレーを見せるのは危険なことです。これは「生兵法は大怪我のもと」という教えでわかります。へたをすると，「出る杭は打たれる」ことになりかねません。

外国人が日本の習慣に疑問を感じると，日本人はよく「郷に入りては郷に従え」と迫ります。日本人はものごとをこまかく説明するよりも，ことわざを使ったり，大前提を示すことによって，問題解決の方法を教えようとします。日本人のことわざ好きは，日本人が帰納法よりも，演繹法のロジックを好むからかもしれま

People try not to be too self-assertive because they know that "A little learning is a dangerous thing" and that "Envy is the companion of honor."

When people from abroad find it difficult to follow Japanese ways of getting things done, they are often told bluntly "When in Rome, do as Romans do." Instead of offering precise explanationas, Japanese use proverbs or general statements to teach how to solve problems. Reliance on proverbs may indicate that Japanese prefer deductive logic to inductive reasoning. (NH)

Quality control It is often said that Japanese-made products are good in quality. The precision machinery and tools, in particular, have good reputation all over the world.

In Japan, it is normally the case that people work together, with job specification and responsibility left unclear with respect to each position or person. It follows that they assume joint liability in case something damaging to their reputation has happened, even though the head of the section involved may take the responsibility in behalf of all the employees working under him.

With the introduction of the QC circle, which is a small group of workers who take care of the quality control of their products, things have changed. Since they serve as the final filter before their products are put on the market and are responsible for everything, they tend to have an enhanced sense of responsibility.

せん。

品質管理　　日本製品は品質が良いとよく言われます。とりわけ精密機器は世界で高い評価を受けています。

日本では共同作業が通常の形態です。職務内容や職責は一人一人についてはっきりしているわけではありません。その代わり，評判を汚すような事態が起きた場合には，関係者全員が責任を負うことになります。もっとも実際には，トップに立つものが部下に代わって責任をとります。

しかし，総合的品質管理の一環として，**QC** サークルと呼ばれる，少人数による自主管理運動の導入を機に事態は一変しました。彼らは，いわば製品が市場に出る前の最後のフィルターとしての機能を果たすこととなり，責任の所在もかなり明確化されるので，一層強い責任感を持つようになったのです。これに伝統的な日本人の美意識あるいは価値観から来るうるさいほどの几帳面さが加わって，今日の品質管理の水準の高さが実現，維持されているのかもしれません。

物事に対しうるさいくらいに細かいこの性質は，日本から仕事を下請けすることがますます多くなってきている他のアジア諸国にとっては迷惑なものとなることがあります。たとえば東南アジ

To this is added the fact that the Japanese are methodical or even meticulous, a characteristic deriving from the traditional Japanese sense of beauty and value. The high standard of quality control in Japan may be a result of these combined factors.

This meticulous nature of the Japanese may be an annoyance to other Asian nations, who undertake increasingly more subcontracted work from Japan. According to a newspaper article that dealt with Southeast Asian sewing subcontractors, the terms of the contracts they made with Japanese companies were generally quite satisfactory, but there was one thing that annoyed them. It was that if a seam was found to be a little crooked, or a stitch or two were not in line, then the clothes were sent back to them. This kind of thing may strike them as nitpicking, but it is not so for the Japanese. (MAT)

Religion   On New Year's Eve many Japanese visit Buddhist temples for ringing out the 108 evil passions such as greed, enmity, and foolishness. Then, with the coming of New Year's morning, they pay the first visit to *Shinto* shrines to pray for good luck throughout the year. Also, these days an increasing number of young women wish to celebrate their weddings in Christian churches . Funerals are most often observed in a Buddhist fashion.

Japan has a long history of observing various ceremonies of different religions. *Shinto*, the native reli-

アにある縫製の下請け企業を扱ったある新聞記事によると，彼らは日本企業と取り交わした契約条項にはおおむね満足しているのですが，一つだけ困ったことがあるというのです。彼らが言うには，縫目が少しでも曲がっていると（たとえば一針か二針線からはずれたりすると），それだけで返品されてくるそうです。これは彼らにしてみれば，重箱の隅を針でつつくようなことにしか思えないのでしょう。しかし，日本人にとっては違うのです。そしてこの細かさが品質管理に生かされているのです。

宗　教　　大晦日には大多数の日本人はお寺に詣でて除夜の鐘をつき，貪欲，怒り，愚かしさの三垢をはじめとする 108 の煩悩を祓います。やがて元旦を迎えると，今度は，神社に初詣でをして一年の幸運を祈願します。さらに最近では，結婚式は教会でしたいと希望する若い女性は増える一方で，それでいて，今なお葬儀は，仏式で行うのが最も一般的なのです。

　日本では，こうした多種多様な宗教的慣習が，長い間続いてきました。民族宗教である神道は今も人々の間に生きていて，例えば，『古事記』（712 年）に現れる太陽神の天照大神は，皇室の氏神として伊勢神宮に祀られ，また，一般にも長く信仰の対象とされてきました。さらにこの国では，歴史上の優れた人物も，祭

gion of Japan, is still a popular religion. Its chief deity, the Sun Goddess Amaterasu, is enshrined at Ise as an ancestral deity of the Imperial family. The Ise Grand Shrines have long been worshiped by Japanese of all classes. Beside the ancient deities in *Shinto*, great historical figures can be enshrined as deities assigned specific mystic powers. Most typical is the famous ancient scholar Sugawara no Michizane (845-903) enshrined at Temmangū shrines throuhgout the country. He is highly revered as a deity of learning and worshiped especially by college entrance examinees and their parents. This open or unconcerned attitude of Japanese people to religious doctrines together with their inherent reverence for all things in nature and their prayer for worldly benefits seems to have originated in Japan's rice-growing agricultural society.

Historically, the openness can also be related to Buddhism from China and Korea in the middle of the first millennium A.D. The conflict between the native *Shinto* and the imported Buddhism led to such resolutions as the *honji-suijaku* doctrine which originated in the 9th century and remained dominant until the Meiji Restoration in 1868. The doctrine, integrating the two religions, held that the *Shinto* gods were nothing but incarnations of Buddhas and Bodhisattvas. Japanese religious awareness can be said to be closer to pantheism, rather than to polytheism, in that it allows syncretism of various religious doctrines. This explains why Japanese people report multiple religious affiliations. Japan's

神として祀られることがあります。その好例は，平安初期の公卿・学者であった菅原道真（845〜903）で，学問の神として津々浦々の天満宮に祀られ，特に受験生やその親たちの間で崇敬されています。このように日本人は，現世利益を祈願したり，自然崇拝をする一方で，種々の異なる宗教に対しても鷹揚なのです。日本人のこうした宗教観と信仰心は，恐らく米作を中心とする農耕文明の中で培われた，自然との強い結びつきと愛着とによるものなのでしょう。

　複数の宗教を受け入れる日本人の異教に対する寛容さは，6世紀半ばの仏教伝来と，それに伴う神仏習合とも無縁ではありません。土俗信仰である神道と，のちに伝来した仏教は，9世紀頃，本地垂迹説のような形をとり，神仏調和の習合思想となって明治維新（1868年）まで続きました。これは，神道の神は仏菩薩（本地）が権に姿を変えて現れた権現であるとして，これら二つの宗教を融和しようとするものなのです。このように日本人の宗教観は，多様な異なる教義でも，それらを併呑融合してしまうという点で，多神教よりも汎神論に近いといえましょう。日本人が同時に複数の宗教に属しているとみなされるのはこのためなのです。事実，1985年の宗教人口は2億2千4百万人で，これは日本の総人口の186%に相当します。そのうち，神道が51.7%，仏教徒41.1%，キリスト教徒は0.8%です。

religious population in 1985 was 224 million, which is 186% of the total population. Of them 51.7% were Shintoists, 41.1% Buddhists, and 0.8% Christians. (ON)

Responsibility, how to take　　Recently there happened an incident which would have never occurred in a Western country. The chairman and president of a large Japanese company "took the responsibility" and resigned their posts when it was revealed that one of the company's subsidiaries had engaged in illegal dealings with foreign countries. The resignations were said to be the deepest possible way of expressing the firm's apology.

In this incident, we see an extended parent-child relationship. In Japan a father often feels responsible for his son's or daughter's wrongdoing and resigns his post even when his child is an adult. In a company too, a boss resigns his post, taking responsibility for one of his men's misconduct.

This way of taking responsibility may be inconceivable to Western people. But Japanese give up what they possess—their honor, social position, income, and sometimes even their own life—and by suffering the loss they feel they can make amends for their or their in-group member's wrongdoing. In other words, by inflicting punishment on themselves, they hope for a reduction of further charges. When one takes "social" responsibility, he resigns his post; when he takes "moral" responsibility, he sometimes takes his own life. In

責任のとり方　　最近，欧米ではまず起こらないような事件がありました。子会社の外国との不正取引が露見した大会社の会長と社長が，その「責任をとって」辞任したのです。その辞任は親会社の謝罪の最たるものだと言われています。

この事件には親子関係の延長された姿が見られるように思います。日本では，息子や娘が罪を犯すと，たとえその子が成人していても，その父親が責任を感じ，会社を辞めることがよくあります。会社でも，部下の不正の責任をとって，その上司が辞めたりすることがあります。

このような責任のとり方は欧米の人には信じられないことかもしれません。しかし，日本人は自分や身内の不始末の償いをするために，自分が持っているもの——名誉，社会的地位，収入，時には自分の命までも棄てることがあります。そしてその損失で苦しむことによって，その不始末の償いをすることができると考えるのです。つまり，自らに罰を科すことで罪が軽くなることを望むのです。「社会的」責任をとる時には会社を辞めます。「道義的」責任をとる時には，時として，自らの命を断ちます。そうすることで，自分は責任から自由になると思うのです。現在の立場に留まって，または生きて，自分や身内の不始末の償いをしようという発想はほとんどないようです。

so doing, he thinks he becomes free from the responsibility. It hardly occurs to his mind that he should keep his position or stay alive in order to make up for what he or his subordinate has done. (YY)

Rights and duties   Traditionally duty-conscious, the average Japanese have been somewhat insensible of their own rights. The political history of Japan, with the absolute monarchy extending over ages, may explain why they even now tend to conceive of law as mere listings of musts and must-nots rather than as the guarantor and protector of their rights. The concept of a right itself had to be borrowed from Western political philosophy when the Japanese government was modernized in the 19th century. People's fundamental human rights and civil rights were partly acknowledged, but under very rigid restrictions. These rights were in effect guaranteed after World War II by the democratic Constitution of Japan (enforced in 1947), which has brought forward a variety of political and social movements among the general public.

However, Japanese reservedness in exercising their rights seems to be deep-rooted. For example, a landlord may refrain from urging his delinquent tenant for the payment of rent for fear of being considered too exacting or crusty, even though it is wholly within his right to do so. On the other hand, Japanese are sometimes so insensitive to the violation of others' rights that they may very innocently trespass on others' private

権利と義務　　日本人は昔から義務感が強く，権利意識にいくぶん乏しかったようです。今でも法律というと，自分の権利を保障し保護するものというより，しなければならないこと，してはいけないことを単に羅列したものと考えられがちです。これはいくつかの時代にわたって，長い間，絶対権力が支配してきた日本の政治史に原因があるのかもしれません。権利という概念そのものも，19世紀に日本の政府が近代化されたときに西洋の政治哲学から借用したものです。国民の基本的人権や公民権は部分的に認められたものの，非常に厳しい制限がついていました。これらの権利が実際上保障されたのは第2次大戦後（1947年）に民主的な日本国憲法が制定されてからで，それ以後一般民衆のあいだにもさまざまな政治的，社会的な運動が盛んになってきています。

しかし，日本人が自己の権利を主張するのを控える傾向は根強いようです。例えば家主は借家人が家賃を払わない場合，督促する権利は十分あっても，あまりにも杓子定規だとか，けちけちしていると思われやしないかと，そうするのを遠慮することがあります。他方では，他人の権利の侵害には鈍感で，他人の私有地にまったく無頓着に立ち入る人もいます。

多分，法律や規則よりも義理や人情のほうが行動規範として拘束力を持っているのでしょう。協定はそれを守る誠実さや信義が重要だとされています。最近まで，保険の場合を除いて契約書でさえ当事者の権利や義務を詳細にわたって明記してはいませんでした。明記されていないことは後に必要に応じて話合いで解決できると考えられていたからです。一般的に，紛争を解決するのに

grounds.

Perhaps *giri* and *ninjō* (mutual obligations and human feelings) are more binding as behavioral codes than laws and regulations. Importance is attached to sincerity and faith in fulfilling an agreement. Until recently, even in contracts (excepting insurance contracts) rights and duties of the parties concerned were not specified in complete detail, because things not stipulated could be discussed and settled later as occasion demanded. Generally, mediations are preferred to law-suits in settling disputes, and a conciliatory attitude is always expected of the parties in the case of an out-of-court settlement. (TS)

Satire   Some critics say that rigid censorship enforced throughout the Edo period (1603-1867) and during World War II has almost destroyed the traditions of satirical literature, which had flourished in the forms of *kyōgen* (comic interludes performed between *nō* plays), *kyōka* (satirical short poems in *tanka* style), *senryū* (comic short poems in *haiku* style), and *kibyōshi* (illustrated storybooks in yellow covers). This notion is open to question, for satires are often seen to thrive in ages and in countries where most strict control over speech and writing is exercised so that writers are in constant danger of being indicted for their articles or books. However, there is little doubt that modern Japan, for all its freedom of speech, has produced comparatively few dramatic and literary works in satirical

は訴訟よりも調停が好まれ，示談の場合には当事者が和解的態度をとるよう期待されます。

風刺　日本の風刺文学は，狂言，狂歌，川柳，黄表紙といった形で何世紀にもわたって栄えていましたが，江戸時代と第2次大戦中の厳しい検閲のためにその伝統がほとんど途絶えてしまったという批評家がいます。この考えには疑問があります。風刺というものは，記事や本のために作者が拘禁される危険がいつもあるような，厳しい言論統制がしかれている国や時代にかえって盛んだからです。しかし，現代の日本は言論の自由があるにもかかわらず，風刺という形での劇作品や文学作品が比較的少ないことも確かです。

　風刺が不振な一つの原因はまだ儒教の影響が残っているからかもしれません。儒教は笑いを不真面目で卑しいものとみなしました。本当に社会を変えようとするなら，風刺の常套手段である揶揄や嘲笑に訴えるよりも強硬な抗議や率直な批判をするほうが失政や社会不正を糾弾するのに有効であると考えられています。もう一つの原因として，権威に屈服しやすいという大衆の根強い傾

forms.

One reason for the decline of satires may be that people are still under the influence of Confucianism, which looked down upon laughter as insincere and vulgar. A strong protest or a straightforward criticism is considered a more effective way of censuring misgovernment and social follies than ridicule or derision, the usual method of satires, if one really intends to bring about any change. Another likely reason is people's deep-rooted resignation and readiness to yield to the authorities. It may be that harsh satirists or malcontents revolting against the mainstream cannot be very popular in a society where a conciliatory or conformist attitude is so highly valued.

However, in the hearts of the common people there still lingers the satirical spirit; literary, theatrical, or TV parodies of current follies and vices are now gaining popularity; newspaper cartoons mocking the absurdity of certain government policies appeal to a large readership; also popular are topical and satirical epigrams contributed by readers to newspapers and magazines. (TS)

Saving and spending　In recent years Japan has been sharply criticized by other nations for its huge trade surplus. They complain that the Japanese work too hard and save too much instead of spending enough time and money to enjoy their lives. They also insist that Japan should take more responsibilities appropriate

向をあげられるかもしれません。主流に反抗する毒舌の風刺家や不満の徒は，協調的態度が高く評価される社会では人気が出ないということなのかもしれません。

しかし，庶民の心にはまだ風刺精神が残っています。現代の不正や悪徳をパロディーにした文学作品や演劇やテレビ番組が人気を得ています。政府の政策の愚かさをからかった新聞の漫画も多くの読者を引きつけています。また，新聞や雑誌に読者が投稿する時宜を得た風刺的な一言時評も人気があります。

貯蓄と消費　　近年日本は，大幅の貿易黒字に対して外国から厳しい批判を受けています。外国の不満は，日本人は働きすぎであり，生活を楽しむために時間とお金を使うのでなく，貯金をしすぎることです。また日本人は経済大国の地位にふさわしい責任を果たすべきだと言われています。

このような要求に応えて，日本は内需拡大と対外経済協力促進

to its status as an economic power.

In response to these claims, Japan has taken measures to expand its domestic demand and promote economic cooperation with the rest of the world. For example, it has decided to reform the tax system, abolishing in principle the tax-free savings system under which saving rather than spending was encouraged.

Indeed, Japan may now be rich as a country, but on an individual basis, ordinary people do not feel they are prosperous. Even when they agree that their country is a financial giant, they are afraid its economic success is evanescent. They are very anxious about the future of their rapidly aging society in a country with poor natural resources. They think they have to save as much as possible in their earlier years to provide for their old age or their children's education. They hope to have a house of their own, though it has become extremely difficult due to the soaring land prices, particularly in big cities. Land prices alone may reach 1,000 dollars per square foot in Tokyo's middle-class residential areas.

The average Japanese household puts about 20% of its disposable income each year into savings. This is one of the highest saving rates in the world, far higher than in any other major nation. In Japan, "hard work, frugality, and saving" is something like a motto handed down from age to age. Consumption is not a virtue, especially in the eyes of the older generations. As a result, it is no easy task for the Japanese to change

の対策を講じました。例えば，税制改革を実行し，消費よりも貯蓄を奨励するような貯蓄優遇制度を原則的に廃止しました。

　確かに日本は国としては豊かになりました。しかし個人のレベルでは，一般の人は自分が金持ちだとは思っていません。日本が経済大国であると認める者も，今の経済的繁栄が長続きするものではないと感じています。資源が乏しく，急速に高齢化が進んでいる国の将来を大変不安に思っています。老後の生活や子供の教育に備えて，早い時期からできるだけ貯金をしなければならないと考えます。自分の家を持つことを望んでいますが，地価の高騰のため，特に大都市では極めて難しくなりました。東京の中流の住宅地域で，土地だけで1平方フィート当たり1,000ドルはするでしょう。

　平均的な日本の家庭では，毎年可処分所得の約20%を貯蓄にまわします。この貯蓄率は世界で最も高いものの一つで，他のどの先進国よりもかなり高い率です。日本では「勤勉，倹約，貯蓄」が昔から伝わるモットーです。消費は，特に年輩の世代から見ると，美徳ではありません。そのため，日本人が貯蓄と消費に対する考え方を変えるのは容易なことではないのです。きりぎりすの生活よりも蟻の生活を高く評価する傾向があるからです。

their ideas about saving and spending. They tend to value the ant's life above the grasshopper's. (MT)

Scolding   The Japanese concept of disciplining a child by scolding is dominated by the consciousness of shame (disapproval by others) rather than guilt (subject to discipline because of a sin or crime). In former days when paternal rights were quite rigid, prodigal sons were scolded and often repudiated for bringing shame on the family.

From that time, the father has had the task of scolding his child with lectures or disciplining by corporal punishment, while the mother's role is soothing the crying child. In daily life the mother reproaches the child for his/her bad manners or ill conduct by saying that she will tell the father about it.

Until a decade ago the mother or even the father used to threaten to call a policeman or a schoolmaster in scolding a young child. Even now scolding is not done in such a logical way as to convince the child of his/her misdeed or mistake. Rather, it is done emotionally and often for the purpose of keeping up public appearances. For instance, if a child is running around in a crowded train or bus, the mother often reproves him/her by saying, "Stop it or you'll be scolded by others," "Stop it. I am ashamed of you," and so on.

In social organizations like government offices, companies, and schools, scolding is performed formally if the offense or the fault is considered grave. It ranges

しかる　　しかることによって子供を訓育していくという日本人の考え方は，罪の意識というよりは，他人から非難されることを恐れた恥の意識を基にしています。親権がかなり強かった昔，放蕩息子は家の名を汚したとしてひどくしかられ，しばしば勘当されることもありました。

　その当時から，子供に説教をし，あるときは体罰を与えて訓育をするのは父親であり，そのために泣いている子供をなだめるのがもっぱら母親の役目でした。普段母親は，「お父さんに言い付けますよ」などといいながら，行儀の悪い，悪態をついている子を叱責します。

　一昔前まで母親は，またあるときは父親まで子供をしかる際に，「おまわりさんを呼びますよ」「校長先生に言い付けますよ」などといって，子供を脅かしました。今でも子供の悪事や過ちに対し，子供を納得させるような論理的なしかり方は，あまりやられていません。むしろ感情的な，しばしば親の体面を保つようなしかり方がされます。例えば混雑した電車やバスの中を自分の子供が走り回っていると，母親はしばしば「やめなさい。ほらしかられるでしょう」とか「およしなさい。ほら恥ずかしいでしょう」などといって，子供をしかります。

　役所，会社，学校などでは，もしその罪や過失が重大である時は，訓戒から免職に至るまでの，さまざまな処分が下されます。このような場合，罪をおかした人の上司も，部下に対する監督不行届きということで，おそらく懲戒を受けるでしょう。過ちに対してこのように責任の所在をはっきりさせるやり方は，社会のあらゆる面に見られるもので，こうすることがまた一般に受け入れられてもいるのです。

from oral admonition to dismissal. In these cases the offender's superiors are likely to be reprimanded also for a lack of control over their subordinates. This way of placing responsibility for a fault is seen in every aspect of social affairs and is accepted by the society in general.

Nowadays, because of the decline in the traditional social values, change in people's attitudes toward discipline, and hesitation in interfering with other person's affairs, scolding is losing its social function of training the rising generations. The father seldom scolds his child to teach him/her manners. Adults no longer scold their neighbor's children as they used to even if it is part of their social obligation to do so. Superiors are often hesitant to scold their subordinates. The increase of bullying at schools and corruption of discipline in offices may have much to do with the decrease of the traditional use of scolding at home and in society. (KA)

Self-sacrifice for the benefit of a public cause

Historically, Japanese people were almost always ready to sacrifice themselves for the sake of a public cause. Confucianism, Tennoism (the Emperor system), *bushidō* (the feudal-military Japanese code of behavior) teachings, and later militarism, invariably advocating one's selfless devotion to the country, much contributed to the permeation of the idea of self-sacrifice into the Japanese mind. The cooperative work system prevalent

今日伝統的な社会的価値というものが衰退していること，しつけに対する人々の態度も変化していること，また他人の事柄に干渉するのを避けようとする風潮によって，しかることがもっていた，これからの世代を育てていくという社会的な機能が失われてきています。父親はしつけを目的に，子供をしかることも滅多にしません。以前は，大人は社会的な義務としてよくしかったものですが，今ではこういうことはしなくなりました。会社でも役所でも，上司も部下をしかるのにはためらいを感ずるようになってきたのです。学校でのいじめや職場での規律の低下は，家庭や社会で昔のように人々がしからなくなったことと，大いに関係があるのかもしれません。

　滅私奉公　　歴史的にみると，日本人は公益のためには自己を犠牲にすることをいとわない国民だったと言えます。儒教，天皇制，武士道，それに軍国主義はどれも，私心を捨てて国に仕えることを唱道し，自己犠牲の精神を日本人の心に浸透させました。自己犠牲は，意志の問題ではなく，義務だったのです。共同作業を主体とする農民や漁民は，公益を優先し，個人主義を戒めることを知っていたでしょう。軍国主義，全体主義一色に包まれた戦時中には，自我は完全に抑制され，上官に盲従し，それが即公益につながると考えられました。第2次大戦中の神風特攻隊の攻撃

among people engaged in agriculture and fishery may also have served to emphasize common good on the one hand and suppress individualism on the other. Thus, the idea of self-sacrifice became somewhat compulsory or obligatory rather than voluntary. With the military and totalitarian trend of the wartime, it culminated in total self-annihilation and blind obedience to one's superiors who were believed to represent public good. One typical example may be the suicidal attacks made by *Kamikaze* corps during World War II.

The pendulum swung in the opposite direction after the war. People were by then well aware that the war had been fought under the cloak of a general and noble cause. Schools abolished patriotic education and began to attach more importance to one's self. However, a traditional way of thinking embedded deep into people's mind dies hard. Sturdy individualism or a self-asserting attitude never gains popularity in Japanese society, where a conciliatory or cooperative attitude is highly respected. In the business world, for example, many people are still sacrificing their personal interests to the general interests of their company, which seem to have become synonymous with public 'causes.'

It should be remembered, however, that an increasing number of volunteers are working for the welfare of the aged and the handicapped. Some eager young Japanese, though small in number, are reported to be helping the destitute, the displaced, and other sufferes in African and Southeast Asian countries. Their activities

は自己犠牲の極端な例です。

　ところが戦後は時代の趨勢が180度の転換を見せます。国民は戦争の欺瞞性に気付き，学校は愛国主義教育を捨て，自我を重視する教育を採用しました。それでも，人の心に深く根ざした思想はたやすくは消えるものではありません。和を尊ぶ日本社会では，個人主義や強い自己主張は決して皆の賛同を得られるものではないのです。たとえば，ビジネスの世界では，今だに会社の利益のために自分の利益を犠牲にする場合がよくあります。ここでは会社のためイコール世の中のためという公式が成り立っているようです。

　しかし，見逃してはならないことがあります。それは，老齢者や身障者の福祉のために奉仕しているボランティアの人がますます増加していることです。そして，まだ数の上では多いとは言えないものの，情熱に燃える若者が，アフリカや東南アジアで飢餓貧困に苦しむ難民の力となって働いています。このような活動から教えられることは，滅私奉公の真の精神は義務感からではなく愛から生まれるものであり，ヒロイズムや愛国主義とは無縁のものであるということです。

show that self-sacrifice primarily derives from love for others rather than from a sense of obligation and that it has in fact little to do with heroism or patriotism. (MaT/TS)

Seniority rule   One of the practices peculiar to Japan is the seniority system. It ensures your promotions on condition that you continue to work hard for your company for a long time and acquire a certain amount of technical knowledge and skills. The employees of a company are evaluated more on the basis of seniority than on their abilities except in extreme cases.

Some interesting phenomena can be observed, as far as the pay structure is concerned. It so happens that a competent but younger section chief may be given smaller salary than his subordinates who have been working with the company longer than him. Another instance worthy of note is that nearly all the companies in Japan provide their workers with a fringe benefit in the form of seniority allowance, which depends on seniority and grows larger with each year.

Consider next an English proverb "A rolling stone gathers no moss." This particular proverb and its Japanese counterpart have conflicting meanings. The "moss" is taken as something bad in the United States, while it means something good in Japan. Thus, if a person is really able, then he cannot be held back but is bound to change companies. This is the American inter-

年功序列　　年功序列は日本特有の慣習です。真面目に勤務し，それなりの知識と技能を身に付けさえすれば，ある程度までの昇進は約束されるのです。従業員の評価基準としては，特殊なケースを除いて，能力よりもむしろ勤続年数が重視されます。

給与面で面白い現象が見られます。有能で出世が早かった若い課長よりも，部下である平社員の方が，勤続年数が長いため，高給取りだったりすることがあります。もう一つ特徴的なのは，勤続給と呼ばれるものです。これは日本の会社のほとんどが支払っていて，勤続年数に応じて額が決まり，毎年増えて行くものです。こういった慣習は外国ではまず例を見ないものでしょう。

ここで，「転石苔を生せず」という諺について考えてみることにしましょう。面白いことに，この諺に見られる「苔」は日米で相反する解釈を与えられています。「苔」は，米国では悪いものとして，日本では良いものとして，受け止められているのです。アメリカ人の解釈では，もし有能な人であれば，その才能が必ず認められ他の会社に引き抜かれ，一つの会社に埋もれて「苔」が生えてしまうようなことはない，となります。それに対し，日本流の解釈では，一つ所に腰を落ち着けることなく，会社を転々とするようなものは不誠実で信頼できない，となってしまいます。このような考え方の相違を見ると，「社会的移動性」が日本で低く，米国で高いということもうなずけます。

pretation. In its Japanese interpretation, on the other hand, if a person changes companies, he is looked upon as disloyal and unreliable, and has to start at the low end of the promotion ladder all the time. This accounts for the fact that we have much less social mobility in Japan than in the United States. (MAT)

Sex morals In Japanese society, the morals of Confucianism have exerted a great influence on people's ways of thinking and behavior toward sexual matters. Sexual problems and matters used to be considered so shameful and dirty as to be concealed from notice of others, although they excited people's interest and curiosity. The trend of the society made sex a taboo and restricted people's behavior and attitude toward it, condemning sexual promiscuity as morally bad, legally punishable, and socially shameful.

On the other hand, however, unlike the Christian ethic, Japanese religion regarded sex as mere uncleanliness that could easily be purged by ablutions. As a result, the Japanese culture developed a very distorted view of sexual matters. Thus people who frequented houses in the pleasure quarters may have felt shame but would have had little sense of sin or evil-doing, especially if they went in a group. Even now some Japanese male tourists to Asian countries have relations with women of the streets there. It is often reported that they boastfully and shamelessly confess the fact and the result among their friends in the plane on their

274

性道徳　　日本の社会では歴史的に儒教的な道徳観が，人々の性に対する考え方や行動に大きな影響を与えてきました。性の問題や事柄は，内では興味や関心を示しながらも，外に対しては恥ずかしいこと，汚らわしいこととみなされ，ひたすら他人の目からは隠されようとしてきました。そして社会は性をタブー化し，人々の性に対する行動や態度を大きく規制してきたのです。また，性の乱れは道徳的に悪いこと，法の上でも罰せられるもの，社会的にも恥ずべきものとしてとらえられました。

　その一方で，キリスト教の倫理とは異なり，日本人の宗教観は，性は容易に清めることができる単に不浄なものとも考えました。このため日本文化は性に対してかなり屈曲したとらえ方を発展させてきたのです。それゆえ男たちは遊郭に出入りしながらも，特に集団でそこに通う場合，恥の意識は持つものの，それを罪悪だとはみなさなかったのです。現在でも男仲間が集まり，現地の女性目当てにアジアの国々へ出掛けていく買春ツアーといわれるものがしばしば話題になります。恥じらう様子もなく，大胆にも彼らは，帰りの機内で，自分たちの成果を語りあうこともあるといいます。婚外交渉に対しても，ほとんど罪の意識を感じない人もいます。

　しかしエイズの流行と 1985 年に施行された新風俗営業法によって，ポルノや一種の風俗産業は，ある程度まで鎮静化してきたといわれます。しかし見方によっては，これらがなお一層潜在化

way back. Some people feel little guilt in extramarital affairs.

Because of the AIDS crisis and enforcement of the new law in 1985 regulating any business affecting public morals, the flood of pornography and the businesses dealing with sex seem to be subsiding to some extent. However, these businesses have apparently become latent and more tactful. To prevent the youth from being influenced by this corrupted atmosphere and from being involved in degenerated activities, the majority of people advocate sex education at home and schools, but both parents and teachers find it very difficult to give it because they feel too shy or bashful to do so. Problems concerning sex, especially sexual offenses done by juvenile delinquents, have been increasing in number lately. Many educational critics point out the fact that while today's youth mature physically very quickly, they make slow progress mentally, confused or hindered perhaps by an overwhelming amount of information about sex diffused by mass media.

Homosexuality has a long tradition and gay people have been treated as social outcasts. However, their way of life has often been a subject of novels and magazine articles. These days, because of the AIDS crisis, their existence and present situation are often reported on TV, but they are still seen as immoral or abnormal beings. (KA)

Shin-jinrui : new human species The coined

し，巧妙になったともいわれています。これらの乱れた性の環境から若者を守るため，大人の多くは学校や家庭での性教育の必要性を唱えています。しかし親・教師とも真っ向から性の問題を子供と語りあうのは恥ずかしいという意識から，これが難しいということもよく知っています。性に関する問題，特に青少年による性犯罪の件数は，最近増加の一途をたどっています。教育評論家の多くは，今日の若者が肉体的には早熟であるが，マスコミによって与えられる性に関する過度の情報に翻弄され，肉体の成長に心の成長が伴っていけないのではないかと指摘しています。

　同性愛は日本でも長い歴史をもっていますが，同性愛者は社会的には除けものの扱いを受けてきました。しかし彼らの実態は，しばしば小説や雑誌の題材にされてきたことも事実です。今日，エイズの流行やこれに対する危機感から，テレビを中心としたマスコミは，彼らの現状や実態をしばしば取り上げるようになりましたが，いまだに同性愛が一般に反道徳的なもの，異常なものという扱いを受けていることには変わりがありません。

新人類　　「新人類」という造語は，旧い世代の人々には全く

word *shin-jinrui* represents an entirely new human species totally different from the preceding older generations in tastes, views, and values, as if mutantly produced. Raised in material affluence in the 1960's and the early 1970's when Japan boasted of rapid economic growth, they watched TV or played computer games at home while their parents went to work contributing to Japan's high productivity. As a result, they take for granted Japan's present prosperity which their parents' generation has brought about with all their might. They are characterized mainly by the following three points.

First, inward-oriented, they build up their own private world. Today college students spend only 49 minutes a day reading books and 97 minutes listening to the radio and taped music. They value their own individual 'self' more than anything else and yet feel happy in the company of their friends who are on the same wavelength, exchanging information about music, fashions, computers, and girl friends or boy friends.

Second, the young generation is optimistic in their way of living. They are different from the preceding generations in that they are mostly free from the traditional work-ethic values and indifferent to Japan's still vertical-structured society. They act freely in accordance with their circumstances, discard endurance as a fossilized virtue of little importance, and think that eventually things will always work out somehow. Now is a moratorium in their lives in which they can really enjoy

考えられなかったような，異なった価値観や趣味や好みをもった若い世代を指します。この「新人類」とよばれる世代は，日本経済の高度成長期，すなわち1960年代から1970年代初めにかけての物質的豊かさの中で育った世代で，彼らの親たちがせっせと生産性向上に汗水垂らして働いている間，家でテレビやコンピューターゲームで遊びながら，親の留守を過ごした世代でもあります。従って，親の世代の汗の結晶である今日の日本の繁栄も，彼ら「新人類」の目には，ごく当り前のことと映っているのです。この「新人類」の特徴は，次の三点に要約されるでしょう。

　第1に，彼らはその生い立ちに見られるように，自分の私的世界を作り上げて，それを大事に守ろうとします。大学生の1日の平均読書時間はわずかに49分。97分はラジオやテープの音楽を聴いて過ごします。彼らは「自我」という己れの個性を何よりも重んじますが，波長の合う友達とも結構うまくやってゆき，音楽やファッション，コンピューターや異性の友達について，お互いに情報交換したりします。

　第2は，彼らの生き方が極めて楽観的なことです。親たちの世代と違って，勤勉を旨とする伝統的な価値観などには囚われないし，依然として根強い日本のタテ社会にも無頓着なのです。彼らは自由に状況に適応して行動し，忍耐などという価値観は，ほとんど価値のない化石化したものとして顧みません。万事は所詮何とかなるさと考えています。今という時は，彼らにとって人生で最も楽しむことのできるモラトリアムであり，従って，転職ですら大学時代のアルバイトの延長ぐらいにしか考えない傾向があります。当然，会社への忠誠心は稀薄であり，いきおい仕事以外の自分の趣味に生き甲斐を見つけることになります。

　第3点は，今の若い世代が遊び心と自由な発想を持った，スマートな世代だということです。コンピューターをはじめとする機器類の取扱いは手慣れたもので，実に楽しげにこなしてしまいま

themselves. And they tend to look upon even their jobs as an extension of their part-time jobs they experienced in their college days. Consequently, they naturally have little sense of loyalty to their companies, placing a greater stress on personal-interest activities outside of their work.

Thirdly, today's young people are a smart generation with a playful and creative mind. They can easily handle and play with computers and other machines in a pleasant manner. Reportedly, a team of freshman engineers recently developed a best-selling Japanese word processor with its keyboard arranged in the Japanese alphabet. Their managers first thought with some contempt that they were just wasting time, but it was actually a big success.

Thus there exists a generation gap in Japan's present society between the old and the new with regard to the way of thinking and living with the age of Japan's economic growth as a great dividing line. However, it is also true that this generation gap promises a new Japanese people and society. (ON)

Sibling relation　How to address the brothers and sisters in Japanese gives a clue to understanding sibling relationships in a Japanese family. Different terms are used to refer to and address siblings according to seniority and gender. When Japanese refer to their own siblings, elder brothers are called *ani*, younger brothers *otōto*, elder sisters *ane*, and younger sisters *imōto*.

す。最近開発されたヒット商品の日本語のワープロは，キーボードをアイウエオ順に配列したもので，これは入社したばかりの若い技術陣の手になるものだといいます。先輩の上司たちは，当初，彼らの時間潰しぐらいに考えて，少しばかり軽蔑して眺めていましたが，これが実は大いに当たったのです。

このように現在の日本社会には，考え方や生き方をめぐって，新旧の世代間にギャップが存在するのです。このギャップは，高度経済成長期を境として生じたものですが，日本の社会と国民の新しい明日を占うものであることも，また事実です。

　　兄弟姉妹関係　　　日本語で兄弟姉妹を何と呼ぶかを考えると，日本の家庭での兄弟（姉妹）関係を理解する鍵になると思います。年上か年下か，男か女かによって，兄弟（姉妹）に対する呼びかけ方も違いますし，また兄弟（姉妹）について述べる時の言い方も違います。自分の兄弟（姉妹）について述べる時，年上の男性は「兄」，年下の男性は「弟」，年上の女性は「姉」，年下の女性は「妹」と言います。兄弟（姉妹）に対して呼びかける時には，

When talking to siblings, elder brothers are commonly called *onīsan*, elder sisters *onēsan*, and younger siblings by their first names. Asymmetry exists in that only elder ones have special kinship terms and are addressed with deference. Seniority counts in sibling relations as well as in all the other human relations in Japan.

Gender also plays a role. In the Japanese traditional family, parents treat their sons and daughters differently. A first son is treated favorably by them even if he is the youngest. Although the patriarchal, primogenital male-oriented system is no longer rigid under the postwar constitution, it is still a first son who is expected to take great responsibility. For example, when the parents get old and need some care, usually the first son and his family take care of them, whether or not he is living with them. Girls in the family, on the contrary, are considered less in terms of education and career because they are supposed to become brides who belong to different families.

Although sibling relations differ in one family to the other, brothers and sisters usually take care of each other, being of service to each other and acting as a support group independent of parents or friends, even after they have left home and have started separate families. (MH)

Sōgō-shōsha : **general trading company** The *sōgō-shōsha* offer several services such as : (1) the extending of credit, loans, loan guarantees and capital;

年上である兄のことは，「おにいさん」，年上である姉のことは「おねえさん」と呼びますが，年下の弟や妹は男女を問わず名前で呼びます。このように，年上の者だけが特別な親族呼称で呼ばれ，それによって尊敬の気持ちが同時に表現されているというところに兄弟姉妹関係の非対称的な仕組を見ることができます。日本人の人間関係において，年齢がものを言うことはたびたび見られますが，兄弟姉妹関係も例外ではありません。

　性別もまた大切です。伝統的な日本の家庭では男の子か女の子かによって，異なった育て方をすることがあります。長男はたとえ末っ子であってもかわいがられます。戦後の新憲法で男性中心の家父長制度はもはや廃止されましたが，まだ長男の責任は重いと言えます。例えば，親が年老いて介助が必要となった場合には，同居していようがいまいが，親の面倒を見るのはたいてい長男です。一方，女の子は教育や仕事などの面で男の子ほど大切には扱われていません。というのも，女の子は結婚すると別の家族に属してしまうと考えられているからです。

　兄弟姉妹関係はもちろん各々の家庭によって違っています。しかしながら一般に，兄弟姉妹は独立したり結婚したりして生家を離れた後も，お互いに助けあったり，面倒を見あったりしています。

総合商社　　総合商社の仕事はいろいろありますが，以下のことが主な仕事です。(1)信用貸し，借款，借款保障，資本の提供，(2)情報の全世界への提供，(3)銀行と商人の間の危険吸収の役割，

(2) the providing of information about many products all over the world; (3) the playing of a role of risk absorbers between bankers and small customers; (4) arrangement and coordination of various plans, such as the extraction of iron ore from mines, drilling for natural resources, or exporting of plants; and (5) the clerical work involved in business transactions abroad.

Through these services the *sōgō-shōsha* have been helpful in reducing unnecessary costs for many client firms. Besides, they have many employees trained in various posts outside of Japan and these human resources are essential to handling the above-mentioned services effectively. Their world-wide communication network is also vital to quick information and is often said to be more rapid in getting the latest news than the news agencies or the Ministry of Foreign Affairs.

There are nine *sōgō-shōsha*, which deal with every aspect of business transactions in Japan and all over the world. They are Mitsubishi, Mitsui, Marubeni, C. Itoh, Sumitomo, Nissho-Iwai, Tōmen, Kanematsu, and Nichimen.

Mitsubishi, Mitsui, and Sumitomo trading companies developed in 1870, 1876, and 1919 out of the trading sections of the respective former *zaibatsu* (financial cliques), which tried to increase Japan's interests by handling world trade that was almost under the total control of foreign businesses. They also sought to expand the export of manufactured goods all over the world and the import of natural resources from Asia

⑷鉄鉱石の採掘，天然資源のドリル，プラント輸出等の計画案と実施，⑸海外取引の事務手続き，です。

　総合商社はこのような仕事を担ってくれるので，顧客会社の多くは不必要な経費を削減できます。また，総合商社は外国のいろいろな地域に有能な人材を派遣しており，効率よく職務をこなしています。全世界にまたがる情報網は素早い情報伝達に有益で，通信社や外務省よりも迅速であるとの評判です。

　国内と国外のあらゆる種類の事務をこなす総合商社が9社あります。三菱，三井，丸紅，伊藤忠，住友，日商岩井，トーメン，兼松，ニチメンです。

　三菱，三井，住友は旧財閥の輸出入部門から，それぞれ明治3年，明治9年，大正8年に独立しました。当時外国取引はほとんど外国の会社に占められていたので，これらの商社は日本企業の利益を増大しようとしたのです。加工品を全世界に輸出し，アジアから原料を輸入し，ヨーロッパとアメリカから先進技術の導入に努めました。

　他の小さい総合商社は違った起源をもっています。金属，繊維産業が成長するにしたがい，原料の流れを効率よく管理する有能な貿易取引人が現れ，総合商社に発展していったのです。占領期の後，銀行中心の寡占的な総合商社が出現し，旧財閥系企業と商業，資本取引をしてきました。

　総合商社は子会社や関連会社を有していますが，取引はそれらに限らず，個人から，寡占企業にいたるまで商取引を行っています。

and advanced technology from Europe and the United States. The rest of the non-*zaibatsu* *sōgō-shōsha* have different roots. As the metal and textile industries grew, competent traders emerged to manage the effective flow of raw materials, and developed into new *sōgō-shōsha*. After the Allied Occupation of Japan, the bank-centered conglomerate groups arose. These big *sōgō-shōsha* have business and capital relationships with their own former *zaibatsu* groups.

The *sōgō-shōsha* also have their subsidiaries and related companies, but their business is not restricted to their group companies. Their clients range from individuals to conglomerates. (MK)

Sōkaiya : **professional stockholder** The commercial law in Japan stipulates that a company has to hold a stockholders' general meeting a few months after the settling day. Most large corporations settle accounts in March and have the stockholders' general meetings in June. In Japan dividends tend to be stored for the future investment and expansion of corporations instead of being distributed among individual stockholders. Some large corporations, therefore, spend only half an hour or so in reporting the annual report at the stockholders' general meetings.

Sōkaiya are people who have a few shares of stocks in many companies and scare money out of them by threatening to cause trouble at the stockholders' general meetings. Historically, the first turmoil happened at the

総会屋　　株式会社は株主総会を決算日より数ヵ月後に開催することと商法は規定しています。大企業の多くは3月に決算し，6月に株主総会を開催します。日本では利益を個人株主に分配するよりは，企業の将来投資と拡張のために蓄える傾向があります。このためにほんの数十分でもって株主総会で決算報告をするだけの大企業もあるのです。

　多数の会社の株式をほんの数株ずつ所有し，株主総会を混乱させると恐喝して，金銭を脅し取る輩が総会屋です。明治35年に東京証券取引所の総会での混乱が最初でした。この総会は午後3時から始まり，総会屋による議事妨害のために翌朝まで続きました。

　アメリカの議事妨害屋と違って，日本の総会屋は秩序正しく速やかに株主総会の議事を進めるために金銭を求めるのが普通です。昭和56年には全国でおよそ6千人の総会屋がたむろして，約1千億円を手にしました。全企業は1万2千人の弁護士へ約1千億

general meeting of the Tokyo Stock Exchange in 1902. This particular general meeting started at 3 p.m. and went on until the dawn of the following day due to *sōkaiya's* attempts to disrupt the proceedings.

Unlike the professional hecklers in America, *sōkaiya* in Japan ask for money to keep the proceedings of the stockholders' general meetings orderly and smooth. In 1981 there were about 6,000 *sōkaiya* all over Japan and they received about one hundred billion yen. All the corporations paid about one hundred billion yen for the services rendered by twelve thousand lawyers in Japan. This means *sōkaiya* earn more than lawyers.

Most *sōkaiya* are right-wing people and gangs of hoodlums and racketeers. To them this job of *sōkaiya* is the easiest way of funding themselves.

The commercial law was, therefore, changed to make it illegal to supply *sōkaiya* with profits. Competent lawyers in commercial law are employed to handle *sōkaiya* at the stockholders' general meetings. (MK)

Spouse relationship   Fairly fixed roles are played by both husband and wife in the Japanese family—the husband as a bread winner, his wife as a home-maker. The majority of Japanese husbands spend relatively little time at home, working eight hours a day five days a week and a few hours on Saturday, dropping in at one of the bars for a few drinks after office hours with clients or with colleagues, playing golf on Sunday, and so on. The typical Japanese wife stays at home, doing

288

円支払いました。総会屋のほうが弁護士よりも稼ぎがよいということです。

　総会屋の多数は右翼でやくざです。総会屋がいちばん簡単な稼ぎ方なのです。

　そこで，商法が改正になり，総会屋への支払いが不法になり，商法にくわしい弁護士が株主総会対策として雇われるようになりました。

　夫婦関係　　日本の家庭では夫婦はかなり固定した別々の役割を分担しています。夫は外で働き，妻は家族の世話をするのです。日本では大多数の夫は家庭にあまりいません。週日は 8 時間の労働，そして土曜日も午前中は働きます。仕事が終わると得意先や同僚と一杯飲みに行ったり，また日曜日には接待ゴルフに出かける人もいます。妻は家の中で家事を担当し，子育てに専念します。妻が家の外で働いていても，夫やまわりの社会は全体として，妻によい主婦であることを期待しています。最近の統計では，都市部に住む妻の 99％ が毎日家事をしており，夫は 14％ しか家事の

household chores and raising children. Even when the wife has a job outside the home, the role of a good housekeeper is expected by her husband and by society as a whole. Recent statistics show that 99% of wives living in urban cities do the household chores everyday, while only 14% of their husbands help them. Wives feel responsible for the household economy as well as the children's education. It is the wives who control the purse strings in the majority of Japanese families.

A husband and a wife have rather separate social lives in Japan. There are a few social gatherings such as New Year parties, wedding receptions or funerals that a man and a wife attend together. On other occasions, they have their separate gatherings. As a current popular saying much favored by Japanese women goes, "A good husband is healthy and not at home," which implies the Japanese concept of a happy wife.

Among the young Japanese, a somewhat more Western concept of a married couple has become prevalent. Husbands spend a significant part of their free time in family activities, wives get more freedom to enjoy outside their homes either in their careers or hobbies, and both share their social life together. (MH)

Success ladder, Climbing up the　Success stories seem to be much the same all over the world, invariably emphasizing courage, self-discipline, perseverance in adversity, quick-wittedness to seize good luck, and consequent riches and luxury in life. However, in

手伝いをしていません。妻は家計と育児には責任を感じています。大部分の日本の家庭において，財布の紐を握っているのは妻のほうです。

　夫と妻は社交の面でも別々のつきあいをしています。夫婦が揃って顔をみせるのは正月の集まり，結婚披露宴，葬式や法事などで，他の場合には別々に社交の場を持ちます。最近，日本女性の間で人気のあることわざにいわく，「亭主は丈夫で留守がいい」というわけです。

　若者の間では，西洋流の夫婦の考え方が広まってきています。夫はできるだけ家族と一緒に過ごそうとし，妻は仕事や趣味で家の外での生活も楽しもうとしています。若い夫婦では社交生活も一緒にすることが多くなっています。

　出世階段　　成功談または出世物語というものは世界中どこでも同じようなものです。逆境にあっても勇気や忍耐や規律を失わず，好運を逃さない機転を持つことが大切であるとし，そうして成功した人の豊かでぜいたくな暮しぶりを描いています。しかし，日本の社会では肩書きが重要とされ，そのために出世ということ

Japanese society, where titles attached to one's name are considered very important, *shusse* (success in life) is often talked of in terms of one's social position, occupation, scholarship, rank in the managerial hierarchy and the like rather than in terms of one's wealth piled up during one's career. Therefore, government high officials, presidents and executives in large business firms, doctors, lawyers, university professors, movie stars, TV personalities, and other celebrities of various fields are all regarded as successful people, even if they are not really self-made and their incomes are not astounding.

The myth that holds diligence to be the mother of success is seriously challenged by modern society with its complex economic systems, in which equal opportunities and fair competition are not always insured. People are aware that handicaps and disadvantages no longer produce self-made persons. Instead, they believe that a good academic career is a shortcut to success. This is one of the reasons why so many Japanese parents are enthusiastic about their children's education and why entrance examinations for prestigious universities are so competitive. To enter a prestigious university is to step on the first rung of the success ladder, and to find employment at a good company is to climb up to the second.

Those who want to get on the promotional track must stay in the same place of work and have their competence and merits recognized by their higher-ups.

も成功して積み上げた巨額の富よりも職業や学問的な権威や管理職の位置などの社会的地位という面から考えられます。したがって，たとえ独力で立身した人でなくても，またその収入がたいしたことはなくても，政府の高官，大会社の社長や重役，医師，弁護士，大学教授，映画スター，テレビタレントなどの有名人はみな出世した人とみなされます。

　現代社会は経済のシステムも複雑になり，機会は必ずしも均等でなく，競争も公平ではありませんから，勤勉は成功の母という神話は通用しなくなっています。もはや障害や不利な環境から立志伝中の人が生まれることはないと思われています。むしろよい学歴を身につけることが出世の早道だとされています。日本で多くの親が子供の教育に熱心になり，有名大学の入試の競争が激しいのにはこうした理由もあるのです。有名大学に入ることは出世の階段の第一段を登ることであり，よい会社に就職することは第二段に登ることであるというわけです。

　出世街道を歩きたいと思う人は，同じ会社で永年働き続け，自分の能力や長所を上司に認めてもらわなければなりません。同僚と昇進をめぐって競争することになりますが，その場合も出世主義者だという悪評を立てないようにしなければなりません。しかし，最近では特に若者を中心に，出世信仰離れが見られるようになりました。彼らは富や地位や名誉を求めるよりも家族や趣味やスポーツや余暇に楽しみを求め，人生を自分の好きなようにエンジョイしたいと考えています。

They are to compete with their colleagues for advancement, but they must do so without incurring a bad reputation of being a careerist. Recently, however, the cult of success has lost its popularity especially among the young, who prefer to enjoy their lives the way they like, seeking happiness in their family, hobbies, sports, or other leisure activities instead of wealth, status, or honor. (OT/TS)

Superordinate-subordinate relation Position classification systems in Japanese companies are generally simple, having only five or six managerial positions in the hierarchy. There is no explicit regulation defining the duties of each position, but usually a middle manager is required to perform the manifold function of supervising his / her subordinates' work, of educating them, of helping them bring their ability into full play, and of absorbing and conveying their ideas to the top. A task assigned to a department is to be performed by the teamwork of the staff, and the credit for achieving good results goes to the entire department.

The superordinate and the subordinate are basically regarded as co-workers, and not as competitors for better wages or higher positions. Therefore, superordinates having very active and competent subordinates under them would rarely sense a job threat. Seniority carries a lot of weight, but this does not necessarily mean subordinates' unquestioning obedience to their superordi-

上司と部下　　日本の会社における役職の種類は一般に単純で，全体の階級で5～6の管理職の地位があるだけです。それぞれの地位の義務を明確に規定する規則はあません。ある部門に課せられた仕事はスタッフのチームワークですることになっており，よい結果が出れば，その功績は部門全体のものとされます。しかし，中間管理職はたいてい多くの役割を果たさなければなりません。それは部下の仕事を監督したり，部下を教育し，その能力を十分発揮させるようにしたり，彼らのアイデアを吟味して上層部に伝えたりすることなどです。

　上司と部下は基本的には共同作業者とみなされ，よりよい給料や昇進を争う競争相手とはみなされません。したがって，非常に活動的で有能な部下を持った上司も自分の地位が脅かされるように感じることはめったにありません。年功がかなりものをいいますが，だからといって部下は上司に盲目的に従うというわけではありません。意見が対立したときには，まっこうから衝突するのを避けるために双方が心配りをします。職場に必要な協調精神と家庭的雰囲気を保つために，部課長は勤務時間後に部下に一杯おごったりすることがあります。他方，部下は私的な面でも上司の手助けを厭いません。例えば引越しを手伝ったり，休日にゴルフのコンペのお供をしたりします。このように職場での関係は私生

nate. When differences of opinion arise, care is taken on both sides to avoid a head-on collision. To attain the complete harmony and homey atmosphere much desired in the office, the chief of a section often treats the staff to a drink after work. The staff, on the other hand, are ready to be a help on a personal level—lending a hand on a moving day or accompanying the boss to a golf competition, for instance. Thus the relationships in the office are often extended to the private lives of the personnel.

However, the superordinate-subordinate relation can easily be strained, especially when the superordinate fails to earn the subordinate's respect. For many businessmen, criticizing or backbiting their higher-ups at bars is a normal way of letting off steam. (TS)

Tax During the Allied Occupation, Carl Shoup, Professor of Economics at Columbia University, headed the group of seven tax experts with the aim of balancing the budget and stabilizing the economy of Japan in 1949. To ensure stabilized taxation, the Shoup mission recommended that the Japanese government increase direct (that is, personal and corporate income) taxes, rather than indirect taxes.

The Japanese government's internal revenue depends mostly on individual and corporate income taxes, which amounts to 40.2% and 31.3% respectively in 1986. The other revenues are indirect taxes imposed on alcoholic beverages (4.7% of tax revenues in 1986), gasoline (3.

活にまで及ぶことがあります。

　しかし，上司と部下の関係はまずくもなりやすいものです。特に上司が部下から尊敬されない場合はそうです。多くのサラリーマンがバーで飲みながら上役の批判や悪口を言って，うさを晴らします。

　税　　占領時代の昭和24年に，コロンビア大学経済学教授カール・シャープ氏が日本経済安定と予算均衡を目指す7人の税専門家のグループの長になりました。シャープ使節団は日本政府に安定した税収入を確保するのに間接税ではなく直接税，すなわち個人，法人所得税を増やすように勧告しました。

　政府の税収入は個人，法人所得税によって賄われていますが，昭和61年にはそれぞれ40.2％と31.3％になっています。他は間接税によって賄われていますが，昭和61年には税収入の4.7％は酒税，3.8％はガソリン税，3.8％は物品税，1.3％は関税，3.8％は印税，他が7.8％になっています。県市民税は半分以上個人，法人所得税によっています。自動車税，ガソリン税，飲食税も県民税です。市町村は固定資産税，所得税，タバコ税，電気税，ガス税を課しています。

8%), commodities (3.8%), tariffs (1.3%), stamp duty (3.8%) and others (7.8%). The prefectural governments depend on individual and corporate income taxes for more than half of their revenues. They also lay taxes on automobiles, gasoline, and restaurants. Property taxes are imposed only by the municipal governments, which also tax individual income, tobacco, and electricity.

Japanese people pay a smaller share of their income to taxes than Americans, Englishmen, Germans and French people in the ratio of taxation to the national income, the Gross National Product, and per capita income. However, quite a few people complain that they are heavily taxed. Since income taxes are paid on a self-assessment basis, tax evasion can frequently occur especially among business-income-tax payers, whereas employees' taxes are withheld at the source, which makes it virtually impossible for office workers to evade taxes. Good tax accountants have been thought to help their clients find loopholes to evade taxes. In 1985 tax inspectors discovered hidden incomes amounting to 63.6 billion yen ($318 million at the exchange rate of 200 yen to the dollar), which meant that the level of tax evasion had reached 40.8 billion yen ($204 million). Two hundred and one cases were indicted for prosecution. This is one of the reasons why the tax collecting system is criticized as unfair and partial.

The individual income tax scale as of 1987 is as follows; Taxable income from 4 million yen ($27.6 thou-

国民所得，GNP，国民1人当たり所得に対する課税率では，アメリカ人，イギリス人，ドイツ人，フランス人より日本人の所得に占める税率は低くなっています。しかし，重税との不満は根強くあります。所得税は申告制をとっているので，脱税が多いのです。サラリーマンは源泉徴収されているので脱税はありませんが，特に企業主に脱税が多くみられます。顧客に脱税の抜け穴を教えるのが有能な税理士とみなされています。昭和60年に636億円の所得隠しがあり，408億円の脱税がありました。201件が検挙されています。不公平税制と批判されるわけです。

　昭和62年度の個人所得税は以下のようです。400万円から500万円までは約20%，500万円から600万円では約25%，600万円から800万円までは約30%，800万円から1000万円までは約35%，1000万円から1200万円までは約40%，1200万円から1500万円までは約45%，1500万円から3000万円までは約50%，3000万円から5000万円までは約55%，5000万円以上は約60%です。

　中曽根政権はシャープ税制を抜本改正する大型間接税を導入しようとしましたが，国民の強い反対にあって昭和62年初期に税制改革法案を破棄せざるを得ませんでした。しかし，赤字を埋め合わすための国債発行を減らし，不公平な所得税の是正をするために，消費税の導入はやむをえないと考える政治家は多いようです。

sand at the exchange rate of 145 yen to the dollar) up to 5 million yen ($34.5 thousand) represents approximately 20%, from 5 million yen up to 6 million yen ($41.4 thousand), 25%, from 6 million yen up to 8 million yen ($55.2 thousand), 30%, from 8 million yen up to 10 million yen ($69 thousand), 35%, from 10 million yen up to 12 million yen ($82.8 thousand), 40%, from 12 million yen up to 15 million yen ($103.4 thousand), 45%, from 15 million yen up to 30 million yen ($206.9 thousand), 50%, from 30 million yen up to 50 million yen ($344.8 thousand), 55%, and over 50 million yen, 60%.

As of 1988 there is no sales tax or value added tax in Japan. The Japanese government has started to try to revise the fundamental framework of the Shoup mission by introducing a large-scale indirect-tax system similar to sales taxes, but this has turned out to be so unpopular that the Nakasone government had to adandon this plan early in 1987. Some statesmen still maintain, however, that introduction of sales taxes of some kind is inevitable, if the government is to redeem deficit-covering bonds reaching a colossal sum or to reduce individual and corporate income taxes.

(MK)

Teacher-pupil relation　The teacher's position in relation to pupils has traditionally been an unconditional one in which the former is regarded as the one with

先生と生徒　　先生と生徒の関係は，かつて前者が後者に対して絶対的な力や威厳をもつものでした。特に高等教育機関や書道，生け花などの伝統芸術を教える教室では，教師（師匠）と生徒

power and dignity. This holds true of professor-student relations at a higher level of educational institutes or traditional art schools like calligraphy, flower arrangement, and so on. The absolute obedience of the students to the teacher has been expressed in the popular phrases such as *waga-shi no on* ("the favor of my honorable teacher") and *sanpo sagatte shi no kage wo fumazu* ("Don't step on one's teacher's shadow by taking three steps backward"). These ideas, originally deriving from Confucianism, were positively reinforced by the nationalism and Emperor system, especially by the Imperial Rescript on Education in pre-war days. Even today students are always expected to address their teachers by *sensei* ("Teacher") or by their last name plus *sensei*, even after their graduation. A general concept of seniority system and apprenticeship is deeply rooted in the relationship involved in the giving and receiving of instruction. It is generally considered bad manners for students to criticize their teachers.

However, the democratic trend of today and especially the popularity of prep schools called *juku*, providing after-school courses in preparation for the intensified competition of entrance examinations, have caused the decrease of authority and dignity of teachers at public schools. It is also true that classroom teachers often have difficulty in managing their classes and educational environment because of the growing students problems of bullying, school violence, juvenile delinquency, refusal to attend school, and even violence toward teachers

（弟子）の間では，一層強くこのことが意識されるのです。生徒が教師に絶対的に服従する姿は，少し古めかしいけれどよく口にされる表現「我が師の恩」や「三歩下がって師の影を踏まず」によく表されています。これらの表現に見られる教師に対する考え方は，儒教の教えに基づくものですが，第2次大戦前には国家主義や天皇制，特に教育勅語によって，人々の頭のなかに積極的に植え付けられました。今日でも生徒は学校を卒業したあとでも，自分たちの恩師に対して「先生」あるいは名字に先生を付けて呼び掛けます。年功序列や徒弟制度という概念が，「教えを与える」「教えを受ける」という関係に根付いているのです。生徒が自分の先生を批評するのは，一般に悪いことだとも考えられています。

とはいうものの，今日の民主主義教育の風潮や，熾烈な受験戦争の準備のために放課後生徒たちが通う塾の盛況などによって，公立学校における教師の権威と威厳は徐々に失われつつあるといわれています。増加するいじめ，校内暴力，青少年の犯罪，登校拒否，そして教師に対する暴力などによって，クラス担任の教師は，しばしば授業の態勢や教育環境を維持していくのが難しくなってきています。これらの問題は，日本の社会や人々の価値観が複雑化，多様化してきており，これから起こる混沌とした状況の反映であるともみなされています。教育基本法や各種の法令は，学校で教師が体罰を与えることを厳しく禁じていますが，教室の秩序を保つためにこの手段に訴える教師もいます。事細かに規定されたさまざまな校則や内申書が，伝統的な訓育にとって代わり，教師と生徒の関係を維持するために有効な役割を果たしている，という皮肉な見方もしばしばされています。

themselves. These problems are sometimes taken as the reflection of the confusion arising from complexity and diversity of values of Japan's society and people. Though educational laws and ordinances strictly prohibit corporal punishments in schools, some teachers resort to them to keep order in the class. It is often said cynically that many kinds of minute school regulations and school record reports have taken the place of traditional discipline. They seem to be the main effective means of maintaining the traditional relation between the teacher and the student. (KA)

This world and the other world   What symbolizes Japanese thought about life after death is the *butsudan*, a small Buddhist altar set in many homes. It serves as a window through which living persons can communicate with the departed, who are believed to live in the other world. The first boiled rice and fresh water in small ceremonial cups are offered at the altar in the morning. Devout family members, on coming home, offer incense and a prayer to the deceased. They seem to sense the silent presence of the departed, who they believe give advice and comfort to the living.

The *Bon* Festival (a traditional Buddhist festival) held every summer is an occasion to honor the dead. The souls of the departed are believed to return home during the festival to see their families and descendants. The vernal and autumnal equinoxes are also the days to

現世と来世　　仏壇は，死後の世界に対する日本人の考え方を象徴的にあらわしています。仏壇はこの世にいる人々があの世にいる死者と言葉を交す窓の役割をはたしていると言えます。毎朝，仏壇用の茶碗に盛られたご飯とお水がそなえられます。信心深い人々は帰宅すると仏壇にお線香をあげてお参りします。そこには，死んでしまった人がいて，生きている人をなぐさめたり助言を与えたりすると信じられています。

　夏のお盆は死者をうやまうお祭です。死者の魂はお盆の期間中，家族や子孫に会いに家へ帰ってくると信じられているのです。春と秋のお彼岸には，亡くなった先祖のことを想い，お花とお線香をもって先祖の墓参りをします。仏教の儀式と先祖崇拝は非常に密接に結びついているので，亡くなった者の思い出を大切に思う人々の中には，年をとるにつれて仏教に親しむようになる人もいます。しかしながら，余り信心のない人々にとって仏教は，葬式や法事の時の宗教であり，神道はお宮まいりや結婚の時の宗教というほどの意味しかありません。

　霊魂の存在を信じている人々にとって，この世とあの世をつな

remember dead ancestors, and people usually visit their family graves with flowers and incense . Buddhist ceremonies and ancestor worship are so closely related to each other that those who cherish the memories of the departed turn more and more to Buddhism as they grow older. The indifferent tend to think, however, that Buddhism is for praying for the souls of the dead and consoling the bereaved , while *Shinto* is for celebrating births and marriages.

To believers of spiritualism, verbal communication they hold with the departed spirits through a medium during trances would be another link that connect this world and the other world. There are many folk stories about heaven and hell and ghost stories of vengeful spirits or of haunted houses, which are still whispered with wide eyes. This shows also that with the Japanese there is not a great gap between this world and the other world.

Thus to many Japanese, the other world is not "the undiscover'd country, from whose bourn no traveller returns, " as Hamlet says, but it is a domain somewhere between the earth and the heaven with whose inhabitants the living can have contact. (MH/TS)

Ties by blood Japanese have a strong "in-group" consciousness, which seems to be rooted in agrarian society. The consciousness is accompanied by a strong sense of belonging to a group. Most Japanese groups have been formed with the concept of "family" as their

ぐもう一つの方法は，霊にとりつかれている状態の時に死者の霊魂と言葉を交すことです。極楽と地獄についての民間伝説，復讐するおばけやおばけ屋敷の話なども，依然としてささやかれています。こうしてみると，日本人にとってこの世とあの世をへだてる溝は深くはないように思われます。

　従って多くの日本人にとって，あの世とはハムレットの言う「この世から旅立つ者の1人として，帰って来たためしのない見知らぬ国」ではなく，地上と天国との間にある中間地点で，天国へ旅立った人々とこの世に生きている人々がまだ接することのできるところなのです。

　血　縁　　日本人は強い「身内」意識をもっていますが，これは農耕社会にそのルーツがあるようです。この身内意識は集団への強い帰属意識を伴っています。日本の集団はそのほとんどが「家族」という概念に基づいて形成されています。諺に「血は水よりも濃し」というように，血縁による集団はいたるところにあ

basis. As the saying goes, "Blood is thicker than water," and groups based on blood relationship are common.

Unlike an Indian family where blood relationship has an absolute value throughout one's life, a Japanese family values the family members living together under one roof more than those blood relatives living in distant places. Even sons-in-law and daughters-in-law living with the family are more important than children who have married and left the house to live independently and raise their own families.

The frame of "family" is extended to social groups in the Japanese society. In each pseudo-family group the members assume their roles—parents, children, brothers and sisters. For example, the term *oyaji* (one's old man) can mean not only one's father but one's boss in the office and even an elderly man one feels close to as if he were one's own father. (YY)

Trade policy One characteristic of Japanese trade has been its processing trade, in which raw materials are imported and processed products are exported. Though this is necessitated by the comparative scarcity of natural resources in Japan, it has caused excessive competitions among developed industrial countries in the international market. Particularly serious are the U.S.-Japan and EC-Japan trade frictions, which have provoked sharp criticisms against Japan that it is not doing a free trade or a fair trade. The imbalance of trade led

ります。

インドの家族では血縁が一生絶対的な価値をもちますが，日本人の家族は家を離れ，遠くに住む肉親よりも一つ屋根の下に住む今の家族構成員に価値を置きます。したがって，同居している婿や嫁は，結婚して家を出た実の息子や娘よりも大事なのです。

日本の社会では，「家族」という枠は社会集団全体にひろがっています。それぞれの擬似家族集団では，構成員が親，子供，兄弟姉妹のそれぞれの役割を果たしています。たとえば，「親父」という語は父親だけでなく，職場での上司や自分の父親のように親しい年長の男性にも使われます。

貿易政策　これまで日本の貿易の特徴は原料を輸入し，加工品を輸出するという加工貿易にありました。これは日本が比較的自然の資源に乏しいことから必然的なことなのですが，そのために国際市場において先進諸国の間での過度の競争が生じました。特に深刻なのは日本とアメリカ，そして日本とEC諸国との間の貿易摩擦で，日本は自由で公平な貿易をしていないという激しい非難を浴びるようになりました。貿易の不均衡を是正しようとアメリカ議会は「1988年総合通商法案」を可決しましたが，これは保護主義的な意図が強いものです。

1955年にGATT（関税及び貿易に関する一般協定）に調印してか

the American Congress to take a countermeasure by passing the Comprehensive Trade Bill of 1988, which has a strong protective intention.

Since Japan signed the GATT (General Agreement on Tariffs and Trade) in 1955, it has rapidly liberalized its trade except for beef, dairy products, leather goods, and some kinds of agricultural products such as oranges and rice. The number of items under residual quantitative import restriction in Japan has fallen to 27, whereas that in France stands at 42. It exceeds by far, however, those in West Germany 14, in the U.S. 7, and in the UK 3.

Although the foreign demand for further liberalization is great, concerned industries in the country are raising equally loud voices against it. For one thing, Japanese agriculture producing the foods listed above are not competitive enough to cope with imported products. For another, Japan is faced with the high value of yen, which some economists speculate will cause a considerable decrease in export. It is argued, therefore, that a radical change in the trade policy would bring about a devastating effect upon Japanese economy. In 1988, however, Japan made an agreement with the U.S. to liberalize the import of beef and oranges by 1991.

Further efforts have been made on the part of Japan to redress the imbalance of trade. One such project is the plant export in which factories furnished with necessary machines and facilities are exported and employment is given to a large number of people of the

ら，日本は急速に貿易を自由化してきました。除外されている品目は酪農製品，皮革製品，そしてオレンジや米などの農産物です。日本の残存輸入制限品目の数は27にまで下がっています。これに対してフランスは42となっています。しかし，西ドイツの14，アメリカの7，イギリスの3を日本は大幅に上回っています。

　さらに自由化を進めよという海外からの要求は強いのですが，国内の関係産業も同じくらい強く自由化に反対しています。一つには，上記の産物を生産している日本の農業は輸入品に太刀打ちできるほどの競争力がないからです。また，円高という問題もあります。円高によって輸出は相当に減るだろうと予測している経済学者もいます。従って，貿易政策の急激な変更は日本経済に破壊的な影響を及ぼすだろうという議論も出ています。しかし，1988年に日本は牛肉とオレンジを1991年までに自由化することをアメリカに約束しました。

　貿易の不均衡を是正するために，日本の側でさらに努力がされています。一例はプラント輸出です。これは必要な機械や設備を備えた工場を輸出し，貿易相手国の人を大量に雇用する貿易です。また，先進諸国の間で工業製品を相互補完的に輸出入する水平分業を確立する準備が進んでいます。さらに，国内市場を拡大し，国内消費を促進する政策もとられています。

trade partners. Steps are also being taken toward the establishment of horizontal international specialization, which is mutual and complementary export and import of technological products among developed countries. Moreover, a policy for expansion of domestic market and promotion of home consumption has been adopted. (OT/TS)

Tradition and custom   Both traditions and customs are highly honored in Japan. Unwritten laws and rules without penal provisions as well as moral and social codes of conduct and manners are readily observed by the average Japanese. Conversely, they are hesitant to break tradition or go against a long-established custom, whether good or bad, so that any movement toward an abolishment of a certain tradition or custom is almost always resisted, particularly by conservative people.

Historically, however, the modernization that took place in the Meiji period(1868-1912) forced people to discard some of their inherited traditons——the wearing of the traditional Japanese hairstyles and the carrying of the swords for the ex-*samurai* class men, for example. Especially, after World War Ⅱ there arose a general trend toward the Westernization of Japanese ways of life. This furthered the abolishment of old customs that were regarded as empty or useless formalities, and consequently it simplified social courtesies and ceremonies to a great degree.

伝統と習慣　　日本では伝統も習慣も大変尊重されています。たいていの日本人は道徳的・社会的行動規範だけではなく，罰則規定のない不文律もよく守ります。逆に，よいものでも悪いものでも，伝統を破ったり，習慣に背いたりすることを非常にためらいます。ですから，ある伝統や習慣を廃止しようとすると，いつも抵抗があります。特に，保守的な人たちが抵抗を示します。

　しかし，歴史的にみると，明治時代の現代化政策によって人々は代々受け継いできた伝統を捨てることを強制されました。例えば，断髪令や廃刀令による伝統の廃止がそうです。特に，第2次世界大戦後は日本の生活様式の西洋化の風潮が起り，虚礼とみなされた古くからの習慣が廃止され，その結果社会的儀礼はかなり簡素化されました。

　さらに，今日では地方の都市化と人工過疎，家族制度の急激な変化，都市部における貧弱な住宅事情などによって，ある種の伝統や習慣を守ることが困難になっています。暮れに自宅で餅をついたり，ひな祭りに段飾りをしたり，子供の日に鯉のぼりをあげたりする家庭は少なくなっています。

　多くの年中行事を形成し維持してきた宗教的信仰や俗信は今ではほとんど失われていますが，古い習慣に対する庶民の敬意は日本文化の西洋化，合理化の時代を越えて生き残っています。しかし現在では，古い習慣を最も熱心に守ろうとしているのは祭礼や

Moreover, the urbanization and depopulation of rural communities, the drastic changes in the family system, and the poor housing conditions in large cities have made it very difficult for many people today to observe some of the traditions and customs. Only a few families now make *mochi* (rice cakes) at their own home before the New Year, display a full set of *hina* (dolls representing the ancient imperial court members) on the Doll Festival, or hoist *koinobori* (cloth-made carp streamers) on Children's Day.

Though the religious faith or folk beliefs that originally shaped and sustained many annual events are now almost lost, people's respect for the old customs has survived beyond the periods of Westernization and rationalization of Japanese culture. However, the most ardent advocates of old customs today may be industries making or selling goods and foods for festive and ceremonial occasions. (TS)

Train land, Japan as the   Recent decades have seen an explosive growth of automobile transportation in every corner of Japan and, during the past decade, an increasing popularity of air transportation. In Japanese society, the railroad has played a more important role in the daily life of people of all classes for many more decades. Since the completion of Japan's first railway line in 1872, the rail network has spread all over the country. As of 1984, there was a total of nearly 16,800 miles (27,000 km) of track, of which about half are

行事に関係する製品や食品を作ったり売ったりしている業者かもしれません。

　「鉄道の国」日本　　ここ 20 ～ 30 年の間に，日本国内の隅々にいたるまで爆発的に自動車が増加し，最近の 10 年間には航空輸送も拡大しています。しかし日本の社会では，鉄道がずっと長い間あらゆる階層の人々の日常生活において重要な役割を果たしてきました。1872 年に日本で最初の鉄道が開通して以来，鉄道網は国中に延びました。1984 年現在で鉄道線路は全長 16,800 マイル（27,000 km）に達し，そのうち約半分が電化され，残りの半分はディーゼル機関によります。蒸気機関車は長年にわたり親しまれてきましたが，今は観光客向けに，ごく一部の地方で見られるだけです。

electrified, with diesel equipment used on the other half. The steam locomotive, which had long been a familiar sight, is now seen on some local lines only as a tourist attraction and a memento of good old days of trains.

Visitors from abroad are invariably impressed with the punctuality and availability of Japan's railroad transportation. Especially impressive are the speed and efficiency of the superexpress bullet trains on the *Shinkansen* (New Trunk Line), which opened in 1964 connecting the two largest cities, Tokyo and Osaka (345 miles/ 552.6 km), in about three hours. Since then it has been extended northward and westward to many of the more distant cities. Other surprises for foreigners about the Japanese trains are their overcrowdedness during commuting rush hours and the patience of the passengers. It is estimated that a total of 50 million people ride trains each day in Japan.

The government-owned Japanese National Railways (JNR) used to operate about 80% of the nationwide railway network. In April, 1987, it was disbanded into six private companies under the name of the Japan Railway (JR) group, in order to grapple with grave financial problems caused mainly by the tremendous increase of private motor vehicles and consequent decrease in JNR's share of passenger and freight traffic. Despite numerous difficulties, Japan enjoys a high reputation of being a "train land," moving ahead with big projects such as the Seikan Tunnel, the world's longest undersea tunnel,

日本を訪れる外国人が必ず感心するものに，日本の鉄道輸送の時間の正確さと便利さがあります。とりわけ印象深いのは，新幹線のスピードと効率のよさです。新幹線は1964年に開通し，二大都市の東京・大阪間（345マイル／552.6 km）を約3時間で結びました。それ以来新幹線は北へ西へと延び，遠方の多くの都市を結んでいます。日本の鉄道に関して，他の点でも外国人を驚かすことがあります。ラッシュアワーの大変な混雑ぶりと，それに乗客がじっと耐えていることです。全国で1日に延べ5千万人が鉄道を利用していると見積もられています。

　国鉄が国内鉄道網の約80%を営業していましたが，1987年4月にJRグループの名のもとに6つの会社に分割され，民営化されました。これは，自家用自動車の急激な普及と，その結果起こった国鉄の乗客および貨物輸送の減少が主な原因となって生じた深刻な財政問題を打開するためでした。多くの困難があるにもかかわらず，日本は「鉄道の国」として高い評価を得ており，現在もいくつか大きなプロジェクトが進められています。その一つの青函トンネルは，1988年に開通した世界最長（33.6マイル／53.85 km）の海底トンネルで，本州と北海道を結んでいます。

opened in 1988, connecting the Honshū and Hokkaido islands (33.6 miles/53.85 km). (MT)

Treating of others　To give or accept hospitable
treatment nicely or skillfully is an indispensable phase
of Japanese society, especially in maintaining a smooth
relationship between people both in social life and the
business world. The virtue of modesty plays an important role in treating others. In daily life, inviting a
guest or guests to one's house and treating them with
home-made dishes is highly valued, though it has become difficult these days for many people to throw big
parties in their own houses due to housing conditions.

While serving delicious dishes, the hostess usually
says modestly to the guest, "It's a trifling (humble)
thing, but...," "I am afraid the food won't suit your
taste...," "Excuse me for not having been attentive to
you," or so on. The guest often replies with modesty,
"Oh, please don't trouble yourself," even if he knows
that the hostess has been busy treating him.

The guest is asked to take the seat of honor and is
treated in a special way, if he is socially superior to
the host. If the guest is a friend of the host, the hostess is usually busy preparing dishes in the kitchen, and
more often than not only the host (the master of the
family) eats with the guest. It is not unusual to treat
the guest with catered dishes if the hostess does not
want to take so much trouble or does not have enough
time to prepare the dishes.

もてなし　　日本の社会においては，巧みに心のこもったもてなしをし，またこれを上手に受けることは，社会生活でも仕事の面でも，円滑な人間関係を維持するためには欠くべからざるものです。この際，「謙譲の美徳」という考え方が重要になってきます。日常の生活において，自分の家に客を招き，手料理でもてなしをすることは非常に重んじられることですが，最近は住宅事情などから，自宅で大きな宴を開くことは非常に難しくなってきています。

　ごちそうを出すとき，その家の奥さんは客に「つまらないものですが」とか「お口に合いますかどうか」とか「なにもお構いもしませんが」などと控え目に言うことがよくあります。また客もその奥さんが自分をもてなすために忙しく立ち振舞っているのを知っているのに，「どうぞお構いなく」などと遠慮がちに受け答えます。客は上座に座るように勧められますが，特に自分よりも年上である場合や自分の上司である場合には，その家の主人はその客に対して特別な扱いをします。もしその客が夫の友人である場合には，普通妻は台所にいてもっぱら料理を作り，おそらく夫のみが客と食事をともにするのです。奥さんがあまり手間をかけたくない場合や料理を作る時間があまりない場合は，出前をたのんで客をもてなすことも珍しくありません。

　仕事で取引き先を接待するような場合は，料亭や旅館が使われることもしばしばです。食事をしながら，打ち解けた雰囲気のなかで商談に入っていくこともあります。日本の政治家，特に国会議員たちは，密談や根まわしのためにこのような場所をよく利用するともいわれています。

　日本で最も豪華にして高価な客のもてなしは，ホテルや特別な

In the business world, Japanese restaurants or hotels are often chosen to treat the guests or business acquaintances. While eating, the people at the table go ahead with business talk in an informal style and atmosphere. It is often said that Japanese politicians, especially Dietmen, also use these places for behind-the-scenes talks and negotiations to explore various possibilities in the future.

The most gorgeous and expensive entertaining of guests in Japanese society is done for wedding receptions which are often held in hotels or facilities with special ceremonial halls. The guests are expected to bring a monetary present of considerable value to the newly wedded couple and, in turn, are given a cordial reception including free drinking and eating, while watching the bride's many changes of beautiful clothing.

It is customary for a husband not to be accompanied by his wife at parties, although attending together is getting more popular now. In Japan these days, the treating of guests and attending parties is still usually considered a social obligation rather than entertainment or enjoyment. Thus, hospitality in the form of treating often follows rather formal, traditional rules. (KA)

Ultimate freedom and equality   Japanese society has traditionally afforded its members relatively little freedom and equality, keeping them tightly compartmentalized and regimented. This tendency dates back as far as the 17th century. In the Edo period (1603-1867),

式典会場をもった施設で行われる結婚披露宴です。招かれた客は新郎新婦にある程度の金額の祝儀を持っていきますが，引き換えに，飲み物や食べ物を含め心からのもてなしを受けます。さらに新婦のお色直しを眺めることもできます。

　夫は普通パーティーに妻を同伴しませんが，最近では夫婦同伴のパーティーも増えてきました。しかし日本では客をもてなすこと，パーティーに出席することは，まだ楽しみというよりも社会的な義務とみなされることが多く，もてなし自体がかなり形式ばった伝統的なルールに従って行われています。

　仏教的自由・平等観　　日本では，人々は伝統的な厳しい身分差別と支配とによって，自由や平等はあまり許されていませんでした。こうした傾向は，儒教思想が支配的であった江戸時代（1603～1867）に遡ります。当時は「士農工商」という厳格な職階制によって，人々の生活は大きな制約を受け，さらに地縁・血

when the Confucian ethic was dominant, life was rigidly circumscribed according to one's position in the strict "warrior-peasant-artisan-merchant" (*shi-nō-kō-shō*) occupational hierarchy. People were additionally bound by a tight web of social and familial obligations.

An awakening took place in the Genroku period (1688-1703), however, as townsmen (*chōnin*) assumed greater leadership in economic activities and civil life. Surmounting the rigid Confucian code, they started to seek openly for the pleasure of life. *Sonezaki Shinjū* (The Love Suicides at Sonezaki) and *Shinjū Ten no Amijima* (The Love Suicides at Amijima), for example, both written by Chikamatsu Monzaemon (1653-1724), a puppet and *kabuki* theater playwright, were reflections of the new wave of this period. Love suicide represents the rejection of or ultimate freedom from Confucian ethical values.

Yet social barriers continued to impose heavy restrictions on the lives of most Japanese. Regardless of class distinctions, people were inclined to Buddhism, which teaches that all existence is in itself empty, and yet ultimately full: full because inherent in it is the Buddha nature (universal truth), or its potentiality. All physical entities are *ipso facto* free and equal regardless of outer, seeming differences such as appearance, sex, age, class, and the like.

Unlike Christianity, Buddhism does not posit any absolute authority outside of and distinct from one's self. Rather, the meditating believer looks deeply into his or

縁的にも多くの束縛が課せられていました。

しかし，元禄時代（1688～1703）になって，町人が経済活動や市民生活で主導権を握るようになると，新しい動きが起こりました。町人たちは厳しい儒教的規律を侵して，生きる喜びを求め始めたからです。江戸前期の浄瑠璃・歌舞伎作者であった近松門左衛門（1653～1724）の『曽根崎心中』や『心中天の網島』などは，こうした新しい時代の流れを反映しています。町人たちは，心中という形をとって当時の儒教的規律に抗し，真の自由を求めたからです。

しかし，依然として社会の制約や束縛は厳しく，人々は身分の別を超えて仏教に帰依する者が多かったのです。仏教では，一切の存在は縁起なるが故に本来無自性，空であり，逆にそこにこそ本具の仏性（普遍的真理）が満ち満ちていると説きました。また，すべての存在は，外見，性，年齢，身分といった外見上の違いはあっても，一切は本来自由・平等であることを示すものだと教えたのです。

キリスト教と異なり，仏教は，自己の外に，あるいは自己に対峙して何かあるものを絶対的権威として想定することをしません。むしろ自己を深く洞察して既成の自己を否定する体験を求めるのです。

この一見困難に思われる教えは，「色即是空，空即是色」の一句に示されています。例えば，固体といえども，実はその内部では原子が絶えず回っており，また速く回っているコマでも静止しているように見えるようなものなのです。日本人は，対象を知的に分析して理解しようとするのではなく，全体的にとらえようとします。究極的な自由や平等は，こうして二元相対的見方を超えて，存在を一つのものとしてとらえることによって達せられると考えるからです。

her self, and experiences total denial or negation of the established self.

This seeming impossibility is explained in the Buddhist tenet: *shiki soku ze kū, kū soku ze shiki* (Material form is in itself nonsubstantial; nonsubstantiality is in itself material). Thus a solid form is in fact made up of atoms in constant whirling motion, and a rapidly spinning top appears stationary. The Japanese seek to comprehend objective reality not through intellectual processes of discrimination and analysis, but by grasping it as a whole. Ultimate freedom and equality can hence be achieved by transcending a dualistic view. (ON)

Vanity It is said that the Japanese think much of the public image they present to others. One outcome derived from efforts to present a better image appears to be "vanity." Among middle-class Japanese, vanity is institutionalized. No matter how incongruent it may look with their social status or income, they tend to acquire rather luxurious items such as brand-new cars, fully loaded hi-fi equipment, and expensive designer clothes. In addition, they take a tropical holiday in Hawaii, Guam, or Saipan, send their children to good private schools, hold large wedding receptions at one of the major hotels, and so on.

This strong sense of vanity is also a source of much tragicomedy. Young people go into debt buying cars that are far beyond their means and spending most of

見　栄　　日本人は世間体を気にしがちだと言われています。
日本人が見栄を張るのは，人から良く思われたいという意識のあ
らわれであると見ることもできるでしょう。中流階級の日本人の
間では，見栄は制度化していると言ってもいいと思います。社会
的地位や収入からみてどんなに分不相応であっても，彼らは贅沢
な品物を買い，そういう暮らしを手に入れたがります。例えば，
新車に乗り，高級ステレオ・セットを揃え，一流のデザイナーが
デザインした洋服を着，ハワイ，グアム，サイパンなどで休暇を
過ごし，子供は私立の名門校にやって，大きなホテルで盛大な結
婚披露をするといったことが，行われているのです。
　このような見栄が原因で悲劇がおこることもありますが，悲劇
とまでは言わなくても，生活に滑稽なアンバランスが生じること
になります。若者の中には，不相応に高い車を月賦で買ったばか
りに，月給の大部分をローンの返済に追われ生活に窮している者
もいます。また中年のサラリーマンは「うさぎ小屋」の狭い居間

their monthly income to make the payments, at the expense of other necessities of life. Middle-aged salaried workers enjoy their "little peace" listening to compact discs on their luxurious hi-fi proudly set in their tiny living room in a "rabbit hut," which is the way a prominent foreigner once characterized the small, older-style Japanese houses. Their suburban wives go to French cooking classes or tennis schools after the household chores, wearing nice dresses manufactured by famous "labels" which they bought on sale.

In spite of its irrationality, the display of such vanity can be one way of keeping one's self-respect or saving one's face in Japan. (MH)

Way: process rather than goal　Few Japanese are probably aware that in the Muromachi period (1336-1573) *sake* drinking achieved the status of ceremonial art in Japan, nearly comparable to the tea ceremony or flower arrangement. Strict rules governed the serving and sipping of rice wine, as well as the procedures for refilling companions' cups and offering one's own to be filled in turn. This highly structured and refined approach to drinking was apparently intended not only to heighten the pleasures of drinking, but to discourage over-indulgence in and dependence on alcohol. Although this art of drinking *sake* fell into decline and disappeared entirely in the 16th century, it is representative of a deep, continuing tendency among the Japanese to seek out a "way"—a prescribed pattern or ritual for perform-

に鎮座しているステレオでコンパクト・ディスクを聞いてささや
かな平和を楽しんだりしています。彼らの妻はといえば、家事を
すませた後は、バーゲン・セールで買ったブランド物の洋服を着
て、フランス料理やテニスを習いに出かけたりしているのです。

このような見栄を張ることは、非合理的なことではありますが、
自尊心を保ち、面子を立てる一種の方便として日本では機能して
いると言えます。

「道」——目標達成よりもその過程——　今では日本人でも知
る人は少ないけれども、その昔室町時代（1336～1573）には、
「酒道」という酒席の行儀作法があり、茶道や華道に並ぶもので
した。厳格なしきたりがあって、酒の注ぎ方、飲み方、返杯の仕
方などを定めていました。この高度な行儀作法は、明らかに飲む
楽しみを増し、飲み過ぎやアルコールへの過度の依存を戒めるも
のでした。しかし、この酒道も室町末期には完全に姿を消しまし
たが、このことは、日本人の中に今も脈々と流れている「道」を
求める気質を示しています。「道」とは、一定の決められた型や
儀礼に従って特定の行為を行い、それによって昇華された美的喜
びや宗教的覚醒を得ようとするものです。これは、酒道や茶道、
華道など枚挙にいとまがありません。

その好例は茶の湯（茶道）です。茶の湯を嗜む人は、小さな茶
室の中で、渋くて美しい茶碗に点てられた香り高い抹茶をゆっく
りと味わいます。この限られた空間は、主人と客人とが、互いに

ing specific acts in order to gain a transcendent state of aesthetic pleasure or religious awareness. Japanese culture is filled with examples like those mentioned above—*sake*, tea, and flowers.

The tea ceremony (*chanoyu*), otherwise known as the way of tea (*sadō*), is perhaps the best known of all. Devotees learn to savor fine aromatic tea served in bowls of subdued beauty in the limited space of a tea room, where a small, serene cosmos is built up through ritualized exchanges between host and guests. Sen no Rikyu (1522-91), the founder of the *Sen* school of tea and perfecter of the tea ceremony, once stated to a disciple as follows:

> *Chanoyu* in a small tea room is above all a matter of practicing and realizing the way in accord with the Buddha's teaching. To delight in the splendor of a dwelling or in the taste of a sumptuous meal belongs to worldly life. There is shelter enough when the roof does not leak, and food enough when one keeps from starving. This is the Buddha's teaching and the fundamental intent of *chanoyu*.

Two facets of the Japanese mentality are involved in this constant seeking of the Way. One is an ingrained habit of self-discipline in pursuit of some higher purpose; pleasure for its own sake is seen as sinful. The other is a tendency to place greater value on process rather than on goal, on *becoming* rather than on *being*. In any field, the Way is a typically Japanese paradigm

一定の儀礼を守って作り上げる一座建立の静謐な小宇宙です。千家流茶道の祖で茶の湯の大成者でもあった千利久（1522〜91）は，かつて一人の弟子に向かって次のように述べています。

　　小座敷の茶の湯は，第一仏法を以て修行得道する事也。家居の結構，食事の珍味を楽とするは俗世の事也。家は漏らぬほど，食事は飢えぬほどにて足る事也。是れ，仏の教え，茶の湯の本意也。

　この「道」を求めてやまない日本人のメンタリティーには二つの側面があります。一つはより高邁な目標を掲げて自己練磨に励もうとする，日本人の心に深くしみ込んでいる習性です。楽しみのための楽しみは罪とみなされるのです。他の一つは，目標を達成することよりも，達成しようとする過程そのものを重んじる傾向です。それは「ある」ことよりも「なる」ことを重んじる心です。いずれにしても，「道」は，日本人に生き方に対する典型的な枠組みを与えています。目標に到る道のほうが，目標そのものよりも重要なのです。日本人にとって，「道」とは，とりも直さず，人の踏み行うべき道，仏道でもあるのです。

for life itself. The destination is less significant than the way of getting there. The Way signifies the path along which one must walk——the way of man is also the way of Buddha. (ON)

Women's role in the work place   Traditionally, occupational duties and those of homemaking are not easily compatible in Japan. For household chores and child care, male workers spend only 7 minutes per day while female workers spend 2 hours and 36 minutes. For shopping, men spend 5 minutes and women 29 minutes. In early 1988 it was reported that only 14% of Japanese men help with household chores. However, an increasing number of Japanese women now hold jobs outside the home. The increase is due to many factors, including a change in the value system regarding women's employment, a change in the industrial structure which provides more jobs, more leisure time available, higher educational standards for women, economic changes such as inflation, and so on.

The following figures are based on the Ministry of Labor's White Paper on Women's Labor (1987). In 1986, one year after the enactment of the Equal Employment Opportunity Law, female workers including part-timers totaled 15,840,000—a 360,000 increase from the previous year — and exceeded the number of housewives by 420,000. They constitute 36.2% of the nation's workforce.

Structurally, women's roles in the workforce have

330

職場における女性の役割　　日本では伝統的に，仕事と家事が両立しにくくなっています。例えば家事と育児に，男性労働者は1日に7分しかかけていませんが，女性労働者は2時間36分かけています。買物には，男性が5分，女性が29分かけています。1988年初頭に，男性の家事参加はわずか14% となっています。けれども現在，女性の職場進出は増大しています。その理由はいろいろありますが，女性の仕事に対する価値観の変化，産業構造の変化にともなう仕事の増加，自由裁量時間の増大，女性の教育水準の上昇，インフレのような経済的事情などがあげられます。

　労働省の『婦人労働白書』(1987) の統計によると，男女雇用機会均等法が施行されて1年目の1986年に，パートタイマーを含む女性雇用者の総数は15,840,000人で，前年度より360,000人増となっています。この数は，家事専業者の数を420,000人も上回っています。また，労働力人口の36.2% は女性です。

　労働力人口において，働く女性に構造的な変化が生まれています。それは男性なみの就業と，パートの労働との二極化です。伝統的に男性が占めていた仕事につく女性が増えていますが，これには要因がいくつかあります。まず第1に，平均勤続年数が長期化して7年となり，4人に1人は，10年以上働き続けます。第2に，高学歴者の数も，この10年で倍増しており，女性雇用者の19.2% が短大か大学卒になっています。第3に，20歳代後半で，結婚や出産で退職しない傾向が強くなっています。非農林業に従事する女性の58.8% が結婚しています。中高年女性雇用者の数も増加しており，現在女性雇用者の58.7% は，35歳以上となっ

been developing in two directions— "men's" work and part-time employment. Several factors have led to the increase of women engaged in jobs traditionally held by men. First, women now stay with a job longer than before, with an average of 7 years. One out of 10 has been on the job for more than 10 years. Second, the number of women with higher education doubled in 10 years : 19. 2% of the female workers were graduates of junior colleges or universities. Third, there arose a growing tendency to continue work after marriage or child-bearing in the later 20's : 58. 8% of nonagricultural-and-forestry females were married. The number of older female workers has increased, and now 58. 7% of the female workers are more than 35 years old.

Female part-timers totaled 3, 520, 000, which was 22. 7% of all female workers and 70% of all part-timers. Many of them chose part-time jobs so that they could take care of household chores and child rearing more easily. Of the companies which were represented in the White Paper, 63. 1% reported that female workers were good for the jobs they offered to them.

Industry-wise, 50. 4% of the female workers were in service jobs, 18. 2% in manufacturing, and 13. 1% in wholesale and retail sales, including restaurant businesses. (MO)

Work For many Japanese, work itself seems to be a *raison de vivre* (fulfillment), and not just a means of earning their daily bread. Several examples of the

ています。

　女性パートタイマーの総数は，3,520,000人で，これは女性雇用者全体の22.7％，パートタイマーの総数の70％にあたります。家事や育児がしやすいから，パートの仕事を選ぶ女性が大勢います。白書の調査回答企業の63.1％は，採用理由に"仕事内容がパートタイム労働者で間に合うため"をあげています。

　女性雇用者の産業別状況については，サービス業50.4％，製造業18.2％，となっています。卸売，小売業，飯食店は13.1％となっています。

　仕　事　　多くの日本人にとって，仕事は単に日々の生活の糧を得る手段ではなく，それ自体生き甲斐のように見えます。日本人がとても仕事熱心だということを示すものがいくつか最近マス

Japanese dedication to hard working have been seen in the media these days. The working hours in Japan have been 44 or even more hours per week. Even so, many white-collar workers — or "salaried men" — work overtime. Also, a large number of Japanese refrain from taking all the vacation that is due to them. The government has begun to take actions which shorten the work week and encourage workers to take vacations. The Japanese workers have traditionally engaged less in recreational activities than people in other major countries.

There seem to be several reasons for the custom of hard work. First, it has to do with the fact that Japanese society was traditionally agrarian. Paddy-field rice cultivation on a small scale restricted the use of oxen and horses. Farmers had to do all the hard work for themselves. In addition, they had to increase their harvests because land taxes and tenancy rents kept rising. They had no choice except to work hard.

Second, the Meiji Restoration (1867/8) swept away the old, rigid social order and paved the way for anybody with ability to attain a high social position by their individual efforts. As a result, not only farmers but also government officials, members of the military, and company employees began to work hard. Third, Japan's post-war inflation and want of food made people work harder just to survive the hardship.

Another reason is that businesses these days tend to take good care of their employees, providing them with

334

コミに取り上げられています。日本での週労働時間数はこれまで
ずっと44時間かそれを上まわってきました。それでもサラリー
マンの多くが最低就労時間数以上働いているのです。また，多く
の日本人は自分たちの休暇をぜんぶ消化しようともしないのです。
とうとう政府は週労働時間数を短縮し，休暇をとるのを勧める行
動を起こしました。日本人は他の主要国の人々ほど余暇を過ごす
伝統をもちませんでした。

　日本人の一生懸命働く習慣にはいくつか理由があるようです。
まず，日本の社会は伝統的に農耕社会であったという事実と関係
があります。小規模の水田稲作でしたから牛馬は思う存分には使
えず，自分できつい仕事はすべてやらなければなりませんでした。
加えて，年貢や小作料が年々高くなっていったので，一生懸命に
働いて収穫を増やさなければなりませんでした。懸命に働くしか
なかったのです。

　次に，明治維新がいままでの厳格な階級制度を一掃し，能力あ
る者は誰でも努力しだいで高い社会的地位まで登れるような道を
開きました。その結果，農民だけでなく官吏，軍人，会社員など
が一生懸命に働くようになったのです。

　3番目に，第2次世界大戦後のインフレと食料難のために，こ
の苦しい時代を生き抜くためだけにみんな懸命に働かざるを得な
かったわけです。

　そしてもう一つの理由は，今日の会社が終身雇用，年金制度，
年功による昇進などで社員を丸抱えで面倒見ていることにありま
す。これらの要因に助けられて，社員は会社に対する忠誠心を強
め，会社の成功のために懸命に働くのです。これがビジネスの場
で働いている義理と恩の例なのです。また，会社はボトムアップ
式経営で社員に責任感と参加意識をもたせます。

　これら4つの理由が日本人を働き蜂にしたと思われるいろいろ
な要因のなかに含まれていると思われます。

lifetime employment, pension plans, and a seniority system. All these factors in Japan help the employees strengthen their loyalty to the company and work hard for its success. This is an example of *giri* and *on* as they affect the business situation. Also, by "bottom-to-top" management, firms give workers a sense of responsibility and participation. These four reasons are among many which seem to have helped Japanese people acquire their custom of hard work. (YY)

Zaibatsu : financial clique   In prewar Japan, there were several *zaibatsu* (large financial cliques). They emerged as a result of the Meiji Government's sale of some state-owned factories, mines and other industries at reasonable prices and on extended installment payments in the late 19th and early 20th centuries. These passed into the hands of respected powerful families , such as Sumitomo , Iwasaki , Furukawa, Yasuda, Mitsui and the like having holding corporations under control, which were possessed of stocks of various companies. *Zaibatsu* adopted a very exclusive management policy, appointing only their family members and relatives to key positions in the corporations and companies. Through the marriage of their daughters, *zaibatsu* families recruited competent men into their families. It was, therefore, very difficult for outsiders to penetrate into *zaibatsu* executive circles which were cemented by the traditional blood-line system.

財閥　戦前には財閥が数団体ありました。財閥は，前世紀末から今世紀初めにかけて明治政府が，国有工場，鉱山，企業を安い長期払いで民間に売却したことから起こってきたものです。住友，岩崎，古河，安田，三井といった著名で強力な家族の手に渡り，財閥は親会社を支配下において，多数の企業の株式を所有していました。財閥は排他的経営政策をとり家族と親類縁者だけを会社の主要ポストに任命しました。娘たちの結婚を通じて，有能な青年を家族の中に引き抜いていったのです。だから，血縁で固められた財閥のトップに部外者が食い込んでいくのはたいへん困難でした。

　昭和20年に第2次世界大戦が終わったとき，日本の戦争努力の主要な推進者とみなされた財閥は戦後日本の改革を実施していたマッカーサー総司令部によって解散させられました。戦後の財閥は戦前のような中心組織を持っていませんでした。今日では，戦前のように大きな親会社を所有できるほど有力な一族はもうなくなっています。

　しかし1950年代に銀行を中心にして，新しい大企業が出現し，1960年代に急成長を遂げました。特に1970年代に旧財閥系銀行が借款と投資を通じてグループ内の企業に対して影響力を強くし

ZAIBATSU : FINANCIAL CLIQUE

When World War Ⅱ ended in 1945, *zaibatsu*, regarded as one of the chief movers and supporters of Japan's war efforts, were dissolved by General MacArthur's General Headquarters, which carried out postwar reforms of Japan. The postwar *zaibatsu* did not have the core of their prewar organization any more. Today, there are no single families influential enough to have large holding corporations as they used to before World War Ⅱ.

However, new conglomerate groups came into being during the 1950's, centered around the banking industry, and they rapidly expanded in the middle of the 1960's. Especially, in the 1970's, banks in the former *zaibatsu* became strong enough to influence companies in their groups through their loans and investments. It can safely be said that the former *zaibatsu* family system has been replaced by a group system with a bank as its core. By even the most conservative estimates, in 1986, the total assets and shareholders' equity of the Mitsubishi, the Sumitomo, and the Mitsui groups were 66 trillion yen ($507.7 billion at the exchange rate of 130 yen to the dollar) and 3 trillion yen ($23.1 billion), 62 trillion yen ($476.9 billion) and 3 trillion yen ($23.1 billion), and 50 trillion yen ($384.6 billion) and 2 trillion yen ($15.4 billion), respectively. This group system is very similar to big businesses in the United States, such as the Standard Oil Co. or General Electric. (MK)

338

ました。銀行を核にしたグループ体制が戦前の旧家財閥体制にとって代わったと言うことができます。昭和 61 年の数字では，控えめに見積もっても三菱，住友，三井グループの総資産と純資産はそれぞれ 66 兆円と 3 兆円，62 兆円と 3 兆円，50 兆円と 2 兆円です。このグループ体制はアメリカのスタンダード・オイルや GE のような大企業に類似しています。

索　引（太字は見出し項目）
（Index）

i

編者紹介（Editors）

本 名 信 行（ほんな のぶゆき）

1940 年生
青山学院大学大学院卒業
現在 青山学院大学教授
専攻 英語学，社会言語学，異文化間コミュニ
ケーション，アメリカ研究
テキサス・キリスト教大学客員研究員，トリニ
ティ大学客員教授などを歴任，豊富な渡米経験
をもつ。編著書，翻訳，論文多数

Bates Hoffer（ベイツ・ホッファ）

1939 年生
テキサス大学大学院卒業（Ph. D.）
現在 トリニティ大学教授
専攻 英語学，社会言語学，異文化間コミュニ
ケーション，日本研究
東京電機大学客員研究員，ハワイ大学客員教授
などを歴任，豊富な来日経験をもつ。編著書，
論文多数

日本人の考え方を英語で説明する辞典

1989 年 3 月 30 日　初版第 1 刷発行
1997 年 4 月 20 日　初版第 14 刷発行

編　　者	本 名 信 行 ベイツ・ホッファ
発行者	江 草 忠 敬

〒101 東京都千代田区神田神保町 2-17

発行所　株式
会社 有 斐 閣

電　話　(03) 3264-1314〔編集〕
3265-6811〔営業〕
京都支店〔606〕左京区田中門前町 44

印刷　大日本法令印刷　製本　明泉堂
Printed in Japan
★定価はカバーに表示してあります。
ISBN 4-641-07521-2